Latin America

Also of Interest

†Available in hardcover and paperback.

About the Book and Authors

Mass poverty, widespread illiteracy, extreme social inequality, the death of children and the chronic debilitation of adults due to diseases that are minor problems in the developed world, political unrest and repression—all of these conditions are the symptoms of underdevelopment that shape and limit the lives of a majority of Latin Americans today. How did these conditions arise? Why do they persist? What path can lead to development in Latin America?

Some scholars look to the dynamic forces of capitalist development that transformed feudal Europe and colonial North America into modern, postindustrial societies. Others identify the expansion of the capitalist world system as the fundamental cause of Latin American underdevelopment. The latter believe that socialism rather than capitalism is the proper path to development in Latin America.

The authors explore the alternative explanations of development and underdevelopment and the related questions of social class and class struggle in the transition to capitalism. They also examine the issues of political pluralism, internal colonialism, the role of the United States in Latin America, reformist and revolutionary strategies for change, the implications of the transition to socialism in Cuba and Nicaragua, and the prospects for the future of the region as a whole.

Ronald H. Chilcote is professor of political science at the University of California, Riverside. He is the author of numerous monographs and articles in scholarly journals, including *Portuguese Africa* (1967), *Protest and Resistance in Angola and Brazil* (1972), *The Brazilian Communist Party: Conflict and Integration, 1922 to 1972* (1974), *Theories of Comparative Politics: The Search for a Paradigm* (Westview, 1981), and *Theories of Development and Underdevelopment* (Westview, 1984). He is managing editor of the journal *Latin American Perspectives*. His current research, based on fieldwork since 1969, involves a comparative study of ruling class power and underdevelopment in two provincial communities in Brazil.

Joel C. Edelstein is associate professor of political science at the University of Colorado, Denver, where he offers courses on Latin American political economy, especially in Central America and the Caribbean. He has published articles on these subjects in scholarly and popular journals in the United States, Mexico, and Canada. In the mid-1970s he taught at the Universidad de las Americas in Puebla, Mexico. He has done field research in Cuba and Nicaragua and is a participating editor of *Latin American Perspectives*. The focus of his current research is the post-1979 behavior of the private sector in Nicaragua.

Latin America
Capitalist and Socialist Perspectives of Development and Underdevelopment

*Ronald H. Chilcote
and Joel C. Edelstein*

Westview Press / Boulder and London

Latin American Perspectives Series, Number 3

Published in 1986 in the United States of America by Westview Press, Inc.; Frederick A. Praeger, Publisher; 5500 Central Avenue, Boulder, Colorado 80301

Library of Congress Cataloging in Publication Data
Chilcote, Ronald H.
  Latin America: capitalist and socialist perspectives
of development and underdevelopment.
  (Latin American perspectives series; no. 3)
  "This is a complete revision and expansion of our
introduction to *Latin America: The Struggle with
Dependency and Beyond,* published in 1974"—Pref.
  Bibliography: p.
  Includes index.
  1. Latin America—Economic conditions—1945–
2. Latin America—Social conditions—1945–
3. Capitalism—Latin America. 4. Socialism—Latin
America. I. Edelstein, Joel C. II. Latin America.
III. Title. IV. Series.
HC125.C487 1986   338.98   85-13899
ISBN 0-8133-0238-2
ISBN 0-8133-0239-0 (pbk.)

Printed and bound in the United States of America

10   9   8   7   6   5   4   3   2   1

For the peoples of the Americas who suffer
the violent condition of underdevelopment
and for those who struggle against it

To the reader in the hope that understanding
will lead to action

Contents

Preface

This is a complete revision and expansion of our introduction to *Latin America: The Struggle with Dependency and Beyond*, published in 1974. This volume was reprinted many times and adopted in hundreds of university classrooms. When it finally went out of print in 1982, we decided to revise. Although the framework of the original version has been retained, our emphasis has shifted, the consequence of theoretical advances that have carried us beyond the dependency debates of the 1970s. The framework incorporates two interpretations of how capitalism has made its historical impact on Latin America. We criticize both interpretations to suggest that the search for theory is a constant process. Our purpose is to demonstrate that contrasting perspectives lead to different questions, analyses, and conclusions. Once the reader understands this point, then critical thinking is possible. This volume introduces a series of country studies on Latin America; volumes on Argentina, Cuba, and Guatemala will appear shortly. Our hope is that, like our initial effort, the volume will fill a void and provide a book suitable for undergraduate and graduate courses on Latin American anthropology, history, economy, politics, and sociology as well as courses on international relations, political economy, and development.

Latin America usually is thought of as part of the Third World. The term is rather vague. We know what parts of the world are included in it—all the nations of the world except those of North America and Europe, the USSR, Japan, Australia, New Zealand, and perhaps a few others. However, what the nations of the Third World have in common, why they should be placed in the same category, and what the concept implies are more problematic aspects. The term is sometimes used to refer to countries that are poor, primarily nonwhite and nonindustrial. But among the nations regarded as part of the Third World and even within Latin America, some countries are predominantly "white" (Argentina and Uruguay), some have significant industrial centers (Argentina, Brazil, and Mexico), and others have a per capita income closer to that of non–Third World countries than to that of most countries of the Third World (e.g., Argentina's per capita income is about average for the Eastern European countries and is about nine times greater than that of Haiti). The common defining characteristic must be found elsewhere.

The term came into use in the 1950s when the world was divided into two hostile camps. This was also a time when many colonies gained formal independence. Many were admitted to the United Nations, and some observers thought that these "new nations" would be a third force in world politics. Of course, not all the new nations were "new." Most of the Latin American countries had been formally independent for over 130 years; some countries such as Thailand had never been under colonial rule. The idea that the Third World countries would act as a political bloc has fallen over the course of time. Unity has been less frequent than its opposite.

The concept has also been used to imply that the Third World countries are just now emerging from feudalism and that they have the opportunity to create a new, third path of development "between capitalism and socialism." This idea is no more viable than the others we have mentioned, and it is more dangerous because it denies one feature that is shared by the nations of the Third World—their history of economic domination. Each society has been caught up in the expanding international capitalist system. Regardless of formal legal status, the economy of every Third World nation was shaped by the needs of the system's center. All of these nations became exporters of a limited number of primary products, and they became dependent on foreign trade to provide the products their economies did not produce. Responding to international market forces, they developed the distortions of dependent capitalism. In our understanding, the defining characteristic of the Third World concept is this economic structure, which maintains dependency.

Some leaders of ethnic minority movements in the United States have included their respective ethnic groups in the Third World. We consider this interpretation of the concept to be correct, granting that these groups are sufficiently separate from the dominant society to be considered as distinct communities and that dependent economic structures and relationships exist between each minority and the dominant society. The land formerly occupied by native Americans and the territory of the Southwest that was once part of Mexico were expropriated in the course of capitalist expansion. Africans were forcibly removed from their homeland and brought to the United States to provide cheap labor. Although today some assimilation occurs, it almost always requires adoption of the traits of the dominant culture after the fashion of the assimilationist policies of European colonial powers in Africa and Asia. Contemporary economic relationships are essentially neocolonial. Although there are important differences between the historical experiences and contemporary situations of Third World states and ethnic minorities in the United States, they are not central.

Some nations have thrown off the forces of foreign penetration and the domestic ruling classes that cooperated with imperialism. Cuba, following this course, has removed the allocation of resources and labor from the control of the market and the profit motive. By eliminating the private ownership of the means of production, it has been possible to institute planning directed toward independent national development. Cubans have acquired a new respect for their own culture and society, but the economy inherited from the colonial and neocolonial periods has not yet been overcome, given the need to import and to find markets for its limited variety of exports, and it has also received substantial assistance from the Soviet Union. Thus, Cuba is still a Third World nation. However, the Cuban people are now mobilized to create a sovereign economy on which full political independence can be based.

The problem Third World peoples must face in order to overcome poverty and to achieve dignity lies first in regaining control of their resources. This task requires revolutionary struggle against domestic ruling classes and their foreign supporters. Most Third World countries are still governed by a comprador class, some relatively strong and others that would fall in a matter of months if not supported by imperialist military strength. In Asia and Africa, and in the Americas, the struggle continues, more advanced in some areas and using different forms and tactics in different contexts. In many countries the counter-revolution has dropped its democratic facade, placing military regimes in power. The effort to stop the Third World revolution has encouraged similar tendencies in the very center of the system. Nonetheless, revolution continues and in some nations succeeds. It will surely be the dominant force in the history of the world for the balance of this century.

We hope that this volume will contribute to destroying myth and to bringing about a more correct understanding of Latin America. Moreover, it is our earnest hope that understanding will lead to action and change toward the complete reorientation of policies of the U.S. government and to modification of U.S. economic and social institutions, changes that are necessary if North Americans are to play a positive role in the struggle against underdevelopment in the Americas.

Ronald H. Chilcote
Joel C. Edelstein

Acknowledgments

We would like to thank Frances, Stephen, and Edward Chilcote as well as Harriet, Noah, and Josh Edelstein for their patience, understanding, and encouragement as we worked our way through several drafts of this book. We also thank Timothy Harding for criticisms and suggestions that were incorporated into the final draft.

R.H.C.
J.C.E.

1
Introduction

It is costly to be born a Latin American rather than a North American, at least in statistical terms. The average life expectancy in the nations of Latin America is about sixty years compared with about seventy-two years in the United States. If you had been born a Latin American, you would "lose" about twelve years, or one-sixth of your life. As an "average" Latin American, you would receive only a sixth of the schooling you get as an "average" North American—less than two years compared with nearly twelve. The possibility of hunger and starvation would be much greater. A 1968 study (Citizens' Board of Inquiry 1968: 7) estimated that 14 million people suffer from hunger in the United States, about 7 percent of the total population. Although this figure was reduced by income maintenance programs in the 1970s, the curtailment of such programs in the early 1980s has led to an increase in the extent of hunger in the United States—to 21 million, or about 9 percent of the population. Some estimates on hunger regarding Latin America include as much as three-fourths of the population. As an "average" Latin American, you would be sick much more, there are proportionately only a third the number of doctors, and they are concentrated in the cities where only half the people live. Your income would be only one-tenth that of an "average" North American. The probability that you would witness the death of one of your children in the first year of life would be about four times greater.[1]

These facts of human existence are beyond dispute. *Why* these social conditions exist and *how* they can be changed are subjects of heated and sometimes bitter argument. Many explanations have been advanced by observers of Latin America, and the analysis of other regions also has important implications for understanding Latin America. The reader who wishes to examine this large body of literature is confronted by an array of writings. Some describe, others claim to provide a theoretical explanation, some are explicitly focused on particular aspects of devel-

Table 1.1.   Schools of Developmental Thought

Capitalism	Socialism
Stages of development through capitalist accumulation	Capitalist development of underdevelopment
Capitalist development by local bourgeoisies through national orientation	World system emphasizing international trade and impact on national social formation
Associated dependent capitalist development	Internationalization of capital
Imperialist destruction of precapitalist social formations so as to promote capitalist accumulation prior to socialism	Modes of production determined by the labor process and social relations of production

opment, and others try to deal with the subject on a global level. The literature is characterized by many overlapping areas of agreement and disagreement, and often, authors do not even agree on how they disagree! To make matters worse, there is no consensus on the meaning of fundamental terms, such as "development" and "underdevelopment."

There are many ways to group the authors, depending upon which commonalities in the writings are emphasized and which differences are ignored (see Chilcote 1984 for an elaboration and detailed analysis of the following discussion). We have chosen to focus our presentation around the difference between capitalism and socialism as the most appropriate form of political economy for development in the Third World. This method is lacking in academic neatness, and writers on both sides of this divide will complain, not without justification, of the distinctions we have ignored and the company in which we have placed them. We believe, nonetheless, that this method of division is useful because it corresponds to the fundamental political question of our time: Is capitalism or socialism the better form of political economy for Third World development (see Table 1.1).

The people who believe capitalism is the proper path for development in the Third World share a perspective in which the more advanced capitalist countries have and will continue to have a major role in Latin American development. According to this perspective, the conditions of underdevelopment result most importantly from the persistence of feudal stagnation (Rostow 1962, for example). One school of thought projects the interests of imperialism and its local clients. It advocates that Latin American governments permit unrestricted access of the transnational corporations to local resources and markets with tax privileges and other inducements to attract foreign private capital.

A second school of thought speaks for the local capitalist class or bourgeoisie, which often suffers from competition with the multinational firms and foreign monopoly capital in Latin America. This school identifies some negative tendencies of unrestrained capitalist development. Monocultural economies suffer from a long-standing tendency for prices of most agricultural and mineral exports to fall in relation to manufactured imports so these economies are vulnerable to frequent fluctuations in commodity prices. Moreover, the superior financial and technical power of the transnationals enables them to take over the most dynamic industries and sectors in Third World countries, leaving local capitalists with dying industries. These advocates of capitalist development for the local bourgeoisie (Prebisch 1980, for example) seek reforms to create a more nationally oriented development in which foreign capital is regulated and local capital is protected.

A third school understands that the postwar penetration of foreign capitalism in Latin America was accompanied by economic growth. Foreign and domestic capital combined in "associated" dependent or capitalist development so that, despite conditions of dependency on the outside world, capitalism emerged in some countries, such as Brazil (Cardoso 1972, 1973).

The fourth school of thought, an interpretation of classical Marxism, views socialism as a desirable outcome but advocates capitalist development. It emphasizes the portion of Marx's analysis of capitalism that considers capitalism to be a destroyer of precapitalist social formations, so as to permit the evolution of capitalism prior to socialism. This school maintains that the social relations of production are rigidly determined by the level of the forces of production. Therefore, socialism is not possible until capitalist development has taken place. This position was initially enunciated by Moscow-oriented Communist parties, which advocated a united front of workers and local capital against the *latifundista* (large landowner) class and its imperialist allies. More recently, Bill Warren (1980) has argued that capitalism is a force for development and that imperialism is a positive force.

Of the people who advocate socialism as the proper path for Third World development, some have argued that capitalism creates, in André Gunder Frank's terms, "the development of underdevelopment" (Frank 1967a). Frank followed the work of Baran (1957), who argued that imperialism maintains a state of backwardness by reinforcing stagnant economic and social structures as well as conservative social classes in the Third World. Thus, Baran denied the role of contemporary imperialism in destroying precapitalist social formations.

Baran also identified a transfer of economic surplus[2] from agricultural sectors to unproductive commercial sectors and to foreign capital. This surplus, defined as the difference between what is produced and the cost of both production and maintaining the producers, is the potential source of investment that is needed for growth and increased productivity. The transfer of the surplus was seen as a cause of continued backwardness.

Frank applied Baran's thesis to colonial Latin America, arguing that the social formations created after the Spanish Conquest were capitalist, no matter how conservative. Frank and others later identified foreign penetration and the resultant political and economic dependency as the cause of underdevelopment in Latin America, implying that underdeveloped countries can develop only if both their internal structures and their relations with other nations undergo a complete change. This dependency approach argues that foreign penetration has co-opted local capital and denies the possibility of a coalition of the working classes and the local bourgeoisie against imperialism.

Since Baran's pioneering work, some capital accumulation has occurred and a largely foreign-controlled industrial sector has emerged in Latin America. However, dependency on foreign capital, technology, intermediate goods, and capital equipment has increased. Latin America's increased capacity to produce an economic surplus is also a source of a greater loss of the surplus because of increased profit remittances, payments for patents and royalties, interest payments, and imports required for production in the modern sectors.

Over the last decade Frank has adopted the world system approach of Immanuel Wallerstein (1974), which emphasizes international trade and the impact of the world economy on the shaping of national economies and social formations. Unlike Frank's earlier work, world system theory revises the dichotomy between metropolitan and peripheral countries by adding an intermediate grouping of semiperipheral countries, and it recognizes movement within the hierarchy of the world capitalist system. In these terms, the possibility that capitalist development will succeed in some semiperipheral countries is accepted (Wallerstein 1979). However, the capitalist path is rejected as undesirable because of its high costs in hunger, repression, and misery for large majorities in Third World countries. Moreover, Wallerstein maintains that there can be only a single world system, into which all countries are more or less integrated regardless of their domestic property systems. Thus, he argues, socialist revolution in a given country cannot create socialism, though it contributes to shifting the balance of the world system toward socialism (1980: 176–177).

A somewhat different approach, set forth by French political economist Christian Palloix (1977), focuses on the internationalization of capital. Palloix looks at the movement of capital and class struggle on an international level, paying attention to international valorization of commodities, modes of international accumulation of capital, and the internationalization of the productive and financial systems. These ideas are applied by Henrik Secher Marcussen and Jens Erik Torp (1982) in an assessment of dependency in which they recognize that new forms of international capital have appeared since the rise of petroleum prices in 1973 and the subsequent crisis in Europe. They argue that capital has shifted from Europe to the periphery in the search for new investments and markets; this movement permits national capitalist accumulation within some countries (they cite the example of the Ivory Coast, and other writers have noted similar development in Brazil—for example, Evans 1979).

Another school of thought focuses on modes of production (Rey 1973), largely as a response to the emphasis on dependency (Foster-Carter 1978). Although not denying that external relations are significant, mode of production analysts assert that the labor process and the social relations that result in actual production are the principal determinants of the behavior and the development of a given social formation. The means by which economic surplus is produced and appropriated from the producer are more central than the ultimate destination of the surplus. Rejecting the more macrolevel and somewhat abstract nature of the dependency approach, mode of production analysis has opened the way for empirical research on the microlevel, in part to examine the ways in which ongoing social formations interact with each other and with external forces.[3]

We believe that previous explanations of underdevelopment have misunderstood its root cause. They have provided justification for the government policies and corporate activities that have maintained and enhanced political economic patterns and social structures which produce vast human suffering and prevent the realization of individual and social potential.

In 1974 we suggested two alternative models of development and underdevelopment. One viewed the diffusion of capital as the means for promoting development, and the other suggested that this diffusion leads to underdevelopment. At the time we favored the second of these models, despite its inherent defects. The first was popular in mainstream thinking; the second was incorporated in alternative perspectives of the time that interested academics who were struggling with new understandings of the complex development process. Juxtaposing the models stimulated the reader to think critically about the origins and evolution of development and underdevelopment in Latin America. Today, however, both models are part of the mainstream thinking of contemporary social science and history.

For this book, we have modified the models to reflect past debates and criticisms, and we more explicitly contrast capitalism with socialism. There are many forms of capitalism and socialism, however, and proponents and opponents can be found on both sides. Both models have been seriously criticized, and we cite relevant sources to aid readers in formulating their own criticism. Neither model offers a necessarily correct understanding of the origins and evolution of capitalist development. Instead of defending the dependency model, as many people tended to do during the 1970s, we believe that the reader should use the contrasting explanations as a means of seeking a new interpretation. Our preference would be to elaborate an explanation within a Marxist framework, but as Michael Harrington reminds us in his *Twilight of Capitalism* (1976), there are many Marxisms in the thinking and writing of Karl Marx. Consequently, various schools of Marxism have emerged, including the critical Marxism of German philosophers Erich Fromm and Jurgen Habermas, the instrumental Marxism of English political economist Ralph Miliband, and the structural Marxism of Greek political scientist Nicos Poulantzas. Thus, each reader must find a personal position and evolve a theoretical understanding, based on historical reality. In the discussion that follows, it is hoped that by juxtaposing the two now widely accepted models, the student will not feel compelled to side with one or the other but will feel free to explore in new directions.

Our objective in this brief book is to explain the essential premises of these positions and to examine their contrasting perspectives in relation to some prevailing assumptions about the diffusion of capitalist development and the dependency that accompanies capitalist under-development. These assumptions are related to two models that describe the European historical experience, especially the emergence of capitalism in England and the Iberian countries, as well as to that of Latin America. Emerging from our discussion of the models and the historical inter-pretations that are included are controversial issues that permeate past and present literature on Latin America: feudalism and the dual society; the national and international bourgeoisie; the elite and ruling classes; the working class and peasantry; and foreign and domestic classes. We show that polarized positions on these issues are related to one's reliance upon one or another model. We examine three major studies of Latin America to show how these issues have led scholars to different inter-pretations and conclusions. We review various forms of foreign inter-vention in the area and analyze reformist and revolutionary strategies that lead to various outcomes. Then we look briefly at some problems societies that attempt to break with capitalism face, and finally, we assess the prospects for capitalism and socialism in Latin America.

2

A Model of Capitalist Diffusion and Development

In examining the history of capitalist development, the more traditional diffusion model assumes that feudalism and capitalism were forms of economic activity that stimulated a "dual society" with a backward feudal order, on the one hand, and a commercial and industrial bourgeois order, on the other. According to this model, progress will come about through the spread of capitalism to backward and traditional areas. Through the diffusion of technology and capital, these areas will evolve toward a modern state.

Assumptions of the Model

Essentially, the model sees underdevelopment as a condition that all nations have experienced at some time. Although some nations have managed to develop, others have not. In Latin America, according to the model, the feudal structure inherited from the Spanish and Portuguese conquistadores has stifled change. Although modern cities have arisen as a result of contact with the developed world, the countryside has remained backward, mired in the unproductive agriculture of large feudal estates. If conditions are to improve, traditional values must be challenged, and modern diversified industry must replace the current dependence on one or two agricultural products.

Change requires the introduction of outside capital because the region is poor, and foreign investment can also bring modern technology and organizational methods to these backward nations—necessities that were not important for feudal England and other early developing nations but are especially critical for the countries that have started late on the road to development. However, business requires political stability, which is a major problem in Latin America. There are rising expectations, and the masses are impatient. The middle class, though democratically inclined, has been weak and divided. Under these conditions, modernizing military governments appear to be the last resort of progress. It is hoped that the order they provide can stimulate foreign investment which will bring about capitalism and the modernization of agriculture and industry that is necessary to create the basis for a new democratic stability. Thus, the diffusion model encourages increased U.S. investment to advance economic development in Latin America and increased U.S. influence to develop Latin American culture. The model even endorses the granting of aid to the Latin American military in the name of democracy.

Within the model, underdevelopment is denoted by either the single criterion of a per capita gross national product (GNP) below $500 or $600 or that criterion in combination with other characteristics including illiteracy, political instability, inequality, a strong hierarchy and lack of social mobility, and an economy characterized by the dominance of one or two agricultural or mineral products and by a low level of technology and productivity. A region or a nation-state that manifests all or most of these characteristics is regarded as an underdeveloped area. The more pronounced these features are, the greater the degree of underdevelopment. In these terms, most of the nations of Latin America are clearly underdeveloped. There is no doubt about Haiti, which has a per capita income under $300, or Guatemala, where the per capita GNP is $328 and 54 percent of the population is illiterate. Nor is there any question about the status of Brazil as an underdeveloped nation since its per capita income is low and a third of the population is illiterate. It is less clear that Argentina is an underdeveloped country as literacy is nearly universal, the average annual income is over $2,000, and there is a substantial middle class.

The model uses two criteria to define capitalist development. One is national wealth, which is measured by a single aggregate figure, the per capita GNP. The second is the degree of "modernity," a concept that includes social and political characteristics, such as the rate of social mobility; the complexity of the social structure, with emphasis on the progressive role of a middle class; the degree of specialization of political and social roles and institutions; national integration; urbanization; and limitations on government power accompanied by the rise of mechanisms for compromise and for the expression of popular will. [The idea of modernization had various meanings in the literature of the 1960s. For example, David Apter (1965) emphasized the evolution of politics along with industrialization, and Samuel Huntington (1965) stressed that rapid change could undermine the process of modernization and bring about decay in traditional and existing institutions. Although these ideas have been largely discredited (Bodenheimer 1970), Latin American social scientists, including some Marxist scholars, have utilized modernization in contemporary analysis (for example, Graziano da Silva 1984).] According to this definition, medieval England was underdeveloped. National integration was lacking; poverty and illiteracy were the normal conditions of the serf. Compared with current standards, the feudal economy employed a low level of technology, and productivity was low. Today England is considered to have been successful in its gradual progression from being an underdeveloped island to becoming a developed nation-state.

Feudalism, Capitalism, and Dual Society in England and Latin America

In the rest of this chapter, we describe in some detail the early beginnings of development in England, examining the characteristics of feudalism and tracing the transition to capitalism through the growth of commercialization and early industrialization. The discussion focuses on England because of the belief, inherent in the diffusion model of capitalist development, that the experience of that country serves as an example for the development of backward areas elsewhere. In comparing England to Latin America, we acknowledge that many characteristics of early rural European feudalism seem to be evident in Latin America today. Likewise, we also note parallels in the development of urban life in England and Latin America. The emergence of capitalism was the consequence of such considerations as capital for new industry and technology for modern production. Capitalism was accompanied by the rise of a bourgeoisie and a subsequent decline of the feudal lords in England, but in Latin America, two societies, one feudal and the other capitalist, have tended to prevail. Here we are concerned with a traditional explanation of dual society; later we shall identify the contradictions of that explanation.

Feudalism

The diffusion model of capitalist development sees Latin America as emerging from feudalism and stresses a transformation to capitalism as the key to development. This model uses the transition of northern European and English feudalism into capitalism as an example that can and should be followed by contemporary underdeveloped nations. Under the English feudal system, people were spread across the land, and by far the vast majority worked the soil as serfs. Technology was very primitive, and people produced little more food than they and their children needed to live. A portion of whatever food was left over fed the few artisans of the manors who produced and manufactured craft articles—tools, arms, and some household items. The serfs were forced by the power and the position of the nobles who owned the estates, in a sense by the manorial system itself, to produce some surplus and to turn it over to the nobles for their use and for the use of their artisans.

The outlook and the consciousness of the people of the feudal system, serf and nobleman, were very different from those of the modern world.

The concept of change, the sense of acquiring greater wealth and comfort, the thought of moving around to see the world—ideas and aspirations that dominate our own lives—were virtually unknown to the people of the medieval world. Their society was highly structured. If one were born a serf, he or she tilled the soil and belonged to the lord of the manor. The serf's position was fixed by legal custom and could not be changed. There was rarely any movement from one place in the feudal hierarchy to another. One's goal was not to compete for higher positions in society, but to do what one's mother or father did, to till the soil and give part of the produce to one's secular or ecclesiastical lord, to practice the prescribed simple religious duties, and to rest on Sundays. One did not expect more of life because one was not aware of more, nor did one ever receive more. Life was simple, fixed, and predictable.

Feudal economies consisted of very simple agricultural structures that in no way resembled the occupations and industries in which the majority of North Americans work. The service sector, composed of teachers, lawyers, office workers, salesmen, and bureaucrats, hardly existed. This sector forms the economic base for most of what we now call the middle class. Although a primitive class of clerks (clerics) and bureaucrats, which could be considered a managerial class, existed as a by-product of the governmental functions of the universal church and the monarchy, feudal society essentially consisted of two classes—the secular and spiritual lords of the manor and the ecclesiastical estates and the serfs and artisans who were born to those estates and worked in the fields or in the village households that sprang up around the manors.

The responsibilities of the serf included working in the lord's fields, providing a number of other services, and paying rent in cash or in kind for the privilege of farming some land for himself. The arrangements between the serf and his lord, often spelled out in considerable detail (for example, see Cantor 1963: 181–184), were quite extensive, giving the lord power in matters such as marriage of the serf's children.

A serf could not move off the estate without permission. Mobility hardly existed. People spent their whole lives within a few square miles and seldom met strangers of any kind. It would have been unlikely for them to meet more than a few hundred people during their lifetime. Traditional codes and customs amounting to the force of law shaped this way of life and completed the bondage. In this kind of society, urban centers were very slow in appearing because productivity was too low to provide enough surplus to support much urban development. Although there were occasional fairs at which trading occurred, there was not enough produce to create a commercial world out of this simple trade, and transportation was also difficult. The people identified with the immediate locality in which they lived, with the land they farmed, and with its master.

Interpersonal relationships in feudal society were unlike those today, especially in relation to economic transactions. In today's society, a buyer and a seller usually see each other only in these limited roles. In feudal societies, relationships were more personalized. Although the opportunity to buy and sell goods may have been the primary reason for contact, the act of exchange occurred within the context of a long-standing relationship. The dealings between employers and employees today also differ from the more personalized relationship between the lord and the serf.

In feudal societies, there were no unions to provide protection for the serf and no bargaining. There was no economic constraint on the lord of the estate; there was no legal recourse for the serf. The lord was the law in his own territory (the baronial or seigneurial courts). The law governing the lord-serf relationship was rooted in the specific custom and tradition of an area. Two conditions operated to protect the serf from any injurious effects of the lord's arbitrary power. First, the serf and his lord were engaged in more than just a business relationship. In addition to the "employer-employee" or "lessor-lessee" roles, they shared a kind of unequal friendship. The lord was clearly the superior in this relationship, but he had paternalistic responsibilities for the welfare of his serfs. These responsibilities were sanctioned by custom and operated to some extent as a constraint. The relationship included not only the traditional, mutual obligations but also an exchange of favors between the lord and individual serfs. In today's society, the owner of a business and his or her employees are kept together by money. From the worker's point of view, the boss is a signature on the paycheck; for the owner, the worker is a cost of production, nothing more—and the smaller the paycheck, the greater the profit for the owner. In feudal societies, the tendency for a lord to use his power to take nearly all that the serf produced was mitigated by the personalized character of their relationship.

The serf was also protected by the limited nature of the motives for the lord to exploit him: to finance a crusade, the church, and the lord's high level of consumption. However, with only limited trade, the lord was less inclined to extract a surplus from the serfs. In modern society, production is for the purpose of selling in the market. As long as the businessman can sell, he or she has an incentive to force employees to produce as much as possible. The greater the demand for goods, the greater is the motive for increased production. In feudal society, short-term variations in production depended only on the weather—an abundance in good years and low yields in times of flood or drought.

Since most production in feudal society was not for the purpose of profit, production costs were not important to the lord. In a capitalist society, the profit motive dictates not only maximizing production to meet demand but also cutting costs by holding down the share of the product received by the workers. The feudal lord had no motive to attempt to force the serf to work the highest number of hours or at the fastest pace possible, nor to subsist on the least possible portion of his product. This statement should not be interpreted to mean that the life of a serf was a bed of roses. Low productivity made it difficult for the serf to produce much beyond his own needs, and even though the demands of the lord were limited, the serf was often pressed severely to meet them.

The absence of the profit motive had another effect: There was little incentive to try to increase productivity by technological innovation. Production can be increased and costs can be cut by pressing workers to work longer and harder or to consume less, but technological innovation can also achieve these goals by reducing the amount of labor required for a given level of production. Thus, in feudal society, change was so slow as to be virtually absent. Production both in agriculture and in artisan crafts was simple and required few tools. There was little investment in equipment for production. The values of hard work and saving in order to accumulate more wealth, power, or social position had no place in feudalism.

Comparing the traditional sector in contemporary Latin America with early European feudalism, the same individualized, personalistic social relations prevail in the rural life of most countries. Nonetheless, these relations are emphasized in the diffusion model. Peasants living on the large farms and plantations, the *latifundia*, and those who work tiny plots of land, the *minifundia*, seem much like feudal serfs. They, too, are subject to the arbitrary power of the *latifundistas*, who compose only about 1 percent of the landowners but who own over half of the land in Latin America and an even larger share in some of the individual countries. However, since the Second World War there has been a rapid decline in noncapitalist social relations, such as payment of rent for land in kind rather than in cash. In the words of Alain de Janvry, "precapitalist social relations (semifeudal and communal) have disappeared from Latin America" (1981: 120). Although the millions of families living in poverty on small subsistence plots may appear to be remnants of feudalism, their work is structurally linked with modern commercial agriculture.[4]

Politics in rural society are not characterized by competitive bargaining or negotiation. Power is held by the class of owners. Moreover, among the traditional *latifundistas*, the give and take of bargaining is precluded by an orientation toward an interpersonal relationship called *dignidad*. Similar in some respects to the feudal code of chivalry, this relationship places too great an emphasis on honor to provide for regularized confrontation in which one party may lose. Nor is bargaining part of the authoritarian style of even the modern commercial sector.

Technological levels in Latin American agriculture are low compared with those in the advanced capitalist countries. However, the image of an unchanging countryside is obsolete. Although investment in the production of food crops generally remains low, in recent years the use of machinery and fertilizers, for example, has grown rapidly in the production of export and industrial crops.

In approaches that emphasize a diffusion of capitalist development, these changes are interpreted as the vanquishing of feudalism, the demise of the feudal concept of landownership as a source of prestige and of power over the peasants who live on it in favor of the modern, capitalist idea that land is a factor of production used to earn the maximum possible profit. However, the change in Latin America is highly uneven and far more complex than this analysis would suggest (see de Janvry 1981: esp. 68–81, 151–174).

Commerce as a Road to Development

According to the diffusion model of capitalist development, feudal Latin America can and should develop as feudal England did. In England, change occurred when technological progress permitted the creation of an agricultural surplus and its transportation. An increasing urban population could then be supported because the people on the land could produce more than they needed to live and reproduce. Urban migration was also spurred when, with the rise of wool production and trade, the common lands on which the serfs relied began to be enclosed for private use. This process began to increase in the fourteenth century and continued through much of the 1800s.

Trade grew and so did the amount of goods produced for sale in the new market. With these initial changes, several trends were set in motion. The new towns and cities became a haven for serfs starved out by the enclosure system as well as for artisans who gained an opportunity to escape the manorial system to make a living in the new commercial and manufacturing centers. In the towns, the artisans became small businessmen and sold their crafts for profit. The people who assisted the master craftsmen were bound to them as apprentices to learn their trade while being tied to the master in essentially the same kind of relationship they had had with the lord of the estate. As technology advanced, manufacturing became more complex, and the investment in tools became greater. Alongside the master craftsman, there arose a different type of manufacturer, the person who owned and administered the factory but did not work in production.

With the coming of the Industrial Revolution, the steps in manufacturing were divided up and thereby simplified. Whereas it once took an apprentice many years to learn all the aspects of a craft, a person now could do a simple job with hardly any training. The apprentice was replaced by the modern worker, who became dependent upon his wage to buy the necessities of life, which he could no longer produce for himself. Thus, the nature of economic and social relationships changed. The lord-serf and the master-apprentice forms affected many aspects of those people's lives. These relationships were highly personalized under a system of patronage in which an exchange of favors took place. But these forms gave way to the more impersonal and limited relationship of employer and employee, which was based on wages. No longer were workers tied to the land or the households of their masters. They were free to sell their labor for the highest wage it would bring on the market.

As trade increased, more agricultural products were sold in markets. Just as the labor of the worker was assigned a price, the status of land changed. Once the only base of power and prestige in society, inherited by the lord and passed on to his male children, land became just another factor of production and was subject to sale for a price. It became an investment that had a monetary value. a value determined by the profit that could be made through selling what was produced on the land. All of the factors of production—land, labor, and capital—acquired a monetary equivalent and followed the demands of the market.

In the perspective of the diffusion model, commerce was an essential stimulus in the development of England. Capitalism arose out of feudalism through the revival of commerce, and increased trade supplied a motive for creating a larger and more continuous surplus. The new merchant and artisan classes that were created grew and eventually took over existing nonagricultural settlements, which had not been centers of economic activity before the increased commerce. Trade was more important than early manufacturing, and the struggle against the feudal order was led by the large merchants. They consolidated their control over the towns and contended with the feudal lords whose interests, according to the interpretation of the traditional approach, were opposed to their control. Over several centuries feudalism was defeated as the market penetrated the countryside and the political power and the ideology of the new bourgeoisie achieved dominance. The economic, social, and political changes that arose from the resurgence of trade created conditions that made the Industrial Revolution and modern capitalist society possible

The model perceives the cities of Latin America as the focus of modernization and development, reaching out to the countryside just as the medieval towns did centuries ago. Latin America is the most urbanized area of the world outside of North America and Western Europe as it is estimated that 40 to 50 percent of all Latin Americans live in urban areas. Although some of this concentration is due to population growth within the cities, the rate and scale of migration to urban areas in Latin America has not been equaled in any other area of the world. During the period 1930–1960 the population of Latin America doubled, and the twenty-two largest cities more than tripled in population (Ruddle and Hamour 1972: 4). From 1960 to 1980 the trend continued, though at a lower rate. Although the rate of growth of the overall population was 2.6 percent, urban growth was 4.2 percent. At present approximately 64 percent of all Latin Americans live in cities of 20,000 or more, and it is estimated that the proportion will reach 80 percent by the year 2025 (Wilkie and Haber 1983: 88).

In the major cities, one finds tall buildings, superhighways, and traffic jams. There are shops where the finest goods from all over the capitalist world can be purchased. In the business district, there is an appearance of wealth and modernity that contrasts sharply with rural poverty and tradition. The streets are filled with business people and office workers. In the cities, this new sector seems to represent a society that has moved far beyond the feudalism of the countryside toward a developed capitalist society.

Old ways do still persist. Speculation in tangible urban real estate is more attractive than purchasing stocks, which is only an abstract representation of wealth. Manufacturing methods and equipment considered obsolete in the United States are employed alongside modern assembly plants. Small workshops in which the owner works in production with his employees continue to exist. At the same time more large factories are being built. In the new firms, the managers are hired by the owners and own a small share of the firms they manage. The large work force employed by these factories is organized into unions to bargain for better wages and working conditions. Although the cities are ringed by vast slums filled with residents who do not participate in political life, the organized workers and the middle class have an important vote in those nations that hold elections.

It is not only in political and economic life that the city seems to be the agent of change. Cultural values and orientations, especially among the middle sectors, are changing too. The traditional attitudes about the roles of the sexes, embodied in machismo, give men the virtues of aggressiveness and freedom of action while confining women in dependent passivity to the houses of their parents or their husbands. Once alternatives to this reliance carried with them social disapproval and the implication of immorality, but now, in the cities, women working outside the home have achieved greater acceptance. The practice of dating has changed considerably from the time when it used to be required that an unmarried female be chaperoned at all times. In many countries, feminist movements have even arisen. Initially, their ideologies were directed more toward placing increased legal constraints on male chauvinism than on gaining greater freedom for the females, and emphasis was placed on measures that would provide very basic security for the health and safety of children. Since the mid-1970s, groups with ideas that are more similar to those of radical feminists in the advanced capitalist countries have begun to appear, and they are interested in lesbianism and other alternatives to the traditional family. Conditions of urban life have also made some inroads into the strength of the extended family in favor of the nuclear family.

Requirements of modern economic life have begun to affect the typical casualness with which Latin Americans have traditionally regarded the clock. In business, the importance of personal relationships, though still great in comparison with North American practice, has lessened because of the acceptance of more modern orientations of economic life. In the past, Latins had contempt for North American materialism, and they gave more emphasis to aristocratic values of the inner person, personal philosophy, and the personality a person projected. In a society in which social mobility was virtually absent, the traditional poor were not made to feel they were failures because they were poor, and they could maintain a sense of self-respect and inner dignity, regardless of social status. However, in the urban middle sector, a shift has been under way for some time toward attitudes about work, consumption, and getting ahead that are close to orientations prevailing in the United States. Among some members of the middle sector, North American tastes in food and even fads in fashion and popular music have replaced traditional preferences. Partly in reaction to this cultural penetration, the New Song movement arose in the 1960s among progressive Latin American youth. Using traditional native instruments, and sometimes contemporary international electronic ones, the followers of this movement draw upon folk traditions of the past and contemporary periods.

A Dual Society in Transition to Capitalism

The picture we have drawn suggests that many nations may be composed of two societies, one feudal and the other capitalist. Such an assumption has led many observers of Latin America to query if its dual society is essentially feudal or capitalist. Or is the hinterland feudal while the city is capitalist? The tendency among the followers of the diffusion model is to accept the latter suggestion; to understand the conquest of Indo-America by Iberians as a process in which the feudalism of Spain and Portugal was transferred to the New World; to view the cities of Latin America as having been brought into capitalism through commercial contact with more modern nations; and to characterize the countryside as remaining in stagnant feudalism because of its isolation from the dynamic forces of capitalism. The prescription called for by this diagnosis of Latin American underdevelopment is clearly the capitalist penetration of the hinterland to free it from feudalism.

Compared with the countryside, the city is the center of Latin American modernity in political, economic, social, and cultural matters. It seems to be the source of the challenge to traditions that have apparently immobilized the resources of the land and the energy of the people. This perception of the cities in relation to the rest of each respective nation relegates the countryside to the status of a peripheral area, which, because of its poverty and backwardness, is holding back and dragging down the thrust of the vital metropolis within each country. The tasks of capitalist modernization and development are to free the rural population from the arbitrary power of the landowners; propel both land and labor into the realm of the market, where they can be effectively employed to bring about economic growth; increase the middle class to provide upward mobility and reduce the conflict of class polarization; and create an expanding industrial capacity, not only for prosperity but also as a base for labor unions and modern forms of both political and economic representation. It appears that to achieve these tasks—tasks nations such as the United States and Western Europe have already substantially accomplished—it will be necessary to extend to the countryside the wealth, methods, and modern ideas that are growing in the cities.

This view of the relationship of the city to the countryside includes a parallel interaction between developed and underdeveloped nations. The metropolis—with reference to Latin America, the leading center is the United States—provides the capital for new industry, the technology and methods of organization necessary for modern production, and a set of values appropriate to developing modern capitalist society. Since the most direct linkage with the periphery, the underdeveloped nations, is with their major cities, it is to be expected that the seeds of modernization and development will germinate in these cities and spread to even the most remote areas of the underdeveloped countryside.

Just as technological progress brought forth an entirely new form of production and economic organization hundreds of years ago in the history of the now developed countries, the capital and technology introduced by these nations into the underdeveloped world are transforming the underdeveloped economies. And just as the new economic organization created a new class in Western Europe, the growing industrialization of Latin America under the sponsorship of the United States is giving birth to a new middle class of ever-increasing importance. In Western Europe, an industrial bourgeoisie integrated the nation-state; created the mechanism for savings, investment, and capital accumulation; struggled against arbitrary rights in a secular state; and later, supported labor to build an adequate system of social welfare. The perspective we have described has placed the burden of economic, political, and social progress on Latin America's middle sectors, supported by the activities of North American private and government agencies.

Thus, according to the diffusion model of capitalist development, the solutions to the problems and conditions of underdevelopment must originate from beyond the borders of Latin America. Development is to be diffused from metropolis to periphery: from the United States and other industrialized countries to the national urban centers, from this metropolis to regional trading cities, from these centers to the periphery. The process involves the increased integration of the hinterland with its metropolis at each level, a strengthening of the linkages already established. In this view, though the problems are enormous, development following the path first traveled by England centuries ago is under way. But the pace must be accelerated, primarily by expanding the introduction of capital and new technology from the developed countries. What is required is the creation of economic and political conditions that can attract the greater participation of foreign enterprise.

3

A Model of Dependency and Capitalist Underdevelopment

Over the last two decades an alternative view to the model of capitalist development has taken shape in the writings of a number of scholars, both Latin American and North American. It finds that foreign penetration did indeed transform traditional societies in Latin America. However, the result has not been capitalist development leading to stable, high-mass-consumption societies resembling the United States. Instead, in Latin America a dependent form of capitalism emerged, and this political-economic configuration stifled indigenous progressive capitalist forces. As a result, only recently has industrialization taken hold, and even now mainly in the larger countries. Moreover, industrial development has been led, not by indigenous forces in accordance with national development needs, but by transnational corporations pursuing the needs of their global balance sheets. Although economic growth and industrialization have taken place, the benefits of growth have not been distributed. In fact, associated aspects of the process and the loss of both agricultural and urban employment have worsened conditions for the majority of the people. Often, developmentalist policies of austerity and labor discipline have worsened living conditions and brought about severe political repression.

According to this view, poverty and underdevelopment have been the result of a dependency arising from the integration of Latin America into the world capitalist system, and therefore, development through socialism is usually advocated. Instead of supporting the thrust of U.S. policies, this alternate view asserts the necessity of a complete reversal of action if the United States is to become a positive force for development in Latin America.

Theotonio Dos Santos offers a generally accepted description of dependency:

By dependence we mean a situation in which the economy of certain countries is conditioned by the development and expansion of another economy to which the former is subjected. The relation of interdependence between two or more economies, and between these and world trade, assumes the form of dependence when some countries (the dominant ones) can expand and can be self-sustaining, while other countries (the dependent ones) can do this only as a reflection of that expansion, which can have either a positive or a negative effect on their immediate development. [Dos Santos 1970: 231]

Departing from this notion of dependency, we now examine the assumptions underlying this interpretation of development and underdevelopment. We do so through a critical assessment of "dualism" as a dominant characteristic of Latin American society and through an analysis of different classes that may dominate particular societies in Latin America. Finally, using the model as a framework for discussion, we look at the consequences of dependent development in Spain and Latin America.

Assumptions of the Model

The model of Latin American capitalist underdevelopment identifies contemporary Latin American social and economic structures that have been shaped by economic dependency, and it distinguishes underdeveloped Latin America from precapitalist England and Europe. Instead of hypothesizing that underdevelopment is an original state, it asserts that the now developed countries were never underdeveloped and that contemporary underdevelopment was *created*. Ironically, the very same process (the expansion of capitalism) through which the now developed countries progressed brought underdevelopment to many parts of Latin America. Imperialism has dominated Latin America from the extraction of gold and silver through the penetration of commercial capital and, later, financial and manufacturing capital. The most significant result of the colonial heritage is not a system of values or cultural orientations but economies shaped by the needs of the center of the expanding system. When the center of the system has needed to acquire raw materials and to sell finished goods, Latin America has responded as both supplier and market. Although the United States has replaced Great Britain as the metropolis and although Latin American imports now include producers' goods to supply manufacturers of consumer goods within Latin America, dependency has not changed. In fact, it has deepened through greater foreign corporate, government, and foundation penetration of banking, manufacturing, retailing, communications, advertising, and education.

The results of this penetration have not changed in nature. Although the demand for agricultural commodities is limited, the demand for manufactured goods, particularly the goods produced with higher-level technologies, is not. Moreover, agricultural markets are characterized by a high level of competition while there is much more economic concentration in the manufacturing of producers' goods. As a result, the higher level of technology and greater economic power result in high prices for foreign imports while the prices of Latin American exports follow a long-term downward trend. Capital is drained through repatriated profits, interest payments on loans, and fees for royalties, insurance, and shipping. Within each country, the pattern of metropolis-periphery relations is replicated: The economic surplus of the countryside is drained into the urban areas through a process of internal colonialism. The countryside is poor, not because it is feudal or traditional, but because it has enriched the cities. Latin America is underdeveloped because it has supported the development of Western Europe and the United States.

The political result of economic dependency also has not changed. Just as the landowning class and the merchants who over the past century exported Latin America's wealth pursued their interests in maintaining economic relationships abroad, modern industrial managers and higher military officers favor foreign interests. They also fear the demands of the masses within their own nations, preferring a military dictatorship to nationalistic reform or revolution.

The solution to the underdevelopment does not lie in increased penetration. More foreign investment does bring an expanded GNP, but it does not create self-sustaining economic development. Outside control is enhanced; outward capital flows increase. Investment decisions continue to be based on plans for improved profitability and balanced development of multinational corporations rather than on domestic employment and production needs. Economic growth does not even reduce poverty since few jobs are generated by the new technology and less advanced domestic competition is eliminated. Development requires the profound alteration of economic, social, and political relationships in the overthrow of the market and the mobilization of domestic populations in a nationally oriented effort. Thus, development requires the elimination of foreign penetration, which supports the status quo, and the creation of a socialist context for development.

Although this model agrees that the characteristics employed by the diffusion model to define underdevelopment are typical of underdeveloped areas, underdevelopment is not defined by them. Instead, the most significant defining characteristic is the economic dependency that has shaped the economies, social structures, and political systems of underdeveloped regions and countries, producing the characteristics by which underdevelopment is recognized.

In fact, "growth without development is a frequent experience in the past and present of the now underdeveloped countries" (Cockcroft, Frank, and Johnson 1972: xv) so the model does not measure development by per capita GNP or the indices of modernity. Economic development includes the establishment of economic sovereignty (which does not imply isolation) and a level of productivity and a pattern of distribution that adequately provide for the basic (culturally determined) needs of the entire population, generating a surplus for investment in continued national development. The social and political aspects of development are less clearly stated, but they generally include equality, the elimination of alienation, the provision of meaningful work, and forms of social, economic, and political organization that enable all members of society to influence the decisions which affect them.

The two models offer different definitions of underdevelopment. The model of capitalist development is ahistorical, embodying a tacit assumption that underdevelopment is an aboriginal state—that underdeveloped areas have always been underdeveloped. Underdevelopment is the starting point on the road to development, a condition that has characterized every region and nation-state, from which some have advanced toward development. In contrast, the model of capitalist underdevelopment believes that both underdevelopment and capitalist development (which should not be confused with the conception of development stated above) are the products of the same historical process, the expansion of international capitalism. Through this process, the political, economic, and military forces of the system's center have penetrated underdeveloped areas, creating development in the metropolis and underdevelopment in the periphery (Frank 1966a, 1967a). This perspective incorporates the history of the underdeveloped areas as well as their integration into the expanding system. As expressed by Frank: "Neither the past nor the present of the underdeveloped countries resembles in any important respect the past of the now developed countries. The now developed countries were never *under* developed, though they may have been *un*developed" (Cockcroft, Frank, and Johnson 1972: 3).

The model of capitalist underdevelopment finds many interpretations of Latin American development based on England's transition to capitalism superficial. The economy of undeveloped feudal England did not respond to an international market. By the time this market had been established as a major force, England was in a position to meet all challenges to its domination of the market. English economic growth, especially decisions regarding investment in both infrastructure and production, was determined by the indigenous elites whose interests were shaped initially by internal conditions. External markets provided incentives for the growth of a diversified industrial economy.

In contrast, from the first moment of European penetration, the underdeveloped nations of Latin America were dominated by external elites and markets. These forces created monocultural economies, and infrastructural development was oriented toward agricultural export. Competition from already industrialized countries stifled attempts toward indigenous industrialization, and a configuration of political-economic interests within the host nations resulted in a suppression of national capitalist forces favoring independent development by the forces that were benefiting from the existing economic patterns. As the center of an expanding capitalist system, England traded from a position of superiority. Terms of trade were favorable for English goods, so England was not burdened with a foreign debt. The English economy has always been controlled by the English. Thus, the surplus exploited from the English peasants and workers was invested in the creation of a developing capitalist economy. The overseas expansion of this economy has, initially via Spain and Portugal, appropriated the surplus created by the labor of Latin America (Stein and Stein 1970).

Isolated and therefore necessarily self-sufficient societies of Indo-America became dependent on English goods and markets as a consequence of foreign penetration and the influence of Iberian elites. The economic and social structures created and perpetuated by dependence have resulted in contemporary societies that are different from that of feudal England.

The Myth of a Dual Society

In spite of the existence of a feudalistic ideology and social relationships in the countryside, advocates of the model of capitalist underdevelopment reject the characterization of Latin America as a dual society in transition to capitalism. In brief, the feudal images projected by the huge estates only hide a more important reality: Unlike the economy of feudal England, the Latin American economy responds to market influences.

The market system in Latin America creates underdevelopment rather than development. With the advent of commercial capitalism in England, the market operated to mobilize resources for their most productive use. In contrast, land and labor are grossly underutilized in Latin America under the market system. The traditionalism of the countryside is not due to isolation and should not be viewed in isolation. In fact, its poverty and its conservatism are reinforced by its relationship to the city. Moreover, while the growth and expansion of the market in England gave rise to a dynamic entrepreneurial class, which took command of society and led the transformation into the Industrial Revolution, in Latin America the forces of the market system first suppressed and then co-opted this class. Contrary to the diffusion model, development will not necessarily be brought about by intensifying relations between the hinterland and the city, between Latin America and the developed capitalist nations, or by strengthening the capitalist class. Instead, development requires the overthrow of capitalism and imperialism and the creation of a socialist context for development.

Economic development requires the investment of an economic surplus to increase future productivity. The surplus must not only be produced and accumulated; it must also be invested. The potential for producing some surplus has existed in virtually all societies. That is, there have been few instances in which a society could not get from its environment more than the minimum necessary to subsist if conditions existed that created a reason to do so. Feudal serfs were forced to produce some surplus. The days they labored in the fields of the lord and the crops, later money, they paid in rent represented such a surplus, since they managed to subsist and reproduce even though they had to give up a portion of their labor and/or their product. The surplus was for the most part consumed by the lord and his household or the nobles or the church hierarchy to whom the lord owed allegiance. The part of the surplus that was not consumed was accumulated, but it did not thus contribute to raising productivity. It was not accumulated as an investment but as an ostentatious display in castles and churches, which did nothing to bring about economic development.

The rise of commerce in England did lead to the development of an independent capitalist society, but only indirectly. Its direct effect was to accumulate surplus, which was invested in expanding trade to accumulate more surplus. Through this process of commercial accumulation, capital was available to invest in altering the process of production. But this most important development required the ascendancy of a manufacturing class with the motive and the ideology to do so (Mandel 1968: 95–131).

Commerce does not necessarily result in the growth of a manufacturing class, nor does it necessarily destroy the power or the ideology of the feudal nobility (Hilton 1952: 32–43; Hibbert 1953). It provides an incentive for the lord to extract a greater surplus from his serfs so that he can sell it to purchase luxury goods. But this change can be accomplished *within* the manorial system, using the position accorded the lord in feudal society to make possible the increased demands on the serf. Ironically, instead of breaking feudal bonds in favor of a system of free labor, traditional relationships and agricultural methods are preserved, and the only change is a greater extraction of surplus from the serfs.

The commercialization of agriculture in this fashion is in accord with the interests of the merchants whose livelihood comes from purchasing agricultural produce from the landed nobility and supplying them with luxury items. However, for a number of reasons, commercialization is incompatible with the growth of manufacturing. First, the introduction of more productive agricultural methods is limited. Any innovation that might threaten the manorial system will be resisted by the lord, who correctly sees such a change as a threat to the social structure on which he relies to expropriate some of what his serfs produce. The value of the traditional system to the landed nobility also reinforces the conservative predisposition that rejects innovation on ideological grounds. Without great advances in agricultural productivity, most of the labor supply remains tied to the land and is not available to work in manufacturing. Moreover, when rent to the lord is in labor or in kind for use of land, the peasant remains largely outside the money economy.

When payment is in money, he is forced into direct contact with the market by the need to sell his produce to pay his rent, but he receives little more than what he must pay the lord. In neither case are the serfs able to buy manufactured goods, and a potential manufacturing sector is denied an internal market for its products, which is essential to its growth.

Thus, the commercial road out of feudalism can result in an apparently dual society. In the towns, wealth accumulates from both commercial and financial activities, and a white-collar class of clerks employed in these activities emerges. Free artisans produce for the urban market. The life of the towns is founded on buying cheap and selling dear. The urban economy supports an ideology, involving speculation and risk, different from that of the manor. The goal is profit to use in larger transactions to make a still greater profit. Based on the wealth drawn from the countryside, the trading cities become relatively modern prosperous centers of commerce. In the countryside, the manorial system remains. Personalistic social relationships are continued, and the same productive methods are used. The feudal way of life appears virtually unchanged. The heavy extractions on the serfs made by the landed nobility to get the produce they need to pay for luxury goods keep the serfs in poverty. What has changed is the motive for production. Dominance of production for consumption by the serf and the household of the lord with random additional demands for taxes and tribute to outside authorities gives way to production for sale to merchants who transport the product far beyond the manor. As a result, questions arise concerning what will be produced on the estate and in what amounts. The decisions made in response to these questions are influenced by changes in market conditions, which are reflected in the prices and terms that are brought to the manor by the merchants.

The qualification, an "apparently" dual society, is used because of the crucial importance of the link between the city and the countryside. Examined in isolation, the countryside appears to be poor and traditional simply because outside agents of change have not yet arrived on the scene. But as explained above, conservatism is reinforced by the opportunity of the landowners to make a profit by using the traditional system to increase their exploitation of the serfs or peasants. The relationship of external influences to traditional modes of production is not always the same. It is in the exploration of the many and varied interactions that have occurred, and continue to occur, that we are likely to gain a deeper understanding of the historical and contemporary role of imperialism in Latin America. This is only one aspect of the relationship between the apparently feudal countryside and the city.

What Kind of Bourgeoisie?

Both local and long-distance trade have existed for thousands of years. Commercial capitalism in England was a prelude to the development of industrial capitalism, but in Latin America, society could not develop without the existence of a foreign market. That is, the heightened systematic exploitation of the countryside, not through taxation—as, for example, in eighteenth-century France—but through an extension of the market system, occurs only when a market for agricultural products exists beyond the manor. If demand is in the city, then the growth of a manufacturing bourgeoisie can be expected. To pursue its interests, this class must bring land and labor into the market, and it must integrate the nation. Increased domestic trade requires that a system of roads be maintained and that the nation be unified to provide free right of travel on those roads. A body of law must be established that provides for the transfer of property ownership. Policies must be adopted to force unproductive serfs and lords from the estates so that both land and labor may be subject to the efficient allocation of the market. As economic enterprises become larger, mechanisms for joint investment must be established. As manufacturing grows, the nation requires land and naval military power to develop and protect its international trade. An efficient tax system must be established that can finance these ventures without absorbing all the resources it collects.

If the market for the agricultural products is not in the cities but in a foreign nation, then commerce will strengthen the landowners and merchants of the agricultural nation and thus bring about the dominance of an agrocommercial bourgeoisie. This class does not need a good system of roads, except for transport to the sea. It does not require, and in fact is threatened by, a strong central government that raises revenues to finance public projects. And it is not in the interests of this class to carry out development tasks that would conflict with and therefore threaten its relationship to the metropolis. Consequently, it rejects policies that would encourage the growth of an independent manufacturing bourgeoisie. Industries develop only in areas that do not conflict with metropolitan competition, and in these fields, manufacturing tends to arise as an extension of agrarian capital, not in opposition to it.

Under the policies of the agrocommercial class, the agricultural nation acquires the characteristics of a dual society. And it does not develop. Although capital is accumulated in the cities through commerce and finance, it is not applied to production. Therefore, labor does not become more productive. The market for manufactures is confined to luxury goods for the rich and does not grow. The social structure remains static: an upper class of wealthy urban merchants and "feudal" landowners who rule; a fragmented middle class of clerks, bureaucrats, artisans, and independent professionals; and a lower class of serfs or peasants in the countryside and various laborers and apprentices in the cities. The countryside is dominated by the market forces of an international capitalist economy.

Are these agricultural nations dominated by an agrocommercial bourgeoisie? Can a capitalist society arise without a strong national manufacturing bourgeoisie? It is this class that, historically in the now developed capitalist countries, has been given the role of acting sometimes consciously and at other times unwittingly or even unwillingly as the revolutionary agent of social transformation. It is this class of people, pursuing their self-interest at times individually and at others collectively, that has used the surplus accumulated from the labor of the producing class to change the nature of the economy over which it gains power and to alter the way in which that society interacts with nature to gain the means of its subsistence, thereby changing society itself completely.[5]

The question about the nature of the pre-twentieth-century Latin American political economy has been answered in several ways. The model of capitalist development tends to identify capitalism as the sort of dynamic system that is ever-transforming itself toward higher levels of productivity and prosperity. According to this criterion, capitalism has still to penetrate substantial portions of the countryside in Latin America. The model of capitalist underdevelopment finds no contradiction in a capitalist society that is ruled by an agrocommercial bourgeoisie and is characterized by underdevelopment. Although peasants are tied to the haciendas and plantations much as serfs were tied to the feudal manor, they participate in a production process that is characterized as capitalist because its products were destined for international markets. In these terms, a nation may become capitalist through its integration into another economic system that has already achieved the strength and dynamism by which the capitalism of Western Europe and the United States (and more recently, Japan) have been characterized.

Together, these two types of nations, one dominated by a manufacturing bourgeoisie and the other by an agrocommercial bourgeoisie that responds to the demands of the more developed nation, constitute a single system. Just as the underdeveloped nation may appear to consist of two separate societies, this system may appear to be a sort of dual society: one dominant nation, capitalist and developed, and the other dependent nation, feudal and underdeveloped. But this view ignores the linkages described above, which, to repeat Dos Santos's description of dependence, create "a situation in which the economy of certain countries is conditioned by the development and expansion of another economy to which the former is subjected" (Dos Santos 1970: 231).

Spain and Latin America:
The Consequences of Dependent Underdevelopment

Even though it had participated in the conquest of Latin America, Spain itself became a dependent nation because it was unable to use the riches extracted from the New World to promote economic development. To do so would have required that the wealth from the colonies find its way into the production process as an investment in the Spanish economy. Had the proper economic and social basis existed in Spain, this situation might have occurred. That is, if a manufacturing bourgeoisie had been dominant in Spain in the sixteenth century, American silver would have paid for the expansion of Spanish industry, and the interest in industrial expansion would probably have led this group to unify and consolidate the divided country. The price inflation in Spain caused by the arrival of colonial wealth would have enabled the manufacturers to raise their profits by even more than the increase brought about by expanded production since, as occurred in England, wages would have increased more slowly than prices. When the flow of silver declined in the first half of the seventeenth century, Spain would have been left with an established industrial economy and would have been in a strong competitive position in Europe and the Americas. Even without the flow of precious metals, the nation would probably have proceeded on a course of national development characterized by continuous techno-logical, economic, and social change organized by a nationally oriented manufacturing bourgeoisie.

In some respects, the conquest of the Americas was an extension of the earlier reconquest of Spain from the Moors. Conditions in the repopulation of the northern regions of Old and New Castile in the ninth through the eleventh centuries tended to favor the growth of a class of small freeholders, both owners and leaseholders. Early in the period frontier conditions encouraged an independence that was contrary to the development of feudalism. In the later portion of this period settlement took place under different circumstances, which nonetheless encouraged a tradition of small settlers to possess their own lands (Malefakis 1970).

Several conditions contributed to a rather different formation of the later reconquests. In the twelfth century increased fighting with the Moors lead to the development of three powerful military orders in Spain, which played a crucial role in the thirteenth-century reconquest of Andalusia and the other southern lands. As would later occur in the conquest of Spanish America, military chiefs and strongmen were rewarded with extensive land grants. The southern region was large, over three-fourths the size of Old and New Castile. There was no surplus Christian population to fill the land, and the Muslims who remained after the reconquest had an uncertain status that encouraged quiescence. Thus, there was no pressure to break up the estates into smaller holdings. With labor often in short supply, using the land for pasture was more feasible than planting crops. Finally, it is important that the thirteenth century also saw the rise of a demand for wool in northern Europe. According to Edward Malefakis,

> In contrast to Old and New Castile, the rural social structure of Christian Andalusia was shaped from the beginning by foreign demand for Spanish wool exports, a demand which continued for more than three centuries. . . . The joint effect of the servile rural population, the basic economic changes, and the fundamental political transformation that the appearance

of a well-articulated military aristocracy implied was to incline Southern Spain in the direction of a latifundistic system of land tenure. Once established, this system . . . tended to perpetuate itself. [Malefakis 1970: 57–58]

The Castilian economy underwent a substantial economic expansion in the thirteenth through the fifteenth centuries, based largely on the export of wool. This economic prosperity involved the participation of only certain regions of the kingdom of Castile: "It was a peripheral development, with one center in the montala region of Santander and the Basque Country and the other in Andalusia, and both these centers were in close contact with, and even dependent on, foreign activity" (Vicens Vives 1976: 241).

Already economically dependent on the rest of Europe at the time of the conquest of the Americas, the Spanish kingdom was divided sharply into regions. In Castile, commercial capitalism was already well established. In Andalusia the merchants required a trade monopoly and limited trade to the inland port of Seville. But the conquest became a force to heighten regionalism rather than national integration.

After the conquest, the economic pattern based on trading Spanish wool and iron ore to England, France, Holland, and Italy in return for ironware, steel, nails, textiles, and paper was altered only by the Spanish using precious metals as commodities for trade. The Spanish food, clothing, and hardware industries expanded in response to demand from the colonies in the first half of the sixteenth century, but they later were overwhelmed by English, Dutch, French, and northern Italian competitors (Stein and Stein 1970: 4–20, 44–53). The prices of Spanish goods were too high to compete with their products because of the price inflation caused by the silver of Peru and Mexico. Although this wealth might have been used to subsidize Spanish manufacturers and although other trade restrictions might have kept out English competition, the interests of the Spanish merchants lay in a pattern of exchanging precious metals for European goods. Even though the commercial class increasingly became an agent for English capital, its domestic position grew stronger because of the increased importance of trade in Spain.

With the decline of silver, beginning around 1630, Spain's role in the Americas was weakened. Without economic power, Spain could do nothing to hold the colonies, and during the boom, nothing had been accumulated. The benefits had gone to other European nations, especially England, and after the wars of independence they dropped the Spanish linkage to the Americas and dominated the area directly.

Thus, though a great deal of wealth passed through Spanish ports, little remained when the boom was over. The pattern of economic activity and the technology employed in production remained unchanged. The export-oriented commercial capitalists and the commercial landowners had been strengthened, but their interests lay in fulfilling a narrowly defined role in an international economic system. They fulfilled that role and maintained a stagnant status quo in Spain.

It was this same pattern of economic activity, with the same combination of ruling interests, that was established in the Americas. In a most fundamental sense, these patterns were not "imported" from Spain any more than feudalism or Latin values were carried across the Atlantic Ocean. Rather, the Spanish Conquest occurred under conditions similar to those of the reconquest of southern Spain three centuries earlier. Huge land grants were made to military conquerors, who had to contend with a scarcity of labor. More important, there was great demand in Europe for precious metals and for certain plantation crops, especially sugar. The existence of the metals and of excellent conditions for growing crops led to the creation of economies that sustained these demands. The forces were sufficiently strong to overcome obstacles such as a shortage of labor, which could have caused different patterns to arise. Although the conquistadores and those who followed them across the ocean brought with them the cultural orientations of the society into which they had been born, these norms—authoritarianism, hierarchy, machismo, dignity, and the concept that physical labor is degrading— were perpetuated because the Americas were integrated into the expanding capitalist economy that was centered in England, which came to fulfill a role similar to that of Spain.

The early establishment of mining and plantation agriculture directly led to the creation of an essentially two-class society with a narrow oligarchy at the top. This oligarchy, though quickly characterized by several divisions (*peninsulares* versus *creollos*, liberals versus conservatives, federalists versus centralist-unitaryists, prochurch versus antichurch, etc.), was defined by its relationship with the buyers of its products and the suppliers of its goods—with Europe. The indirect consequences of this economic structure and the social class structure it created may be seen in contemporary cultural orientations as well as in economic policies.

As to the cultural orientations, the values that appeared in both the Iberian Peninsula and the Americas were appropriate for societies in which mining and plantation agriculture predominated and in which ownership of the means of production was highly concentrated. The labor system required outright slavery or conditions approximating slavery. Authoritarianism and hierarchy are characteristic of this type of labor system and are in fact necessary to it. With virtually no mobility, the lower classes had to accept their position, so a fatalistic orientation was encouraged.

In this type of economy, the social classes are sharply distinguished by whether or not they engage in manual labor. A small ruling class can avoid all forms of physical work while the lower classes must participate in manual labor to survive. Physical labor thus becomes a sign of lower class status. This sharp class division also leads to a division of women into the categories of, one, those who are honorable and therefore must be isolated from contact with the lower classes and, two, those who are dishonorable and therefore may be exploited by the landowners without guilt. The situation of the plantation owner as a dictator on his own land encourages a rejection of settling disputes through the courts since accepting arbitration suggests that the *latifundista* is subordinating himself to the authority of the court. In a sense, he would be jeopardizing his sovereignty over his domain.

This explanation of the cultural orientations of Latin America as an indirect result of the economic structure of mining and plantation agriculture is strengthened by comparing the Latin American experience with that of North America. Much of the area that is now the United States was conquered by people who did not share many of the cultural orientations of the Iberians. In the area that is now the northern United States, geography and climate precluded the development of plantation agriculture, and precious metals were not found. The growth of family farms and an economic structure that permitted upward social mobility fostered the growth of concepts such as the dignity of work and discouraged authoritarianism and fatalism. The position of women in the family farm unit, though subordinate, was reinforced by the vital economic role they played. The land tenure system did not lead to an avoidance of arbitration and adjudication of disputes. The area that is now the southern United States was conquered by people of ethnic and national backgrounds similar to those of conquerors of the North. The rise of plantation agriculture, slavery, and a two-class system, however, led to a set of cultural orientations that were quite distinct from those of the North. These southern attitudes and values were very similar to those associated with Latin American culture, even though the two areas differed in religion and ethnic and national origins.

The Latin American economies established during the colonial period created a dependence that has still not been broken. Economic activity was oriented toward the production of commercial crops and precious metals for export; domestic food production and crafts grew up around the mines and were dependent upon the prosperity of mining. Thus, the colonial economies required the maintenance of external markets for exports as exports were necessary to provide foreign exchange to purchase all the products not produced in the colonies, both necessities and luxury goods. This pattern of dependence on the export of a few raw materials in order to satisfy the need to import all the commodities not produced has remained, with some changes, to the present day.[6]

It is not surprising that England shifted from a mercantile policy and trade and proclaimed an ideology of free trade, penetrating to the furthest reaches of the planet in search of materials, markets, and profits. The acceptance of this doctrine of laissez-faire by Latin American elites, on the other hand, might seem to indicate shortsightedness, incompetence, or plain stupidity. However, it must be recognized that the English elites brought about national development in their country by following policies that enhanced the individual position of members of the dominant sector. In Latin America, the original establishment of plantation agriculture and mining for export to the metropolis created oligarchies whose members' individual interests coincided with the maintenance and expansion of the trade patterns, even though they prevented development and created dependence. The behavior of the ruling classes in England and in the colonies was the same—pursuit of immediate self-interest—but the result of this policy was quite different in the two cases because of the structural contexts of the respective elites.

For the metropolis, the flow of raw materials from the colonies constituted fuel for expanding industries, and the colonies' demand for manufactured goods stimulated metropolitan industrial growth. The profit derived from this trade pattern provided investment capital for the metropolis. Industrial expansion confirmed and strengthened the domestic position of the metropolitan industrial bourgeoisie, assuring the dynamic role of this class in orienting its own society. In dependent societies, each boom strengthened the internal position of the agrocommercial elites. The temporary prosperity created by the boom further encouraged monocultural tendencies as the demand for the boom product channeled resources into expansion of production in this limited area while the inflation accompanying the boom priced potential domestic manufactures above those of foreign imports. Moreover, in periods of monocultural expansion, the agrocommercial elites received large profits, which enabled them to purchase foreign goods. From their perspective, change was unnecessary. Change could even be dangerous since existing patterns of exploitation of the masses might be disturbed and trade relations with the metropolis could be disrupted.

At various times, particularly in the twentieth century during the First World War, the Great Depression, and the Second World War, when the industrial nations have been unable to supply manufactured goods and been otherwise preoccupied, the issue of competing with industrial imports and foreign shipping has arisen. However, those members of the bourgeoisie whose interests have coincided with independent national development have rarely been strong enough to prevail over the agrocommercial sector. The few victories have not been permanent, dissolving when the advanced nations have been able to resume preexisting patterns.

Since the 1960s the larger countries of Latin America have experienced important growth in the manufacturing of consumer goods, including consumer durables and automobiles. Brazil even produces aircraft. And although the shift from classic dependence toward dependent development is significant, as Peter Evans (1979) points out, it has taken place within, rather than in opposition to, dependence. It represents a more complete merger of the interests of local and international capital. Moreover, there is a continuity in the structural elements of dependence, including a reliance on external capital as well as an ever-increasing need to earn foreign exchange.

U.S. history provides a parallel to the Latin American experience. In the period following the American War of Independence, the agrocommercial elites of the South argued for a low tariff policy while the industrialists of the North sought to further their aspirations by promoting a protectionist policy. In Latin America, the agrocommercial elites were dominant. Granted, there were additional conditions that gave an advantage to North America; for example, accumulation from shipping, smuggling, and the slave trade provided a larger internal market to stimulate domestic manufacturing. Nevertheless, what has since transpired in the two regions raises the question of which nation the rich resources of North America would have developed if the North's protectionist policy had not ultimately won out in the United States. In any case, economic policies in both hemispheres did not spring from cultural orientations or racial characteristics but from elite interests that were shaped by prevailing economic patterns.

The model of capitalist underdevelopment finds the origins of contemporary underdevelopment in capitalism. Not only was England never underdeveloped because it was never dependent, the very same process of expansion of capitalism by which England progressed brought about the underdevelopment of Latin America. The outward reach of the market brought boom periods to the colonies as they were penetrated. In Mexico and Peru the boom product was silver; in Cuba and on the northeast coast of South America it was sugar; in the interior of Brazil, rubber and coffee; in Chile, nitrates and later copper. Each of these boom periods, though different in length and intensity, left virtually nothing behind upon which self-sustaining growth and development could be based. Like the bullion boom in Spain, created by exploitation of the colonies, the beneficiaries were the developing, not the dependent, nations. The spread of commercial capitalism destroyed existing manufacturing in the colonies and prevented the rise of competition with imported products. Each boom created an inflationary period, which made imported goods cheaper in relation to domestic manufactures. Land and other resources were employed to produce the product that was in demand on the international market. Monocultural economies were created. Infrastructure—roads, railroads, housing, and other facilities—was built to permit and facilitate the extraction of resources and their shipment abroad. Networks of internal communication and transportation were neglected. When the international market for the boom product declined, there remained only symbols of past glory—such as the magnificent opera house that still stands in Manaus, Brazil, a leftover from the days of the rubber boom.

4
Issues of Class and Class Struggle in the Transition to Capitalism

The premises of two models have been carefully elaborated. Through each model we have examined the impact of feudalism and capitalism on Europe and Latin America. We have traced a story of precapitalism, capitalism, and monopoly capitalism in the economic history of Europe, and we have referred to the capitalist expansion in the New World as colonialist and imperialist. We have noted that the consequences for Latin America were considerably different than those for Europe, and the discussion has revealed several crucial issues that are evident in the continuing dialogue about Latin American development and underdevelopment: the dual society, the national bourgeoisie, the ruling class, and the proletariat. These issues relate to the nature of social classes in Latin America, to their struggle internally, and to their ties with the outside world. In the light of the Latin American experience, we now briefly summarize the earlier discussion and relate the interpretation of each issue to the two models. Later in this chapter we examine three major books on particular Latin American nations—Mexico, Argentina, and Peru. Our intention is to make clear to the reader that different models and conceptualizations lead to different analyses and conclusions. Our hope is that the reader will be encouraged to seek a framework that will offer a clear understanding of development and underdevelopment in Latin America.

Dual Society: Feudalism or Capitalism

It might seem odd to the introductory reader that we have stated that our central concern is the condition of Latin Americans today and yet we have spent a great deal of time discussing developments hundreds of years and thousands of miles away. Yet some journalists and scholars continue to emphasize the false assumption that most of Latin America today is a feudal society as England was. This assumption leads to the equally false conclusion that Latin America can and should follow the path first taken by England. We have tried to correct both of these misperceptions through a simple, but careful, review of the most important aspects of feudalism and the different ways in which the two models interpret these aspects in contemporary Latin America.

We have focused on feudalism as the formative core of a European civilization based on two classes: the secular and spiritual lords of the manor and the ecclesiastical estates and the serfs and artisans who were born on those estates and worked in the fields or in the village households that sprang up around the manors. The commercial road out of feudalism resulted in an apparently dual society, in which the towns prospered from commercial and financial activity and the countryside appeared unchanged. Based on the European example, the model of capitalist development anticipates a breakdown of this dual society as the landlords demand new luxury goods produced in the towns in exchange for produce that is transported beyond the estate. Production for consumption on the estate gives way to market conditions, which are reflected in the prices and terms that are brought to the estate by the merchant.

In the past, an apparent feudalism existed in Latin America. Although the relations between landowner and peasant were not as formalized or detailed as in European feudalism, two classes prevailed, and power was held by the class of landowners to whom an immobile peasantry remained obligated in a system of patronage. The model of capitalist development interprets this condition as feudal and separate from the commercialization and industrialization that are evident in the cities of Latin America. The cities are developing while the rural areas remain underdeveloped, a condition that will be corrected when the capitalism of the urban areas is diffused to the backward rural areas. The model of capitalist underdevelopment, however, sees a capitalist link between the city and the countryside that accounts for the persistence of and even promotes underdevelopment and an apparent rural "feudalism." This link is characterized by the commerce between landowners and merchants, who form an agrocommercial bourgeoisie that is subject to the market forces of a national and an international capitalist economy. These differences in the interpretations are clearly illustrated in Table 4.1.

It may be helpful to review briefly some of the interpretations of dual society in Latin America. One interpretation, evident among non-Marxist European and U.S. social scientists, is exemplified by the work of the French geographer Jacques Lambert. He has identified two Brazilian societies: "The dual economy and the dual social structure which accompanies it are neither new nor characteristically Brazilian—they

Table 4.1. Interpretations of the Dual Society[1]

Model of Capitalist Development	Model of Capitalist Underdevelopment
Commerce stimulated the development of England. Capitalism grew from feudalism in the tenth and eleventh centuries. The struggle with feudal lords was led by the large merchants, who consolidated their control over the towns and penetrated the countryside with new markets to establish a bourgeoisie and political and economic dominance.	During the period of the conquest of the Americas, Spain, like England before it, was a country in transition from feudalism to capitalism, a nation of uneven development combining feudal institutions with a relatively strong commercial bourgeoisie that was dealing with foreign markets, especially those in England.
The challenge to feudalism in the Iberian Peninsula was not immediately successful. Thus, the conquest of Indo-America by the Iberians involved the transfer of feudalism to the New World.	The discovery, conquest, and colonization of the Americas were natural developments for the Iberian countries that had begun to break their ties with the rural economy of the Middle Ages. The capitalist purpose of the conquest was the exploration and commercialization of precious metals.
A feudal aristocracy evolved in Latin America and was to predominate to the present day. This aristocracy impeded the development of capitalism and the rise of a progressive "national" bourgeoisie.	The Iberian countries (especially Spain) conquered the Americas in order to incorporate the area into a new system of capitalist production, not to reproduce the European feudal cycle.
In the cities of Latin America, mercantile capitalism was introduced by commercial contact with more modern nations.	Latin American countries were ruled, not by feudal lords, but by a commercial bourgeoisie that had no desire to develop the domestic market or national industry because its basic source of income lay in the export trade.
Through capital and technology the development of the modern metropolitan nations was diffused to the national urban centers in Latin America. If this process were accelerated, there would be a breakdown of the two societies through a diffusion from city to countryside; the result would be an integration of the hinterland with the national and international metropoles.	Although precapitalist relations of production may have contributed to backwardness in the countryside, underdevelopment is also a consequence of the market system. The poverty of the countryside is reinforced by its relationship to the city and to the outside world. Development can be brought about only by the overthrow of capitalism and imperialism.

[1]For a fuller statement and critique of the dual society thesis, see Luis Vitale (Petras and Zeitlin 1968: 34–43).

exist in all unequally developed countries" (Lambert 1959: 105–106), and he would attribute the poverty of the Brazilian Northeast to its isolation, archaic nature, or feudalism. Following a similar line of thinking but basing his analysis on a mixture of contemporary bourgeois social science and Marxist notions, Pablo González Casanova (1970a: esp. chap. 5) attempts to relate the dual society in Mexico to his idea of internal colonialism: One society dominates and exploits the other (marginal and indigenous) in a colonial relationship that is characteristically internal and not dependent on the international order. A more orthodox position of feudalism has been maintained by the pro-Soviet Communist parties of Latin America and by traditional Marxist-Leninists such as Argentine Rodolfo Puiggrós who steadfastly insisted upon a dualist-feudalist framework in order to advocate a revolution in which a progressive bourgeoisie would oppose reactionary landed interests.

In assessing such views, Brazilian economists such as the Marxist Caio Prado Júnior and the radical Celso Furtado would discount Lambert's interpretation of the Northeast and relate the region's underdevelopment to mercantile and capitalist cycles in an international system that brought first growth, then depression, as the focus of the Brazilian economy moved from the sugar plantations of the Northeast to the coffee-growing areas of the South. Rodolfo Stavenhagen would recast González Casanova's concept of internal colonialism and relate it to the international order: What Spain signified to the colony, the colony signified to the indigenous communities. According to Stavenhagen, "What is important is not the mere existence of two 'societies' or a 'dual society' . . . but rather the relationships that exist between these two 'worlds' and bind them into a functional whole" (in Petras and Zeitlin 1968: 16). André Gunder Frank, who has carefully negated all dualist arguments, has criticized the orthodox views of Puiggrós (Frank, 1969a: 331–347), and Frank, in turn, has been criticized by George Novack (1970), who insists that both capitalism and feudalism were combined in a process of uneven development in Latin America. Colonialism, he argues, exploited precapitalist conditions of production for the benefit of the rising capitalist system; precapitalist and mercantile relations coexisted on the *encomiendas* (or large estates), in the mines, and on the sugar plantations where the products of forced and slave labor were sold on the capitalist market.

These interpretations are concerned with identifying the prevailing thrust of economic life in England, Spain (to a lesser extent Portugal), and Latin America. Some qualification may be in order, however, given our stress on the feudal beginnings of England, because historians now know that some capitalist development was evident there even before the Middle Ages and many medievalists emphasize incipient capitalism rather than feudalism in their analyses of European development. We also know that there was a landed aristocracy in Latin America which enjoyed the prestige and status characteristic of feudal lords. Andrew Pearce (in Stavenhagen 1970: 15–20) describes the power of this aristocracy as being "maintained *directly* by the acquisition of labor power and its application to the land *without* deep involvement in market relations." He identifies this early pattern as precapitalist, but he also makes clear that the ranches or rural properties (haciendas or *fazendas*) of today are market oriented, even though they make use of share-tenure and service-tenure labor combined increasingly with wage labor. At the same time the estate "attempts to maintain as much internal subsistence as possible," which makes it "a complicated, rigid structure for which adaptation to modern conditions is extremely difficult." In contrast, the plantation organization of estates was an early response to the European demand for tropical products such as sugar, cotton, and coffee. The plantation thus existed to produce for the market and to make profits for its owners; it "came to signify a capitalistic type of agricultural organization in which a large number of unfree laborers were employed under unified direction and control."

The agricultural backwardness of the past colonial and the present national periods generally has been intimately related to the advanced capitalist sectors of Latin American society. The perpetuation of feudal-like underdevelopment in the backward sectors is seen as a consequence of the monopolistic dominance of imperialist foreign capital in the capitalist areas. The critique of dualism focuses on the *interaction* between these advanced and backward sectors. In spite of the existence of feudal ideology and social relationships in the countryside, this dual society is described as having few feudal remnants. In this view, the feudal images projected by the landed estates only hide the more important reality of capitalist influences. Of course, the result is not a dynamic society characterized by continuous growth, which we usually associate with progressive capitalism. The countryside may be characterized by capitalism, but it is not usually a developed industrialized capitalism. The cities are capitalist, but they often lack a powerful manufacturing bourgeoisie.[7]

National or International Bourgeoisie

The rise of commercialism was followed by industrialization in many parts of Latin America. At the head of this process emerged a "new" manufacturing bourgeoisie, which claimed to be progressive in advocating reform and national development. This segment of the bourgeoisie has often manifested a nationalist xenophobia or resentment against the imperialism that had permeated the hemisphere. This new or "national" bourgeoisie represents a force in the struggle against the old, or international or imperialist, bourgeoisie made up of the agrocommercial class that ruled so long and effectively. There are differing interpretations of the role that this domestic bourgeoisie plays in contemporary Latin America so we will attempt to identify the contrasting perspectives of the two models as traced in Table 4.2. Then we will elaborate upon

Table 4.2. Perspectives of the National Bourgeoisie[1]

Model of Capitalist Development	Model of Capitalist Underdevelopment
The national bourgeoisie is interested in breaking the power and dominion of the landed aristocracy because of a profound conflict of interests between the new and old bourgeoisies (modern commercial and industrial entrepreneurs versus the traditional aristocracy or oligarchy).	Agricultural, financial, and industrial interests are often found in the same economic groups, the same firms, and even the same families. Thus, the capital of archaic *latifundias* may be invested in lucrative enterprise in the cities, or the grand families of the city, who are associated with foreign capital, may also be the owners of the backward *latifundias*.
In overcoming the power of the landlords, the national bourgeoisie (the manufacturing class) will provide for the modernization of agriculture and industry. They will lead in the drive for social reforms and political democracy. Imperialist capital will prompt the national bourgeoisie to take an anti-imperialist stand against the alliance of the landowning aristocracy and imperialist foreign interests.	The combined interests of the land-owning aristocracy and the urban commercial bourgeoisie will be aligned with the interests of the manufacturing bourgeoisie. Tied to the dominant class interests and dependent on world imperialism for the manufacture of some goods, for foreign currency, and for foreign capital, the national or domestic bourgeoisie has no choice other than to accept its condition as a dependent bourgeoisie.
The national bourgeoisie will promote development through the diffusion of technology, capital, and enterprising spirit to the backward areas. Inevitably there will be a transition from traditionalism to modernism.	The diffusion of capital and products to the backward zones results in economic stagnation and decapitalization. This diffusion extends monopolies into the rural areas with negative consequences for balanced development as income becomes concentrated in a class of merchants and middlemen.

[1]For a useful discussion of arguments for and against the national bourgeoisie in Latin America, see Stavenhagen (Petras and Zeitlin 1968: 18–26) and Romeo (Horowitz, Castro, and Gerassi 1969: 595–606).

the contradictions and weaknesses of the thesis that the national bourgeoisie is a revolutionary and a developmental force in Latin America.

Reorienting economic policies toward national development in Latin America requires displacement of the agrocommercial rulers and the assumption of power by a leadership that is committed to undertaking development regardless of the hardships. The model of capitalist development looks to the so-called national bourgeoisie, the segment of the capitalist class engaged principally in manufacturing that directed the now developed capitalist nations to empire and capitalism, to overcome the power of the *latifundista* class and establish policies that will lead to more intensive land use and economic diversification. This bourgeoisie has also been perceived as a source of leadership for social reform and political democracy as it has the same preference for constitutionalism that was displayed by its counterpart in England. With support from the urban middle sector and the urban industrial workers, the national bourgeoisie was expected to chart a democratic course to modernization and development and thus overturn centuries of "feudal" hierarchy and stagnation.

Import substitution industrialization, a strategy to reduce the outflow of foreign exchange paid to purchase products that could be produced domestically, has also been seen as a way to promote the development of the domestic bourgeoisie. This strategy involves attracting foreign capital to establish facilities for the domestic manufacture of formerly imported products, particularly consumer goods. In addition to reducing balance of payments problems, import substitution is expected to build the manufacturing sector and thus strengthen the domestic position of the national bourgeoisie vis-à-vis landed interests. The modern urban population is to be enlarged by the establishment of new industries created by foreign investment. Inflation, a problem that is general in underdeveloped economies, is to be controlled by monetary stabilization, increasing tax revenues through more effective tax collection methods, and decreasing expenditures by cutting social welfare programs. Government-enforced wage freezes are also used.

Foreign participation is considered a necessity to provide investment capital and modern technology in agriculture and industry as well as modern organizational methods. The strategy assumes that the resultant economic growth, by creating a "larger pie," will increase the size of the portion received by the masses. Economic growth together with a reduced rate of population growth, is also expected to alleviate chronic and massive unemployment and underemployment.

Attracting foreign investment requires economic and political stability, and the political strategy to achieve such stability has three elements. The assumed democratic leanings of the domestic bourgeoisie and the middle sector are to be strengthened by encouraging representative political mechanisms such as political parties while depoliticizing other institutions. A popular theory recognizes modernity in the functional specificity of institutions. In these terms, labor unions should be economic institutions that enable workers to bargain collectively for wages and working conditions, not political organizations seeking to influence national government policies. Schools are to provide education, particularly technical training, not be organizational bases for mobilizing the political energies of students and the intelligentsia. The military should be an arm of civilian government, responsible for national defense and internal order as directed by the government; it should not have a political role either as a veto group or as the head of a government. The depoliticization of the military is to be accomplished through "professionalization." Providing training and sophisticated weapons is expected to enhance the role of technical competence within the armed services and diminish nonprofessional political inclinations.

The second aspect of the political strategy lies in the capacity of economic growth to provide opportunities for upward mobility. With more jobs for the unemployed and greater opportunities for individual advancement through industrial expansion, the potential for militant opposition is to be undercut. The people who benefit from these opportunities will be satisfied with the existing political and economic arrangements, and perhaps more important, those still unemployed or otherwise dissatisfied with their individual situations will have reason to hope that they will eventually benefit. Finally, to deal with militant opposition that cannot be co-opted, the strategy emphasizes a strengthened military, well armed and well trained so that it has the morale and the capability to deal with internal dissension.

The emphasis on the bourgeoisie as the challenger of the landed oligarchy has been maintained by surprisingly divergent perspectives. It appeals to members of the bourgeoisie itself and to U.S. interests, but it has also been a feature of orthodox Marxist analysis—particularly among the more traditional Latin American Communist parties that have been able to justify policies of opposing feudalism through agrarian reform and imperialism by denying foreign capital while cooperating with the industrial bourgeoisie—in the hope that organized urban workers will help industrial capitalists create national capitalism and the conditions for socialist revolution.

Since the mid-1960s theories relying on the national bourgeoisie have suffered a decline. It is now generally accepted that this segment among the Latin American ruling classes is weak and that monocultural economies do not provide an economic base for a strong national bourgeoisie. In the early 1960s several writers noted that owners and managers of manufacturing enterprises were also qualitatively different from their English counterparts. Claudio Veliz (1965: 1–8), discussing Latin America generally, and the Chilean economist Osvaldo Sunkel (in Veliz 1965: 130) observed that the manufacturing class had been co-opted by the traditional agrarian oligarchy; the links between these two sectors are analyzed by Maurice Zeitlin (1984). Dale Johnson's research (Cockcroft, Frank, and Johnson 1972: 165–217) on this manufacturing class indicates that it lacked self-identity and a coherent policy. In his study of the development of Argentine industrialization, Gustavo Polit (in Petras and Zeitlin 1968: 399–430) found that the industrialists had never been independent of landed interests and that they had arisen as an extension of agrarian capital. In her study of Mexico, Nora Hamilton (1982) showed how a certain degree of autonomous capitalist development appeared under President Lázaro Cárdenas during 1934 to 1940 but that ultimately, traditional forces and foreign capital undermined this trend.

Peter Evans (1979) analyzed the alliance of multinational, state, and local capital in showing how Brazilian development was largely dependent on the international system. In contrast, Luiz Carlos Bresser Pereira (1984) emphasizes the evolution of capitalism in Brazil after 1930 and its consolidation after the 1964 military intervention; he discusses the role of the technocrats in promoting development through the capitalist state, and he is optimistic about the potential progressive role of the industrial bourgeoisie. A degree of industrialization has occurred, particularly in Brazil, Mexico, Argentina, and to a lesser extent, Chile. However, it has been the result of the disruption of characteristic trade patterns caused by the inability of the metropoles to supply manufactured products during the world wars and the failure of trade during the Great Depression. These events, rather than a conscious policy of industrialization directed by an independent national bourgeoisie, stimulated import substitution.

The domestic bourgeoisie has generally been unable to promote economic policies leading to national development. In all Latin American countries except Mexico, it has lacked the power and independence from the agrocommercial elite to establish its dominance. The Mexican bourgeoisie, though eventually coming to power through a process that began with the 1910 revolution, has not maintained the level of mobilization of the masses necessary to undertake policies that would break the ties of economic dependence because it has not been in the interests of the bourgeoisie to do so since its control would thereby be threatened. The Brazilian military coup in 1964, which was approved by a large segment of the national bourgeoisie, dramatically illustrates this point. When it appeared that continued support of the reformist coalition that was attempting to work out a program of national capitalist development would lead to reform that would damage the national bourgeoisie's interests, the latter became a "consular" bourgeoisie (Jaguaribe in Veliz 1965: 162–187) and supported military coups that led to a policy of submission to international capitalism. It was not a force for national development, but neither was it a social aggregate lacking identity or policy. After 1964 the Brazilian bourgeoisie had a clear and effectively executed policy to achieve political stability and economic growth as a dominion within the U.S. empire.

The Brazilian experience has also destroyed the assumption that democracy is a dominant value of the domestic bourgeoisie. In England, the abolition of the arbitrary, unlimited power of the crown and the establishment of elections transferred power to the national bourgeoisie. The right to vote was initially very restricted, and it extended throughout the population only after the masses had become involved in industrial employment and could be counted on to support the national bourgeoisie against the agrarian elite. In Latin America, however, the manufacturing bourgeoisie has been in a weak position politically between the *latifundistas*, who control the vote of the peasants who work for them, and the urban masses, who pressure for radical change to solve their desperate problems. Although constitutionalism is favored by the British national bourgeoisie because elections have come out the "right" way, corresponding groups in Latin America have not hesitated to support the overthrow of elected governments that have gone "too far" toward reform.

In Latin America generally, electoral mechanisms for the transfer of power have not been firmly entrenched, and governments that are highly dependent on a foreign power have commanded little respect. Only in Chile did the ruling class show enough independence and competence to establish legitimacy for itself and the political system by which it maintained its power. However, even the bourgeoisie in Chile became like the other bourgeoisies in Latin America, and the 1973 coup affirmed that it supports elections only until its power is threatened.

In the years from 1962 until 1976 military regimes came to power in Argentina, Bolivia, Brazil, Chile, the Dominican Republic, Panama, Peru, and Uruguay. During at least a portion of these years military regimes continued in El Salvador, Guatemala, and Honduras. In the smaller countries, the military has generally been an instrument of oligarchies seeking to perpetuate the status quo; in the others, the people who once looked to the bourgeoisie and the middle sector to bring about development have turned to the military. (For an analysis of the middle class's dependency on the military, see José Nun in Petras and Zeitlin 1968: 145–185).

Military officers generally come from these middle segments of the population, and military governments express their perspectives and receive their support. These governments offer the promise of stability, which encourages foreign economic participation. Moreover, modernization theorists find in military institutions characteristics, such as promotion through merit and appreciation of technical competence, that justify a high regard for the military as an agent of modernization. When this book was written, the military ruled directly only in Guatemala and Paraguay, where elections had been scheduled, and in Chile, where the Augusto Pinochet regime faced broad and growing opposition. In some countries, the change from military to civilian rule is superficial. In Honduras and El Salvador, as well as Guatemala, a civilian facade facilitates U.S. collaboration and support, but the military remains the ultimate arbiter of power. In countries where the military has attempted to act as a development agent in place of or alongside the bourgeoisie, the armed forces have relinquished power in the midst of economic failure.

Clearly, the national bourgeoisie finds itself in a predicament. Thus far in the Latin American experience this group has chosen to rely upon the military for political support and upon U.S. imperialism for economic assistance. If it were to break its dependent relations with other segments of the ruling class and with imperialism, as many observers believe is possible, it would probably be eliminated as a class. A weakened national bourgeoisie did not survive the impetus of revolution in Cuba, and under the Salvador Allende regime in Chile, its prospects were dim. In Peru under Juan Velasco, the military's manipulation forced some land-owners to shift their capital to manufacturing while the regime nation-alized some foreign enterprises. But even in Peru, the emergent national bourgeoisie remained subservient to the military's dealing with foreign interests. Although the domestic bourgeoisie has not demonstrated a capacity to lead development in Latin America, in recent years an opportunity for participation, not merely as a client of foreign interests, has arisen. When the Nicaraguan revolution came to power in 1979 by defeating and then dismantling the National Guard, the bourgeoisie was invited to contribute to national reconstruction and development with the state in a mixed economy. In January 1984 the opposition in El Salvador, which was struggling for power, made a similar offer.

Elite or Ruling Class

This analysis has stressed the dominance of a ruling order in Latin American society. We have suggested that this order comprises several segments, including the landowning oligarchy or aristocracy, the com-mercial bourgeoisie, and the manufacturing bourgeoisie; their dominance is assured by a collaborative military. These segments may be old or new, nationalist or internationalist, but they all seem to be dependent in some form upon international capitalism and imperialism. The model of capitalist development would question some of these assumptions; therefore, we first look at this interpretation of the ruling class and compare and contrast it with that of the model of capitalist underde-velopment as outlined in Table 4.3. Second, we discuss the implications of ruling class relations with imperialism, specifically looking at the impact of the multinational corporations on politics and economics in Latin America.

According to Marx, every society beyond the most primitive is characterized by a ruling class and one or more subject classes. The dominant position of the ruling class is explained by its possession of the major means of economic production and of political power. Perpetual conflict is evident between the ruling class and the subject classes. Under feudalism, this conflict is obscured somewhat by personal bonds between lord and serf, but under capitalism, a radical polarization of classes is encouraged by the sharp divergence of economic interests whereby there is a concentration of wealth in the dominant class and of poverty in the subject classes. Influenced by these assumptions, Vilfredo Pareto and Gaetano Mosca offered a modification of Marxian theory. They

Table 4.3. Perspectives of Elite and Ruling Class[1]

Characteristic	Model of Capitalist Development (*Pluralist Elite*)	Model of Capitalist Underdevelopment (*Ruling Class*)
Power	Dispersed with many centers	Concentrated and unified
Scope of Authority	Specialized, narrow	Wide, general
System	Open	Closed
Base	Dispersion of interests	Coincidence of interests
Outlook and Interest	Diverse, competitive	Unified, cooperative even when fractions are evident
Recruitment	Achievement	By ascription (birth, wealth, etc.)
Duration of Control	Short	Long
Loss of Tenure	Incompetence	Decline in wealth
Consequences	No group favored over the other; decline in politics as self-interest; elites somewhat autonomous but encourage foreign capital and technology	Enhancement of interests of corporations and financial institutions, armed forces, and executive; increased dependence on foreign interests; loss of democracy

[1]These differences are based on the categories in William Kornhauser (Domhoff and Ballard 1968: 50).

noted that in every society there is a minority that rules, and they called this minority the governing elite, which is composed of the people who occupy the posts of political command. Pareto noted that this elite undergoes changes in its membership over time, so he called it a "circulating elite." Subsequent efforts to conceptualize the terms "ruling class" and "elite" evolved into two schools of thought and a polemical debate that has preoccupied social scientists since the late 1950s. An array of terms, from ruling class and governing class to ruling elite, power elite, and circulation or pluralist elite, has sometimes obscured analyses of power.

T. B. Bottomore (1964) suggests that these different terms might be seen as complementary concepts, which may refer to different types of systems or to different aspects of the same system. There might be, in some societies for example, a ruling class *and* elites that represent different interests. There might be societies without a ruling class in which a political elite would be in power through administrative or military control rather than through property ownership and inheritance. Likewise, there might be societies that are ruled by several elites but that have no cohesive group of powerful individuals or families.

In working toward a conceptualization of who rules in Latin America, it should. be noted that "class" is an economic term and "rule" is a political term; i.e., a ruling class is an economic class that rules politically. David Nichols, after carefully reviewing the literature on power in the United States, concludes that there is a directorial class that rules politically. This class is "an upper class which is socio-economically distinct, continuous, and cohesive, and which controls the corporate economy of America" (Nichols 1972: 44). It shares common interests: maintenance of capitalism and maintenance of monopolistic power and its benefits. With its control over the corporations and financial institutions, it dominates the economy. Further, it appears to dominate the government because its members occupy key positions at the executive center of the state; it finances the electoral process; it controls the national media.

This interpretation of ruling class emphasizes an instrumentalist position, that is, the state is considered to be the instrument of the ruling class along the lines outlined by Marx and Engels in *The Communist Manifesto*, where the "executive" of the state was envisaged as a committee for managing the common affairs of the bourgeoisie. This stance is assumed by the English Marxist Ralph Miliband (1969) and opposed by the Greek Marxist Nicos Poulantzas, who takes a structuralist position by arguing that the state and its ideological, repressive, and other apparatuses tend to serve the interests of, but are not necessarily manipulated by, the ruling class itself. Poulantzas, with his structuralist position, does not dissociate his theory from the idea of dependency but instead incorporates it into his analysis of the changing state of affairs in Spain and Portugal and their break from fascism in the mid-1970s (Poulantzas 1976: chap. 1). As to Latin America, Rodolfo Stavenhagen (in Petras and Zeitlin 1968: 23–25) notes that such terms as "middle class" or "national bourgeoisie" are often euphemisms for the capitalist "ruling class." Some authors, he argues, find these terms more neutral, yet their analysis often is directed to the power structure of entrepreneurs, financiers, and industrialists at the apex of society. Another problem is that the members of the middle class of professionals and bureaucrats are usually economically and socially dependent upon the upper strata of Latin American society; they are tied to the ruling class, they are conservative, they defend the status quo, and they seek individual privileges.

Two interpretations of power were referred to earlier. One utilizes the concept of ruling class, in the tradition of Marx and the elaboration of Nichols. In Spanish or Portuguese, this concept is translated as *clase dominante* ("dominant class"), suggesting an analysis of rulers and exploiters, on the one hand, and of ruled and exploited, on the other. It should be clear that we refer not only to a monolithic ruling class but also to a class of varied interests that tends to become cohesive under capitalism and that tends to be intimately related to imperialism. As noted in Table 4.3, a ruling class, even when fractions are evident, tends to be unified in a closed system with a broad scope of authority and concentrated power. The other interpretation views power as pluralist and is based partially on the formulations of Mosca and Pareto. According to the pluralist position, there are multiple groups in society that represent diverse interests and orientations and that compete with each other. These groups accept a set of rules regarding social change, and they tend toward compromise in representing the views, not of any single group, but of the more varied interests of society. Competing elites are evident in a pluralist framework, so pluralism involves a more or less diffuse distribution of power within a sociopolitical framework.

What are the consequences for Latin America according to these two interpretations of power? The diffusionist notions of pluralism suggest that no group is favored. Interests are dispersed, and competing elite groups are able to function independently of foreign interests; the national bourgeoisie would be such a group. At the same time, it is assumed that the capital, technology, and know-how of the advanced nations, within certain limitations, can be diffused to less developed nations just as the modern urban metropolises can influence the backward hinterland of Latin America. In contrast, the model of capitalist underdevelopment sees in Latin America an ever-increasing consolidation of interests— among corporations and financial institutions, the armed forces, and the executive branch of government. These institutions reinforce the ruling class interests of the agrocommercial and industrial bourgeoisie. In turn, there is increased reliance on, and collaboration with, imperialist interests.

Working Class or Peasantry

Our discussion suggests that two classes prevail in an advanced capitalist society, as envisaged by Marx, but that other classes and class fractions are also in evidence, especially in Latin America. At the end of the third volume of *Capital*, Marx identified three great classes— landowners, industrialists, and the working class. Today both landowners and industrialists compose the ruling class in Latin America, and the working class, known also as the proletariat, is made up of wage earners in the industrialized work force both in urban and in some rural areas. Subgroups within the proletariat are identifiable, including employed, underemployed, and unemployed people; usually outside the proletariat but not associated with the bourgeoisie are lumpen elements such as people who are idle. Unproductive workers, in the sense that they do not contribute directly to the material production process under capitalism, include clerks, managers, etc., who are known variously as the middle class or the new petty bourgeoisie and usually are not associated with the proletariat.

Marx and Lenin emphasized the potential revolutionary role of the organized proletariat. The dictatorship of this group meant the control of state power and the means of production by the working class in the transition from capitalism to socialism. The working class is easily identifiable in urban areas by the fact that its members are wage earners who produce commodities so as to meet their own needs and the needs of the capitalist owners of the means of production; the latter exchange commodities in the market and thereby exploit the surplus value of the workers whose labor power they control. These wage earners are usually found in the factories and workshops of light and heavy industry, and the antagonisms between them and the ruling class are such as to provoke tension, conflict, and class stuggle.

The revolutionary potential of the exploited class in the countryside is less clear. This class is commonly referred to as the peasantry, but it has many subgroups. Rodolfo Stavenhagen identifies the following peasant types in Latin America (1975: 102–104): peasants in the highland communities who engage in intense cultivation of food products, mostly for their own consumption but also for the market economy; individual peasants, tied to the capitalist system through financing, who reside on the lower slopes of the mountain ranges and who cultivate such commercial products as sugarcane, coffee, and bananas; medium-sized independent landowning farmers; workers who may be sharecroppers or tenant farmers on large commercial plantations owned by patriarchal families who rely on close relations between patron and cultivator; and workers on capitalist, mechanized plantations whose labor is based on salaried and contractual arrangements. This last type characteristically resembles the worker of industry because production is clearly of the capitalist mode and compensation is explicitly in the form of wages.

The essential questions are to what extent has there been or will there be a proletarianization of the peasantry in Latin America and what are the implications of the dissolution of the peasantry as it gradually becomes proletarianized. These questions have been explored by Richard Harris (1978) in a review of Marxist thought on the nature of agrarian society in Latin America and especially in Mexico. Roger Bartra (1974) writes that the development of capitalist agriculture in Mexico has produced a landless, wage-earning proletariat in the countryside. Accordingly, three-fifths of the population is in this situation, and another third lives in a state of semiproletarianization and poverty. The implication of this finding, of course, suggests the eroding away of precapitalist modes of production in one area of Latin America, which would appear to reinforce an interpretation based on the penetration of capitalism and its subsequent consequence of underdevelopment in the period since independence. Bartra, however, is not simply applying the model to the changing conditions of the peasantry in Mexico but instead is concentrating his analysis on modes of production and their consequences for Mexican agriculture. He also implies that the proletarianization of the peasantry means an expansion of the rural work force and an increase in working class consciousness and struggles among the rural population.

This position is countered by Gustavo Esteva (1978) who argues that the rural population remains tied to the land and that its collective resistance to the forces of capitalism has strengthened its peasant class consciousness. This "peasantization" of the rural population accounts for the increasing number of land seizures by landless peasants, the rapid growth in peasant organization, and the influence of the peasantry in national politics. Esteva believes that the consolidation of the peasantry will reduce the movement of rural people to the cities and mitigate pressures on industrial workers and the huge marginal population of unemployed workers. He feels the peasantry will eventually seek the support of the urban working class.

These contrasting theses about the peasantry illustrate the importance of analyzing class forces and struggles, and while the dependency model would appear to be reinforced by Bartra's position, in fact the model rarely leads to any serious in-depth class analysis. Instead, the model allows for focus on the exploitative conditions that characterize the peasantry in much of Latin America, but it does not necessarily reveal the nature of the class struggle itself.

Foreign Capital and Domestic Classes

Import substitution for industrialization has not created a basis for sustained growth. Moreover, growth has not trickled down to the masses. The ruling class has not shown itself to be democratic, and the industrial bourgeoisie has been transformed into an agent of foreign capital, playing a functional role similar to that of the agrocommercial bourgeoisie, which it has joined or defeated. As for development, it has failed, but it has succeeded in maintaining and increasing the availability of Latin America as a field of operations for foreign corporations, particularly the multinationals.

Earlier in this century foreign activity was limited to plantation agriculture and utilities. In recent years a major movement into manufacturing, banking, and retailing has occurred. Discussing this development in his work on Chile, Osvaldo Sunkel cites a study of the operations of 187 transnational corporations (Vaupel and Curham 1969) that shows the rapid increase of their subsidiaries in Latin America. Sunkel notes that this process accelerated in the mid-1950s, but in the late 1960s "it reach[ed] the stage of the wholesale process of buying up local firms and integrating affiliates closely with headquarters and with each other" (Sunkel 1972: 523). He observes a characteristic pattern of expansion: "first, they export their finished products; then they establish sales organizations abroad; they then proceed to allow foreign producers to use their licenses and patents to manufacture the product locally; finally, they buy off the local producer and establish a partially or wholly owned subsidiary" (Sunkel 1972: 521).

This process removes still more decisions from the scrutiny and possible control of the host country since international trade takes the form of intrafirm transfers within the multinationals. And since the multinationals integrate their own activities and tend to cooperate with each other, the change also represents the introduction of foreign monopoly power throughout the host country's economy, where earlier it was restricted to the export of primary agricultural and mineral products. Along with this trend, foreign influence in areas such as advertising, communications, and education has also increased.

If the growth of foreign participation brought a corresponding increase in the importation of foreign capital, the argument in favor of the multinational firm as an agent of development might be more plausible. However, figures for the period 1960–1964 indicate that only 4 percent of "foreign" investment represented capital actually transferred to Latin America from the United States (Frank 1969b: 2, 9). The period 1963–1968 was little better with a real foreign contribution of only 9 percent (Sunkel 1972: 526). Thus, the growth in foreign holdings in Latin America has been generated primarily by the investment of profits produced within the host countries. Poverty is general throughout Latin America but not because of an inability to produce wealth. Although a portion of the profits of foreign enterprises is reinvested, repatriation of the balance denies the people of Latin America the use of the capital they have produced. Between 1950 and 1965 income on foreign investment transferred to the United States ($11,300 million) exceeded U.S. investment in Latin America ($3,800 million) by $7,500 million (Magdoff 1969: 198, 202). By 1979 the net capital outflow had grown to more than a billion dollars per year.

Repatriation of profits is only one channel for capital drain. Repayment of loans is another. The granting of loans became a part of U.S. policy in 1934 when the Export-Import Bank was started to provide Latin American countries with credit to purchase North American goods. It was a program designed to get the U.S. economy out of its stagnation, not to help Latin America. Loan payments now surpass new loans and absorb a significant portion of the foreign exchange earnings of many countries, especially Argentina, Brazil, Chile, and Mexico. A variety of other charges for shipping, insurance, licenses, and royalties account for still more capital flowing north. The situation is further exacerbated by the continuous drop in the amount of industrial imports that Latin American primary products will buy on the market due to the long-term increase in prices of the former coupled with the decline in the prices of the latter.

Inter-American economic relationships are characterized by exploitation, meaning that Latin Americans do not receive the benefit of what they produce. The economic patterns are "natural" in the sense that market relationships always benefit superior technology and economic power. However, it is worthwhile to note that international trade had its origins in piracy and plunder. Robbery has been recognized as a way of making a living from at least the time of Aristotle, and expeditions for trade and for conquest have not been clearly distinguished. Privateers have been protected and contracted by established governments from early times to the association of the British and French monarchies with privateers (Mandel 1968: 83)—British piracy, for example, was one means of increasing accumulation from the Spanish Empire. Over the centuries more subtle instruments of coercion have supplemented military power to maintain trade in which one "partner" is understandably reluctant to participate. On another level, in addition to aid to regimes and military establishments it supports, the United States provides experts in counterinsurgency and "public safety" (which has included training in torture methods) and the Central Intelligence Agency (CIA) bribes politicians and journalists as part of programs of counterinsurgency and the overthrow of progressive governments. A program sponsored by U.S. corporations, the government, and the AFL-CIO trains Latin American labor leaders and keeps them on the payroll for extended periods after they have returned home.

All of this activity functions to maintain the nations of Latin America as an area open to extraction of resources by foreign corporations, the export of U.S. products, and the draining off of profits derived from a variety of business activities within the host countries—in other words, to maintain capitalism and capitalist regimes that cooperate the most with foreign corporations. It is a political policy of domination which, combined with economic activities and programs that affect Latin American culture, maintains Latin America within a North American empire. We have noted the penetration of U.S. firms and some aspects of decapitalization because these factors represent a heavy burden on efforts to develop. However, we do not wish to suggest that the domestic capitalists would act in a manner more beneficial to the Latin American masses if the multinationals permitted them a greater opportunity to function. The multinationals are part of the imperialist system; indeed, they are the chief actors in both Latin America and the United States. But the problem is the inability of dependent capitalism to mobilize and direct the energies of the people and the resources of Latin America to meet basic needs. The political role of imperialism in maintaining dependent capitalism is as important as the direct economic exploitation in which the multinationals engage.

Although capitalism does not satisfy the needs of the majority of Latin Americans, the system does tend to co-opt many groups that are operating spontaneously to maintain themselves. The bourgeoisie, for the most part unable to compete, is integrated into foreign enterprise. Since the technology of industrial production is capital intensive and does not create much employment, industrial workers have not grown as a proportion of the labor force. In this century manufacturing output as a portion of the domestic product in Latin America has grown from 11 to 23 percent while the proportion of industrial workers in the labor force has remained constant at 14 percent (Frank 1969a: 4, 9). In relation to the masses of peasants and the urban unemployed, the industrial workers are a privileged group. Both salaried workers and organized labor are generally caught in a race against persistent inflation, but they are fearful of a revolutionary change that would favor the unemployed and the superexploited and that could bring retaliation from foreign interests. The very poverty of urban marginals and the precarious existence of poor peasants serve as a means of control, incapacitating them from acting as a political force for change.

In spite of the systematic forces that are supportive of the status quo and in spite of imperialist manipulation, change is occurring. When it reaches the level of governmental change, brought about by armed struggle or by election, the multinational corporations and the U.S. government react strongly. The full repertoire of economic warfare and terrorism has been employed against Cuba as well as armed intervention. The response of the United States to the Nicaraguan revolution has followed a similar pattern of government hostility, though there has been less objection on the part of corporations.

Fifteen years after the Bay of Pigs, the failure of the attempts to bring down the Cuban government and the increasing acceptance of Cuba by other Latin American nations led the Carter administration to a willingness to coexist with socialist Cuba. However, normalization of relations was not achieved, principally because of U.S. demands to set parameters on Cuban foreign policy. Since the middle of President Carter's term of office, U.S. hostility toward Cuba has grown steadily stronger.

The destabilization and overthrow of the Allende government provides another example of U.S. conduct. In Chile, Salvador Allende was elected to the presidency in 1970, leading a coalition committed to fundamental change. Many of the government's measures to stop the capital outflow and to establish a planned economy (including the nationalization of the copper mines, Chile's largest source of export earnings) were supported by nearly all segments of the population, but the distortions of capitalism placed Chile in a vulnerable position. An agricultural country of approximately 10 million people which physically bears a resemblance to California, Chile spent over $120 million a year to import food; foreign exchange was also required to purchase industrial equipment, spare parts, and medicine; and a good share of Chile's annual foreign exchange earnings had to be used to service a foreign debt of over $4 billion inherited from previous governments. The lack of foreign exchange and U.S. pressures which resulted in limits on credits and boycotts of trade, damaged the economy and engendered unemployment. Political unrest also was encouraged at a time when large landowners were sabotaging domestic agricultural production as an act of resistance to the government.

In this critical situation, the U.S. government and the multinational corporations attempted to overthrow the Chilean government through economic warfare. In a speech before the United Nations General Assembly in December 1972, President Allende enumerated the most important consequences of this attempt:

- Cessation of about $80 million in loans annually that had been granted by the World Bank and the Inter-American Development Bank
- Cessation of about $50 million in loans annually that had been granted by the U.S. Agency for International Development
- Suspension of short-term credit to finance foreign trade, which had been available from private U.S. banks and had amounted to $220 million
- Halting of credit normally available from the Export-Import Bank to purchase U.S. goods
- Blocking of short-term operations with private banks in Western Europe, mainly based on payment for copper, resulting in more than $20 million in credit lines not being renewed and in the suspension of financial negotiations for more than $200 million
- Blockage (by Kennecott Copper) of payments for Chilean copper sold in France, Holland, and Sweden (under U.S. pressure, French courts placed a temporary embargo on payments to Chile)

In addition to these economic reprisals, Allende cited the efforts of the giant International Telephone and Telegraph (ITT), known widely through the publication of secret ITT memoranda in 1972, to overthrow the Chilean government by political subversion. The coup of September 1973 resulted in Allende's assassination and the fall of his government.

The expansion of multinational firms is now the most significant economic phenomenon in the capitalist world. Growing at an annual rate of 10 percent in the period 1950–1970, they withdrew over $1,700 million a year from the Third World, and nearly two-thirds of this amount came from Latin America. In the underdeveloped nations, they often act in concert, creating an oligopolistic base of economic and political power. Their policies in both underdeveloped and developed countries are directed to achieve maximum profitability over the entire range of their respective empires, not for the benefit of any of the nations in which they operate. Even the developed countries have not brought these multinationals under control. They have been able to defy attempts to merely require detailed reporting on their activities to host governments, and movements to challenge them have had to confront vast concentrations of power.

Development in Latin America, which is understood to include political and economic independence, requires that existing political and economic relationships undergo radical change. It is clear that the power of U.S. corporations engaged in foreign activities will resist this change. Profit rates on U.S. operations in Latin America are far higher than profits on domestic investment, and control of Latin American resources through ownership and lack of competition among the limited number of purchasers of Latin American products result in high profits on imports to the United States. Although increasingly threatened by Japanese and European competition, North American exports to Latin America enjoy monopoly power in many areas, which results in high prices. Moreover, the operations of U.S. businesses in other nations are growing at a much higher rate than domestic business. Socialism in Latin America would sharply curtail most direct private foreign investment and end foreign control of the production of raw materials. Profits on trade would be reduced since the monopoly and monopsony power of the multinationals would be broken, although joint ventures of state and private capital might be possible. Foreign control of Latin American resources and markets, a goal often as important as immediate profits to North American firms, would be ended.

Implications of Class Analysis:
Case Studies of Mexico, Argentina, and Peru

A further understanding of the issues of class and class struggle may be gained through a critical examination of interpretative analyses of particular Latin American nations. For this purpose, three important studies available in English and written by three major social scientists from Latin America have been selected: *Democracy in Mexico* by Pablo González Casanova of the University of Mexico generally has been considered a classic in its own right; *Los que mandan* by José Luis de Imaz of the University of Buenos Aires has been received as a pioneer work and a best-seller in Argentina; and *Nationalism and Capitalism in Peru: A Study in Neo-imperialism* by Aníbal Quijano of the University of San Marcos served as a major critique of the developmental nationalist policies of the Peruvian military junta that came to power in October 1968.

Each of these works focuses on the issues of dual society, the role of the bourgeoisie, and the impact of a ruling class and a proletariat, yet each draws upon different methodologies and conceptualizations and therefore leads to different conclusions about the prospects for development and underdevelopment in the respective countries. These contrasting perspectives are instructive to the student, for interpretations and findings are closely tied to whichever model has been stressed by the author. Our discussion will demonstrate that the studies by González Casanova and Imaz are largely diffusionist in orientation whereas Quijano's work is cast within a critique of Peruvian dependency.

Mexico and González Casanova

González Casanova's study of Mexico is interwoven with assumptions, factual information, and statistical data. He deals first with the structure of power, examining constitutional government in theory and in practice as well as differentiating between formal and actual power. Then he relates social and political structures and examines political decisions in the light of economic development. Finally, he assesses the future of democracy in Mexico, offering first a "Marxist" analysis, then a "sociological" analysis. A synthesis of his arguments follows:

1. The polity in Mexico is unbalanced with a hierarchical concentration of power flowing downward from the presidency to the executive branch to the central government. At the same time there is the pluralist influence of competing elite groups of bases of power, including the regional and local *caudillos* or *caciques* ("chiefs" or "bosses"), army, clergy, *latifundistas*, and national and foreign entrepreneurs.

2. Even though foreign capitalist influence in Mexico is extensive (more than half of the 400 most powerful enterprises are either under foreign control or have strong foreign participation), the nation remains stable with a strategy of national independence and development. In the face of international pressures, Mexico continues its policy of liberation and nationalization (evidenced by the takeover of the petroleum industry in the late 1930s and the more recent purchase of the power utilities) as well as its independent international policy based on nationalist traditions (exemplified by the country's refusal to accept military pacts with the United States or to break diplomatic relations with Cuba).

3. The state is the largest entrepreneur, providing stability and a rational utilization of resources within a free enterprise framework. With its economic power reinforced by the concentration of political power in a presidential regime, the state controls external pressures, such as imperialism, that produce inequality, negotiates with the large monopolies, and promotes the "takeoff" of national development.

4. Mexican society is dualist: The dominant society consists of the Spanish, Creoles, and mestizos and is characterized by a high degree of participation; the other consists of the Indians and is marginal and dominated. One society dominates and exploits the other in a colonial relationship called internal colonialism. Although internal colonialism is similar to the colonialist relationship between nations, it is directly

related to the internal relations of the two societies: the participant and the marginal, the haves and the have-nots. Although the marginal Indian populations represent the "residue" of a colonial society, internal colonialism is not explained by Mexico's past foreign colonialism or by the nation's dependency on foreign powers. Internal colonialism, however, is evident when a ruling center or metropolis exercises a monopoly over the peripheral Indian community's commerce and credit *or* when social classes of the dominant society exploit the Indian population through forced and salaried labor, share farming and peonage, and demand for free services. The cultural alignment of dominant and dominated populations is a reflection of prejudice and discrimination as well as of colonial types of exploitation and control.

5. The large majority of Mexicans are outside the ruling class; within the ruling class are lawyers, bureaucrats, and other groups who manipulate the people through the political parties. The parties, however, reflect the disconformity of the different sectors of the ruling class and the more advanced strata. The ruling class and these conformist sectors do not view the democratization of institutions as an urgent necessity. Instead, stability, control, and co-optation are favored, and protest is discouraged.

6. Mexico is "precapitalist" and "predemocratic" because of its internal colonialism. A bourgeois democracy and a fully developed capitalist system must be achieved, and conditions of socialism do not exist. Thus, the ruling class must join with the proletariat to mold a progressive bourgeoisie and to put an end to internal colonialism. These aims will be achieved through capitalist development. National integration will incorporate all classes, including the ruling class which will join the other classes in an evolving democracy. Employing our earlier criteria, it is clear that González Casanova has generally taken a *diffusionist* position because he acknowledges the existence of feudalism and a dual society, he advocates the formation of a national bourgeoisie, and he analyzes the ruling class in terms of various segments which pluralistically exercise decision making that is independent of foreign influences. He sees remnants of feudalism or semifeudalism in the marginal populations. Further evidence that Mexico is precapitalist, in his view, is that there are two societies which are nearly mutually exclusive one from the other. One is dominant and participating with access to salaried labor, credits, and investments and has an ability to manifest demands through the organization of the political economy—indicators of an evolving democracy. The other society, dominated and marginal, is isolated; it has no organizations, no rights, and no intermediaries through which it can pressure for resolution of its problems. A kind of ruling class dominates over the participating society, and its decisions favoring stability and the status quo ensure its economic well-being. In turn, the stable participating society is held together by a highly centralized institutional framework within which a pluralism of interests is represented by

different power groups. An expansion of these democratic tendencies along with the evolution of capitalism will break down the existing dichotomy of societies and classes. National integration will be achieved through the molding of a new bourgeoisie that will confront foreign domination and ensure a controlled internal capitalist growth. Mexico's development in the form of political democracy and economic progress will thus occur under the leadership of a national bourgeoisie that will absorb both the proletariat and the ruling class.

In contrast to this perspective, the model of capitalist underdevelopment would interpret Mexico's political economic history in a different context: Feudalism probably never existed in any dominant form, and there was no dual society; a national bourgeoisie did not fully evolve and in any event could not have successfully promoted significant autonomous development; and the ruling class, while composed of many diversified segments and politically nationalistic, nevertheless economically, culturally, and socially had much in common with its foreign counterparts and therefore could not function independently in the interests of the nation. In rebutting the interpretation of González Casanova, Frank argues that since the sixteenth century, Mexico rapidly formed as an integral society fully inserted into the world system of mercantile expansion and capitalist development (Frank 1969a: chap. 20). He demonstrates that the so-called marginal areas were once integrated with the more advanced center around Mexico City. Indeed, the core of the regional and national markets was tied to the world economy—tied to worldwide demand for gold and silver. But reduction in the production of these commodities, coupled with a simultaneous demand for luxury goods by the prosperous classes, produced an economic depression and a decline in the outlying areas, and the consequence was uneven development. Further, the prevailing metropolis-satellite relationships acknowledged by González Casanova preclude the existence of a dual society; the Indians have never been outside the market economy although they are poor, dominated, and discriminated against. Thus, internal colonialism exists but in a different form. The emphasis of González Casanova on political, social, and cultural relations ignores the fact that internal colonialism also has economic ramifications because it is tied to the outside world. Capitalism in Mexico ensures that nation's integration into the world economic order while generating capitalist underdevelopment at home.

Argentina and Imaz

José Luis de Imaz deals almost exclusively with a detailed analysis of who rules in Argentina. Like González Casanova, Imaz speaks of a ruling class, and his ruling class has a variety of power bases—the executive branch of government, armed forces, landowners, entrepreneurs, church, and professional politicians; he even has a chapter on labor leaders. His focus on elites is particularly useful since the question of power in Argentina often has been obscured by interpretations that examine populism as manifested by Peronismo, or the followers of Juan Perón, and the organized labor movement or through the Radical party as responses to industrialization in the early twentieth century. The question of power has been clouded also by stress on an apparent pluralism in the Argentine multiparty system. Then, too, military intervention on numerous occasions since 1930 has resulted in misleading interpretations. Below we briefly examine the arguments in Imaz's *Los que mandan* and then determine to what extent his conclusions are related to diffusionist or dependency perspectives.

1. Imaz believes that a complete ruling class existed under General Augustín P. Justo from 1936 to 1943. This ruling class was a socially cohesive group restricted by such membership criteria as personal relationships, family position, and club affiliations. One belonged in government by right of ascription, and the foremost criterion for high office was business ability or legal capacity. This ruling class operated on the upper and intermediate levels of government, and its dominance via machine politics was assured by electoral fraud and the apolitical stance of the armed forces.

2. Although there must always be an elite in the sense of individuals who command, Imaz affirms that today there is no longer a ruling elite in Argentina. There is a nominal elite, an aggregate of individuals who hold the highest positions and head the basic institutions, but there is no real elite or group of individuals who "act in concert, lead the community, direct it with a view to achieving certain ends and objectives, and accept approximately similar normative frameworks" (Imaz 1970: 242).

3. This nominal elite is still largely the old elite of large landowners that ruled until 1943 and regained control in 1956 after the fall of Juan Perón, and it has continued in that position. In hopes of obtaining the backing of the old elite, the holders of political power usually have surrendered control over the economic and financial system. Thus, the upper class maintains control of certain strategic economic and government sectors. Judges and diplomats usually are recruited from its ranks as well.

4. The old elite permitted a "circulation of elites," which presented difficulties as a "new" upper class became inflexible in the face of reform. Although the old members extended the voting franchise to the whole population, the new members resisted such change, and a crisis ensued, thereby provoking the replacement of the former by a completely different group led by the Peronistas.

5. The entrepreneurial elite comprises members of the well-to-do bourgeoisie, foreigners serving their native corporations as managers or representatives, and immigrants of humble origins. These people do not seem to have been active in public life, nor does their economic prestige seem to ensure them a place in the upper class. The power of the

foreign entrepreneurs is limited because they fail to identify with the national interests. In general, the entrepreneurial elite lacks unity because of a diversity of interests, personal and group conflicts, and different national origins.

6. The weaknesses among the landowning and entrepreneurial elites have produced a leadership crisis: A whole generation of leaders has failed as a consequence of an evolving complex society and the lack of a base for ruling a modern nation-state. This base can only be built if Argentina escapes from its present precapitalist stage of development.

Clearly, there are important differences between Imaz and González Casanova. The latter advocates the formation of a national bourgeoisie, the former a ruling class. Does Imaz's orientation therefore move him away from the weaknesses in diffusionist interpretations? We think not, for a number of reasons. First, Imaz, like González Casanova, places Argentina in a precapitalist stage of development. Capitalism in the hands of a competent leadership will lead Argentina toward modernization; the prescription is growth by stages through an evolutionary process. His position implies that a cohesive ruling group will be able to exercise independent decisions to lead Argentina along the path of development. Although Imaz is aware of foreign influence upon the Argentine political economy, he tends to underestimate its significance. Nowhere does he discuss the possible collusion of domestic clientele classes and foreign elites, nor does he offer insights into the obstacles created by foreign capital—for example, decapitalization caused by high profit remuneration or interference in politics such as that advocated by ITT to prevent Chilean President Salvador Allende from taking office in 1970. As is true of González Casanova's analysis, Imaz's emphasis upon a contemporary precapitalist society suggests the possibility of a dual society—dominant and marginal, elites and masses, and so on— but he does not explore this conceptualization. Nor does he discuss in detail the meaning of precapitalism, and one can only infer that he assumes the existence of a feudal society. Perhaps his stress on political power has unconsciously led him to skirt this important question.

Then, too, Imaz's concept of elite is confusing. The English translation of his work jumps in terminology from ruling class to governing elite to circulating elite; the ruling class of one historical period becomes a nominal elite in another time. In an appendix, Imaz acknowledges his preference for the use of "ruling categories" rather than "ruling class," and it is clear that Imaz intended to deal, not with classes, but with groups on an elite level. His pluralistic framework stresses functionalism and specialization as a society modernizes. He expresses this diffusionist ideal in terms of a pluralistic society, with a complex of interests and ideologies.

Finally, Imaz is distressed at the failure of leadership, essentially in the middle class, which is weak and unstable. Factionalism in Argentine politics and weaknesses in the economy produce destabilizing and antidemocratic tendencies within the middle sectors; thus, military rule occasionally is necessary to stabilize society. Somehow, while not explicitly advocated, we sense that Imaz is counting on the fact that a new bourgeoisie will rise to power to fill the vacuum left by the nominal elite and the weakened middle class. He may label it a new ruling class, but it sounds suspiciously like the national bourgeoisie envisaged by González Casanova.

We conclude therefore that Imaz's argument is essentially diffusionist: His notion of elite is diffused in pluralistic politics; his identification of Argentina as precapitalist suggests a dual society; and his advocacy of a new class implies some sort of technocratic, modern-oriented, and centralized ruling group that will lead Argentina along a continuum of development. It is our feeling that if Imaz were to incorporate a critique of dependency into his discussion, his analysis would be more focused, new questions might be raised, and new interpretations might be offered. For example, his analysis primarily concerns power as a political phenomenon, and he only cursorily examines the relationship of industrial and agrarian interests, their linkages, and their impact on political and economic decisions. Although it is not certain that his interpretation incorporates the notion of a dual society, there are likewise few clues as to any interaction between rural and urban life. One problem is that these diverse interests are examined within institutional frameworks, such as agrarian and industrial societies. Yet Imaz offers some provocative facts. Of eighty-two family groups with land of more than 25,000 acres, fifty-six bear names of members of the upper class of the city of Buenos Aires. Large-property-owning families also tend to control agricultural corporations, and the old oligarchy participated in establishing the industrial union and the industrial bank. Viewing Argentina within the context of an alternative model might have led to an investigation of the impact of foreign influence upon the domestic political economy. To suggest, as does Imaz, that the managers of the great foreign corporations do not identify with the country in which they live because decisions are made elsewhere by their boards of directors may be misleading; at least his evidence is inconclusive. Other analyses might have examined the interrelationships between middle and upper classes. Then, too, there might have been some discussion of the military and industrial interests as the military is known to be involved in industrial enterprise. To what extent is this military activity a consequence of middle class instability?—of collaboration between classes? Imaz's book is provocative and interesting, and it definitely contributes to an understanding of Argentina. Yet its shortcomings lie in a vague conceptualization, a diffusionist emphasis on elites and classes, and a framework that results in some weak conclusions.

Peru and Quijano

The military regime that came to power in Peru in 1968 was involved in restructuring the country along lines advocated explicitly by González

Casanova and implicitly by Imaz: that is, molding a cohesive national bourgeoisie that, guided by the state, would promote development while containing the dominance of foreign economic and political influence. Aníbal Quijano carefully analyzes these events in Peru and offers criticism that shatters the illusion that the regime achieved its objectives. Like González Casanova and Imaz, Quijano examines the strengths and weaknesses of the social class structure in his country, but he also relates the nature of the class relations to the outside world. His analytical framework is based on the dependency model. He is not concerned with a dual society but instead places emphasis upon the interrelationships among social classes within Peru and upon their relations with interests outside the country. He sees the former Peruvian military regime as guided by an ideology of class reconciliation (combining interests of workers and capitalist enterprise) and of limited nationalism within an imperialist order. He concludes that in the absence of any ability to fight for independent power or historic national interests, a small national bourgeoisie is unlikely to be capable of eliminating imperialist domination. Let us examine his argument in more detail and then assess its usefulness.

1. Quijano begins by relating conditions in Peru to the general situation in Latin America. Presently in Latin America, imperialist domination is characterized by two overlapping and contradictory models: one being "traditional imperialism," with the United States as the hegemonic power operating through enterprises totally controlled by foreign capital, and the other, in effect since the Second World War, "consisting of a progressive shift in the axis of domination from agro-extractive sectors to the urban-industrial sector" (Quijano 1971: 4). This shift accompanied economic, political, and social changes: The power of the old oligarchies declined but did not disappear, new groups such as white-collar workers and the petty bourgeoisie began to assert their demands, an industrial proletariat expanded in the cities, and peasant movements emerged in the countryside. These changes produced "the crisis of oligarchic hegemony," that is, the actions of the new bourgeoisie became moderate and indecisive in the face of an oligarchy whose bases of power were declining too slowly while being threatened by a popular revolution. There ensued a crisis of legitimacy of bourgeois domination, a fragmentation of power that could be controlled generally only by the armed forces, which were well organized and held decisive power.

2. Before the 1950s foreign domination over the Peruvian economy was held through control of agro-extractive resources. Thereafter foreign penetration of mining increased, and capital began to flow into industrial production. Since this "erratic and mixed" process was dependent on foreign capital, "it exemplifies a combination of old and new patterns of imperialist control: the appearance of new imperialist bourgeois interests with different ties to native bourgeois groups over and above those already existing between foreign capital and the agricultural and

cattle-raising sectors of the native bourgeoisie." Thus ended the era of domination based on "the alliance between the native landholding-commercial bourgeoisie and the imperialist bourgeoisie" (Quijano 1971: 13).

3. After coming to power in 1968, the military junta tried to end foreign control of the production of agricultural exports as well as of mining and petroleum while simultaneously strengthening the role of foreign and domestic capital in the urban industrial sector. By expropriating the property of landholders and compensating them with payment that must be invested in a new industrial plant, the regime's policy was "to convert agrarian capitalists into industrial capitalists" (Quijano 1971: 16). The state would control basic industry, and private companies (generally international monopolies) would control manufacturing. The new arrangement would not eliminate dependency, however. The state was to become stronger, more efficient, and better organized, but its ties to a network of "imperialist" monopolies "presupposes that it is less national than before" (Quijano 1971: 49).

4. The Peruvian ruling class has always been a dependent bourgeoisie, but the reforms of the military junta made it a less homogeneous bourgeoisie, the consequence of declining power in the landholding sector and the growing importance of the urban industrial groups. Quijano breaks this class into groups: an upper landholding bourgeoisie, residing along the coast, responsible for agricultural exports, and not directly under the control of foreign companies; a middle-level landholding bourgeoisie, located in the Andean Sierra and owners of agricultural resources producing for the domestic market; an upper-level industrial bourgeoisie, wholly dependent on foreign investment; and a middle-level industrial bourgeoisie, diversified with meager financial resources. Financial and family ties bind these sectors together, and the landholding sector has played a central role in banking and commerce, industry, mining, and petroleum.

5. The regime proclaimed that the new order would replace capitalism and at the same time preclude socialism; it described this order as "nationalist," "humanist," and "communitarian." However, the new order strengthened the existing state capitalism in basic industry and in the trade of agro-extractive products, areas that are controlled by large autonomous state enterprises. The new order also strengthened the dependent bourgeoisie, which nevertheless remains in alliance with the imperialist bourgeoisie and subordinate to the more decisive alliance between the latter and the state. Quijano concludes that imperialist participation is sufficient to assure it a dominant position in the country's economy, even though it may be subject to state supervision (Quijano 1971: 87–90).

This description of Quijano's argument offers only a glimpse of his sophisticated analysis, and although our discussion is not conclusive, it should be immediately clear to the reader that his analytic framework, which is closely tied to the theory that posits a dependent relationship to the outside world, offers in-depth perspectives that are not usually generated in diffusionist-oriented analysis. Rather than reiterating the belief of many scholars that two societies persist in Peru (feudal and capitalist, agrarian and industrial, oligarchic and bourgeois), interrelationships between these sectors are carefully identified and empirically verified. Rather than assuming that the consolidation of a national bourgeoisie will resolve Peru's development problems, Quijano examines this class's weaknesses and contradictions. Rather than interpreting domination as the consequence of a monolithic ruling class, he reveals the diversified nature of this class and identifies the bonds among the different elements. Rather than assuming that development is the natural consequence of a regime that professes national independence, he looks carefully at an economic policy that reinforces dependent relations with outside nations. Thus, internal conditions are directly related to external influences, and the contradictions of the military regime are clearly exposed.

Thus far, this book has tried to assess the old and new political economic orders in Latin America. The assumption has been that most of Latin America is bound by its dependent relationship to the capitalist world, the United States in particular, and that imperialism has contributed to the persistence of underdevelopment in Latin America. What then are the prospects for nations that strive to break their imperialist relations with the outside world? In recent times, only three Latin American nations have moved in such a direction. Chile, in an attempt to bring about a transition from capitalism to socialism, made considerable advances by gaining control over most of the foreign-held interests, but with the ouster of the Allende government, these attempts were put aside. Cuba is perhaps the most interesting example of a nation that has broken its ties to the capitalist world. Having done so, Cuba has attempted to solve some of its problems of underdevelopment. Its concerns have involved the elimination of individual alienation and the building of a collectivity. Indeed, Cuba has found itself building a new society. Finally, Nicaragua is consolidating its revolution following the overthrow of the Somoza dynasty.

5

Implications of the Models for Understanding Latin America

The Premises for the Models

Models are heuristic means of structuring ideas and information. The assumptions of the models discussed in this book rest on contrasting premises, values, questions, and explanations of the historical experience of Europe and Latin America. Each model has been elaborated so as to impose upon the reader the obligation to consider alternative perspectives. Presumably, a process of critical thinking has been stimulated, and the reader must now begin to make some choice as to which model may be useful in the study of Latin America. Therefore, it is important to discuss some of the implications of each model and, in particular, to examine some consequences of the historical experience in Latin America.

Both models focus on the impact of capitalism in backward countries. The model of capitalist development has been promoted by many U.S. academics and policymakers, and the model of capitalist underdevelopment, advanced after the Second World War by Latin American intellectuals, was embraced by many mainstream and radical North American academics during the 1960s and 1970s.

On the diffusionist side, there were the ideas and theories of development stages, suggesting that stepped-up knowledge and accumulation of data would signify a trend toward "modernization." That is, development in the capitalist world is part of a continuous, irreversible, and linear progression from traditionalism to modernization, an idea drawn from Max Weber's writings and sketched in the work of Walt W. Rostow (1962) and A.E.K. Organski (1965). Some North American writers, as exemplified by Daniel Bell (1960) and Seymour Martin Lipset (1963), advocated the notion that modernization and technological society accompany consensus and the end of ideology. This idea is tied to prevailing conceptions of pluralism, especially in U.S. political science, which envisaged that a developed polity is related to competition through bargaining and compromise of rival pressure groups and to the belief that pragmatic coalitions transcend a changing class structure. Thus, capitalist political economic development was premised on the spread of capital, technology, political and cultural patterns, and material benefits from developed to underdeveloped areas. In this process, traditional ideologies such as conservatism, liberalism, and socialism would disappear.

On the dependency side, of course, writers like Paul Baran (1957) admonish bourgeois economists for obscuring the issues of underdevelopment. Together with Paul Sweezy (1966), he links backward conditions to monopoly capitalism. André Gunder Frank (1966a and 1967a) focuses on the capitalist development of underdevelopment and emphasizes how commercial monopoly rather than feudalism and precapitalist social formations accounted for the exploitation by national and regional metropolises of their economic satellites. He argues that capitalism on a world scale produces a developing center and an underdeveloping periphery, a process that can be reproduced within nations, for example, between a metropolitan area or city and the surrounding satellite cities and regions.

Methodologically, the two models are premised on radically different assumptions. Diffusion promises progress and growth under capitalism. By associating capitalism in the periphery first with the reinforcement of backwardness and then with a growth characterized by poverty and repression, dependency has shaken the foundations of knowledge and understanding that run through traditional interpretations of Latin America. Obviously, the theoretical assumptions have influenced policy decisions relating to the area and have had very serious consequences on the level of practice and historical experience, especially in regard to U.S. relations with Latin America. On the one hand, there is the view that the United States has and indeed will bring progress to Latin America. On the other hand, there is the view that the United States has negatively altered the course of development in Latin America. Let us look at the historical experience and note its consequences.

Diffusion of Capital and Politics from the United States to Latin America: Three Perspectives

Ever since the mid–nineteenth century, when John L. O'Sullivan formulated the term "manifest destiny" in advocating the territorial expansion of the United States, most North American writers have held that solutions to problems in Latin America must come from the outside. Much of the ensuing social and political thought assumed the existence of a continuous process in which humanity would evolve from savagery to a civilized state. Initially, the condition of the Latin American masses was attributed to racial inferiority. Based on transformations of Darwin's theory of evolution, predictions and prescriptions for Latin America called for a takeover by the United States. People who were regarded as inherently inferior could be improved or reformed only under the rule of those who were naturally superior. Below are some manifestations of this view.

Josiah Strong, Congregational clergyman (*Our Country: Its Possible Future and Its Present Crisis, 1885*):

> Then this [Anglo-Saxon] race of unequaled energy, with all the majesty of numbers and the might of wealth behind it—the representative, let us hope, of the largest liberty, the purest Christianity, the highest civilization—having developed peculiarly aggressive traits calculated to impress its institutions upon mankind, will spread itself over the earth. If I read not amiss, this powerful race will move down upon Mexico, down upon Central and South America, out upon the islands of the sea, over upon Africa and beyond. And can anyone doubt that the result of this competition of races will be the "survival of the fittest"? [Pratt 1959: 6]

John W. Burgess, founder of the first Department of Political Science in the United States (*Political Science and Comparative Constitution Law,* 1890):

> By far the larger part of the surface of the globe is inhabited by populations which have not succeeded in establishing civilized states; which have, in fact, no capacity to accomplish such a work; and which must, therefore, remain in a state of barbarism or semi-barbarism, unless the political nations undertake the work of state organization for them. This condition of things authorizes the political nations not only to answer the call of the unpolitical populations for aid and direction, but also to force organization upon them by any means necessary, in their honest judgement, to accomplish this result. There is no human right to the status of barbarism. [Pratt 1959: 9]

President Theodore Roosevelt, in his annual message to Congress, December 6, 1904 (the Roosevelt Corollary to the Monroe Doctrine):

> If a nation shows that it knows how to act with reasonable efficiency and decency in social and political matters, if it keeps order and pays its obligations, it need fear no interference from the United States. Chronic wrongdoing, or an impotence which results in a general loosening of the ties of the civilized society, may in America, as elsewhere, ultimately require intervention by some civilized nations, and in the Western Hemisphere, the adherence of the United States to the Monroe Doctrine may force the United States, however reluctantly, in cases of wrongdoing or impotence, to the exercise of the international police power.

Such views reflect the policy positions of the United States during the nineteenth and twentieth centuries, and they have been manifested in the actions and dominance of the United States in Latin American affairs in three conspicuous ways: overt intervention, diplomatic maneuvering to ensure order, and recent shifts in policy involving multiple strategies ranging from intervention to collaborative programs in which U.S. assistance was supposed to stimulate a "new development" for Latin America.

Overt Intervention

On April 28, 1965, U.S. President Lyndon B. Johnson ordered the invasion of Santo Domingo "to protect the lives and property of U.S. citizens residing in the Dominican Republic." In October 1983 President Reagan sent U.S. troups to occupy the little island of Grenada. Nearly a century and a half earlier, President James Monroe promulgated the Monroe Doctrine in an annual message to Congress on December 2, 1823. That doctrine challenged the incursion of European powers into the Western Hemisphere and established the "principle in which the rights and interests of the United States are involved, that the American continents, by the free and independent condition which they have assumed and maintained, are henceforth not to be considered as subjects for future colonization by any European powers." (For details on the Monroe Doctrine and contrasting perspectives, see Dozer 1965.)

According to Mexican economist Alonso Aguilar (1965), the motivations behind the Dominican invasion were the same as those that had led Theodore Roosevelt to provoke a revolt in Panama to seize control of Colombian territory and build a canal across the isthmus; that had justified William Howard Taft's protection of U.S. monopolies that sought raw materials in Latin America; and that had prompted Calvin Coolidge to assert Washington's obligations to protect the rights of U.S. investors in that region. Even earlier the Monroe Doctrine had been applied by President James K. Polk in the dispute with Mexico in the 1840s that gave the United States extensive Mexican territory.

On numerous other occasions the Monroe Doctrine has been applied in the hemisphere. For the sake of "American interests," armed intervention occurred in Nicaragua in 1853, 1854, 1857, 1894, 1898, 1899, 1910, 1912–1925, and 1926–1933; in Cuba in 1906–1909, 1912, 1917–1922, and 1933; and in the Dominican Republic in 1903, 1904, 1914, and 1916–1924. The Somoza dynasty in Nicaragua and the dictatorships of Fulgencio Batista in Cuba and Rafael Trujillo in the Dominican Republic emerged as a direct result of U.S. occupations. These were regimes whose military forces were able to contain revolutions and protect U.S. interests. Interventions in Panama in 1856, 1865, 1885, 1903–1914, 1918–1920, and 1925 assured not only political changes resulting in the construction of the Panama Canal but also stability for the U.S. economic and military presence in the Canal Zone for several decades thereafter.

U.S. involvement has been conspicuous elsewhere in the Caribbean and Central America, notably in Haiti (1888, 1891, 1914, and 1915–1934), in Honduras (1903, 1907, 1911, 1912, 1919, 1924, and 1925), and in Guatemala (1920). These events were followed by the establishment in the 1950s of a dictatorship in Haiti under François Duvalier, dominant military rule by the Honduran armed forces, and a CIA-financed coup in Guatemala during 1954. U.S. forces also became involved in the affairs of Mexico (1859, 1866, 1870, 1873, 1876, 1913, 1914–1917, and 1918–1919) and in the South American nations of Uruguay (1855, 1858, and 1868), Paraguay (1859), Colombia (1860, 1868, 1873, 1895, 1901, and 1902), Argentina (1890), Chile (1891), and Brazil (1894).[8]

Diplomatic Maneuvering

The interpretation that the United States could bring benefits to Latin America was at least implicitly tied to U.S. involvement in the movement toward Pan-Americanism. Simón Bolívar, the liberator of much of South America, promoted Pan-Americanism at the Congress of Panama in 1826. His vision was the consolidation of the former Spanish colonies into one great body politic independent of the United States. Yet the United States was invited to the conference, its delegation arriving late because of disinterest and hostility. Although the Pan-American movement itself languished throughout the nineteenth century, there was unprecedented U.S. expansion in the New World. In addition to the acquisition of territory that today comprises Oregon, Washington, Idaho, and parts of Wyoming and Montana as well as Alaska, the United States annexed Texas in 1845 and seized half of Mexico's territory in 1848.

By the latter half of the century, Bolívar's plan of creating a defensive confederation had been abandoned by Latin America. In 1881 James Blaine, secretary of state under President James Garfield, called for a continental conference because "the United States could displace Europe in trade with America." The conference finally took place in 1889 at a time "when the vast domestic market inside the United States began to be insufficient and the rate of profit began to decline, when the powerful industrial trusts, the mining and railroad interests, and the banks demanded new spheres of influence" (Aguilar 1965: 38). The Pan-American system was pushed to ensure U.S. industrial domination throughout Latin America. With its headquarters in Washington, D.C., the inter-American organization offered little resistance to U.S. determination to control the Gulf of Mexico and the Caribbean, especially after the war with Spain in 1898, establishment of control over Puerto Rico, and intervention in Panama at the turn of the century. Under the Platt Amendment, the United States secured the lease of a naval base on Guantánamo Bay, Cuba, thus ensuring a strategic position in the Caribbean. The consequences were analyzed by General Leonard Wood, commander of U.S. forces there:

Of course, Cuba has been left with little or no independence by the Platt Amendment. . . . It cannot enter into certain treaties without our consent, nor secure loans above certain limits, and it must maintain the sanitary conditions which have been indicated. All of this makes it evident that Cuba is absolutely in our hands, and I believe that no European government would consider it otherwise: a real dependent of the United States and, as such we should consider it. [Le Riverend 1967: 210]

Panama was "the product of the decision to get the Panama Canal immediately, and never before had such quick action been taken. The Panamanian 'revolution' was announced in Washington practically before it broke out" (Aguilar 1965: 48). President Roosevelt proclaimed: "I took the Canal Zone." Later he justified his action by the mandate of "civilization" to "coerce a nation which by its 'selfish' actions stood in the way of measures that would benefit the world as a whole" (quoted in Lewis 1963: 78). Such actions became formalized in 1904 in the Roosevelt Corollary to the Monroe Doctrine, which called for the intervention by "civilized" states in any disorderly country.

Latin American resentment to Roosevelt's Big Stick policy was clearly evident at subsequent Pan-American conferences. Yet during the first six meetings, from 1889 to 1928, the United States managed to restrict debate on controversial political affairs and to focus discussion on commercial matters. (For a detailed analysis of this period, see Bemis 1943.) By 1929 direct U.S. investment in Latin America amounted to $3.5 billion, most of which was in railroads and mines. This investment composed two-fifths of worldwide U.S. investment (see NACLA 1971).

The crisis of 1929 and subsequent depression and world war provoked reconsideration of U.S.–Latin American relations. A policy of nonintervention evolved during the Coolidge and Hoover administrations. Hoover ordered the withdrawal of U.S. Marines from Nicaragua and Haiti and repudiated the Roosevelt Corollary. At the same time trade barriers were raised against Latin American products to protect industrial groups in the United States. In 1933 President Franklin D. Roosevelt initiated his Good Neighbor policy, declaring that the United States was opposed to armed intervention and that intervention would be only a joint concern of the whole continent. Such principles were affirmed at the Seventh International Conference of American States in Montevideo in December 1933. A series of agreements was reached, providing for mutual cooperation and consultation within the inter-American system and protection against aggression from outside the hemisphere.

These agreements were secured in spite of Latin American reaction to U.S. meddling in Cuban affairs that had brought down the Ramón Grau San Martín government, which had followed the Gerardo Machado dictatorship, thus ushering in the dictatorial reign of Fulgencio Batista. Once stability and order had been achieved, Roosevelt agreed to the abrogation of the Platt Amendment while retaining the right to the naval base at Guantánamo. Agreements with Cuba, however, resulted in a sharp increase in trade and assured U.S. hegemony over the Cuban economy (see O'Connor 1970). In fact, such hegemony continued as a pattern throughout Latin America as the Roosevelt administration did not modify the monopolistic structure of the United States. Such a structure assured that "the countries south of Rio Grande remained subjugated to the great power in the north and very soon the illusion vanished that things would change radically" (Aguilar 1965: 69).

Nonetheless, the inflow of new capital was negligible between 1929 and 1945 because of a lack of surplus capital during the depression and the later preoccupation with war production. Frank contends that such conditions resulted in a decline of dependence on the world metropolises and allowed for a temporary spurt in economic development in some countries. But, he argues, after the Second World War the Latin American satellites could only be "rechanneled into underdevelopment by the subsequent recuperation and expansion of the metropolis or by the restoration of its active integration with its satellites" (Frank 1967a: 28). Thus, while U.S. investment may not have expanded during the Roosevelt years, it was maintained as a basis for a massive penetration of U.S. capital into Latin America during the postwar years.

The Roosevelt era had initiated multilateral agreements on hemispheric solidarity. A consultative pact signed in 1936 at an inter-American conference in Buenos Aires was partially a response to rising fascism in Europe. At the Eighth International Conference of American States in 1938, the Declaration of Lima reaffirmed the principle of collective defense against all foreign influence in the hemisphere. After the outbreak of world war, the United States established close relations with Latin American military officers and secured a series of military agreements providing for air and naval bases in some sixteen Latin American nations.

Such agreements set the precedent for military and economic assistance in the postwar years, which consolidated the U.S. hold on the continent. By 1947 the Rio Treaty of reciprocal assistance obligated the American nations to assist in repulsing armed attacks from within or outside the hemisphere. This treaty led to the establishment of an elaborate defense network as a deterrent to the Communist threat, and ensuing developments made it clear that the new arrangement was advantageous to U.S. interests in Latin America. During the Ninth International Conference of American States, held in Bogotá in 1948 to establish the Organization of American States (OAS), the popular Colombian liberal Jorge Eliécer Gaitán was assassinated, probably by terrorists linked to conservative groups; the ensuing spontaneous demonstrations of violence, known as the *bogotazo*, were attributed to a Communist "plot."

In 1954, at Caracas, the Tenth Conference declared itself against the intervention of international communism. The immediate concern was Guatemala whose government had expropriated the banana holdings of the United Fruit Company, and U.S. Secretary of State John Foster Dulles argued for action against Guatemala and international communism.

"At the start of the conference the Dulles proposal was supported by only six countries, all of which were dictatorships: but other nations bowed reluctantly to Dulles' threats of economic and political retaliation" (Gil 1971: 211). The March 1954 vote in favor (seventeen to one) of his declaration was followed by the CIA-supported invasion of Guatemala in June. By the end of the month the leftist government of Jacobo Arbenz had been overthrown.

The OAS was called upon to support U.S. intervention in Latin American affairs during the 1960s, specifically the abortive CIA-backed Bay of Pigs invasion in April 1961, and Cuba was eventually expelled from the organization. (Six countries, representing three-fourths of Latin America's population, abstained—Argentina, Bolivia, Brazil, Chile, Ecuador, and Mexico—but the others fell into line because of political and economic pressure.) In April 1965 the United States sent U.S. soldiers and marines to the Dominican Republic under the pretext of protecting Americans threatened by progressive elements. Without OAS consultation, this unilateral action by the Johnson administration was similar to the interventionist era of Teddy Roosevelt. Once U.S. Marines had broken through rebel positions and established order, the OAS met in Washington, and a two-thirds vote finally endorsed the U.S. proposal of establishing an inter-American peace force. (Chile, Mexico, Ecuador, and Uruguay opposed the idea, Venezuela abstained, and the Dominican "delegate" was permitted to vote in favor of the resolution.)

Aid and the "New Development"

Whether involving overt armed intervention or pressures through the OAS, U.S. policies of the past few decades have clearly been oriented to economic considerations. Under the Good Neighbor policy, few gains were made as a result of the modest efforts to break down artificial trade barriers, which discriminated against Latin American goods and perpetuated a highly protectionist U.S. market. Federico Gil affirms: "The extension of economic assistance as a conscious governmental policy to help raise standards of living in foreign areas was a novel idea in the 1930s. Much more study and a clear definition of objectives were needed before this policy could be successfully implemented" (Gil 1971: 167). However, the Export-Import Bank was established in 1934, and after 1940 it became deeply involved in the economies of Latin American nations. In 1944 the World Bank and the International Monetary Fund (IMF) were created; both institutions would have a decisive impact on the hemisphere. The World Bank would offer detailed study, technical assistance, and credit for the implementation of long-range development plans for nations whose economies had been shaped by IMF-supported stabilization and anti-inflationary programs. The IMF would insist on the halting of inflation through price-level controls and the elimination of certain direct controls. (For an elaboration of these programs see David Felix in Hirschman 1961: 81–93.)

Following the Second World War and particularly after the rise to power of Fidel Castro in Cuba, the United States moved aggressively on the economic front. Multinational corporations turned to foreign markets and profits while the U.S. government stimulated the growth of U.S. investments abroad through investment guarantees and tax incentives. At the same time U.S. foreign aid contributed to a "stable" business climate and new markets for the private investor. However, the loss of U.S. investments in Cuba was a major reason the United States promoted the Alliance for Progress in 1961. The Alliance purported to offer a formula of gradual evolution and reform in housing, health, education, and other sectors. Publicized as a revolutionary program, it was in fact a facade for the old diffusionist strategy. Although U.S. Secretary of State Dean Rusk declared that the Alliance "rests on the concept that this hemisphere is part of Western Civilization which we are pledged to defend," his Latin American counterparts made it clear that the intentions of the program were to preserve the status quo. Venezuelan Rómulo Betancourt affirmed that through the Alliance, "We must help the poor . . . in order to save the rich." And the U.S. coordinator for the program, Teodoro Moscoso admitted, "In supporting the Alliance, members of the traditional ruling class will have nothing to fear" (quotes in Aguilar 1963: 31).

The Alliance was a failure for Latin Americans and North Americans alike. In assessing this failure, Federico Gil noted that "the new program floundered at first in a swamp of bureaucratic organization. Administration of the Alliance was entrusted to the Agency for International Development (AID), which was not structured to undertake such an essentially revolutionary task" (Gil 1971: 245). Indeed, AID was established to promote U.S. interests in the region, and clearly these were not revolutionary, no matter what visions the Kennedy administration may have had in the early 1960s. In his analysis of the Alliance, James Petras has noted that at the outset, there was an apparent appreciation of the need for agrarian reform that redistributed both land and power. However, redistribution was gradually replaced by an understanding of the objective of reform to be increased production rather than redistribution (Petras and Zeitlin 1968: 253). As Mexican agricultural economist Edmundo Flores noted in an early critique, the Alliance would face the choice of opposing or favoring revolutionary change. "If, following current misconceptions, the United States backs the quasi-feudal and militaristic governments in power, there will be a pretense of economic development and *Alianza* funds will be misallocated and wasted without changing the conditions responsible for political unrest and economic stagnation. This will lead eventually to the establishment of military dictatorships of the extreme right" (Flores 1963: 13).

It was precisely this situation that developed during the Johnson administration. In March 1964 Johnson's assistant secretary of state for inter-American affairs, Thomas Mann, was quoted in an off-the-record talk to Latin American diplomats as suggesting that the United States would not in the future take an a priori position against governments' coming to power through military coups and that in some cases, military governments were necessary to ensure security. His statement was affirmation of a policy that had evolved earlier in discussions among specialists on Latin America in U.S. universities, the Rand Corporation, the State Department, and the Pentagon.

A conference on militarism, coordinated by Professor John J. Johnson of Stanford University and sponsored by the Rand Corporation in 1959, was concerned primarily with "those officers who have used armies for extra-military purposes" and with "the question of why military governments have promoted national development and democratic practice in some countries" (Johnson 1962: 3–4). Later, Johnson (1964) elaborated upon his proposition that the military, rather than politicians, bureaucrats, and businessmen, would serve their nations as a modernizing force for change. This view paralleled the development of programs for the training of hundreds of Latin American officers in the United States or the Panama Canal Zone in the techniques of civic action and counter-insurgency. Subsequently, the United States supported a series of military coups throughout the hemisphere: Argentina and Peru in 1962; the Dominican Republic, Guatemala, Ecuador, and Honduras in 1963; Bolivia and Brazil in 1964. Later military intervention occurred again in Argentina and Peru and also in El Salvador, Panama, and Uruguay.

The official U.S. reaction to these events became known as the Mann and Johnson doctrines. The former endorsed military intervention by Latin American armed forces in order to ensure stability. When a weak or divided Latin American military could not resolve internal instability, the Johnson doctrine became the order of the day. The conspicuous case was the intervention into the Dominican Republic in 1965. In a message to Congress, President Johnson stressed that there was no one else who could ensure "the right of all people to shape their own destinies," and before a labor conference in Washington he stated, "where Americans go that flag goes with them to protect them." In commenting upon the Dominican intervention a *New York Times* editorial (May 6, 1965) suggested that "the United States gives the appearance of heading toward the unenviable, self-righteous and self-defeating position of world policeman. . . . Ours is the most powerful nation on earth, but there are things that even the United States cannot do in this period of history." The number of U.S. troops in the Dominican Republic totaled nearly 20,000—more than half the number in Vietnam at that time.

Although ultimately the U.S. failure in Vietnam was to ensure the political demise of Johnson and the futility of his doctrine, the Mann doctrine signaled the recognition that the moderate reforms of the Alliance for Progress had also failed. Rather than aid, U.S. policymakers now emphasized trade as the means whereby the United States would strengthen its control over the internal markets of other nations, promote capitalism as the basis for economic development of underdeveloped nations, and maintain stability at any cost. The promotion of capitalism as an alternative to the Cuban revolution continued to be the major impetus of U.S. policy and activity in the area.

The Nixon administration quickly adopted this thrust as the foundation of its policy toward Latin America. Appropriately, Nixon's initial appointee for assistant secretary of state for inter-American affairs was Charles A. Meyer, a director of the United Fruit Company—long notorious for its autocratic dealings in the "banana republics"—and an executive of Sears, Roebuck & Company, which has stores throughout Latin America.

Under President Carter, policy shifted in the direction of protection of basic human rights. Officially repressive regimes such as that of General Pinochet in Chile were pressured to release political prisoners, stop torture, and tolerate opposition. In practice, however, despite its rhetoric and image of goodwill, the Carter administration achieved very little in Latin America. Toward the end of his term, Carter began to hedge on his stance in Central America, specifically bowing to pressure from conservative forces and finally restoring military aid to the government in El Salvador, aid that had been suspended because the paramilitary forces of that regime had raped and murdered four religious women who were U.S. citizens.

President Ronald Reagan moved quickly to place Central America at the core of his foreign policy. Military advisers were dispatched to El Salvador immediately upon his assumption of office early in 1981, and economic aid to revolutionary Nicaragua was halted. Cuba was indicted for its "connection" to Central American revolutionary situations; Nicaragua was chastised for its alleged support of insurgent forces in El Salvador; but Guatemala, scene of torture and repression, was courted by U.S. officials and promised a revival of U.S. aid. A White Paper issued by the State Department attempted to prove allegations of Communist subversion in Central America, but it was criticized for its inaccuracies and Cold War rhetoric by academicians and the press, including the *Wall Street Journal*.

When governments intervene in the affairs of other nations, they rarely explain their actions exclusively in terms of self-interest. The U.S. government has portrayed its Latin American policies for the benefit of the North American people as the result of a happy coincidence of North American and Latin American interests. U.S. citizens have been told by the government that their tax dollars are being spent for a policy that protects their national security and interests while bringing them economic benefit—a policy that at the same time promotes national independence, self-determination, democracy, economic development, and social progress for the peoples of Latin America. As we have seen thus far, the claim that U.S. policy has simultaneously advanced all of these objectives relies on several theories and perceptions of the world that are questionable and others that are clearly false.

A new understanding of Latin American underdevelopment is necessary as well as a critique of the assertion that the penetration of Latin America by North American political, economic, and cultural influences contributes to Latin American development. This assertion has provided the intellectual underpinnings of U.S. policy. The ideas of Manifest Destiny held that U.S. intervention was often necessary to maintain "civilization." Recent U.S. policy not only reaffirms that credo but also contends that North American penetration is essential to the elimination of underdevelopment.

6
Reformist and Revolutionary Strategies

Latin America's struggle for change has been associated with reformist and revolutionary strategies. The independence revolts of the nineteenth century led to the apparent liberation of the continent from the colonial rule of Portugal and Spain, but the influence of these European countries has prevailed until today. Further, England was successful during the nineteenth and early twentieth centuries in obtaining a foothold on the continent. In Argentina, for example, England established an infrastructure of roads, railways, and power to ensure its control over exports of valuable wheat and meat products. English capital also penetrated the Chilean economy through domination of the nitrate industry. After the First World War, U.S. capital established itself in these countries, ensuring that country's hegemony over the burgeoning copper exports in Chile and industrialization in Argentina.

Latin American national capital, which seems to have benefited from the Great Depression of 1932 and the two world wars (Frank 1967a), was unable to meet the challenge of capitalist expansion from Europe and the United States. Thus, it was not uncommon for that region's businessmen and merchants to manifest sentiments of xenophobia, concern for the protection of national resources, and hostility to imperialism. Such feelings were conspicuous in Latin America as early as the late nineteenth century, but they were especially evident during the 1920s (Johnson 1958: 4–5) and on to the present day. Thus, Latin Americans of varied political persuasions have sought changes through reform or revolution.

Authoritarianism and Corporatism

Latin Americans long have been recognized for their propensity to tolerate authoritarian rule. The wars of independence attempted to break the bonds of colonialism and empire Spain had imposed upon the area, and generally these wars were led by liberals who advocated decentralized government and moderate reforms. While liberals and conservatives struggled for power throughout the nineteenth century, conservatives who favored close ties between state and church as well as a centralized form of government seemed to hold the upper hand. The twentieth century witnessed the prevalence of dictators, the most prominent being Batista in Cuba, the Somozas in Nicaragua, Trujillo in the Dominican Republic, Duvalier in Haiti, Getúlio Vargas in Brazil, Juan Perón in Argentina, Gustavo Rojas Pinilla in Colombia, Marcos Pérez Jiménez in Venezuela, and Alfredo Stroessner in Paraguay. The victory of Fidel Castro in 1959 inspired revolutionaries everywhere to rid the continent of these men, but the instability and chaos that followed in the wake of changes necessitated that U.S. policymakers and people with vested economic interests in Latin America find a new authority. Thus, military regimes reemerged in the 1960s and 1970s to ensure tranquillity and order. The foundations of their rule rested on what political scientists have called "modernizing authoritarianism" (O'Donnell 1973, Collier 1979), but the political roots of the recent era stemmed from corporatism.

The populist authoritarianism of Juan Perón in Argentina (1946–1955; 1973–1974) and Getúlio Vargas in Brazil (1930–1945; 1951–1954), the military populism of Peru (1968–1975), and the bureaucratic authoritarianism of Brazil after 1964 are examples of authoritarian regimes in Latin America. James Malloy associates these regimes with corporatism:

> The critical point of similarity is that each of these regimes is characterized by strong and relatively autonomous governmental structures that seek to impose on the society a system of interest representation based on enforced limited pluralism . . . the recognized groups in this type of regime are organized in vertical functional categories rather than horizontal class categories and are obliged to interact with the state through the designated leaders of authoritatively sanctioned interest associations. This mode of organizing state and society has aptly been termed "corporatism." [Malloy 1977: 4]

Corporatism thus is a term that explains a relationship between an authoritarian state and some interest representation, for example, the labor movement in Latin America (see Erickson 1977 for attention to the Brazilian labor movement). However, political scientists in a more general way extended their analysis "toward a corporate ordering of interest politics and of state-society relations around non-competing groups which are officially sanctioned, closely supervised, and often subsidized by the state" (Collier and Collier 1979: 967). In this way, specialists were able to combine an interest in pluralism, influenced by their understanding of Anglo-American politics, with authority patterns that appear to undermine the democratic perspectives usually associated with pluralism. At the same time they introduced new propositions to explain the rise of armed forces to power, the interest in accelerating industrial growth based on foreign investment and capitalist penetration, and repression of popular politics. In turn, the new interpretation allowed for the discarding of old notions of modernization in which industrialization was accompanied by democracy and equality.

This new formulation, however, was inspired fundamentally by the tradition of corporatism in the experience of fascist regimes in Germany, Italy, Portugal, and Spain. Corporatism, of course, has its roots in such thinkers as Aristotle and Saint Thomas Aquinas, and in the middle of the nineteenth century some European writers developed corporatist theories in order to analyze changes in the old social order and the problems brought about by capitalism, industrialization, and urbanization (Wiarda 1977: chap. 3). In contemporary Spain and in Portugal, corporate thought bestowed upon the state the role of arbiter of the national interest. The corporatism of the Iberian nations was founded on two traditions: Roman law, which generally ignores autonomous private interests and favors the general national interest; and the Roman Catholic church, an authoritarian, centralized, and hierarchical institution, which desires to establish itself as the official church (Erickson 1977: 4).

Corporatist theoreticians in the fascist countries based their thinking on the papal encyclicals of Leo XIII (Rerum Novarum) and Pius XI (Quadragesimo Anno). The latter encyclical advocated that class conflict be mitigated by guilds or associations according to functions performed by workers in society. In Portugal, such guilds, along with corporations, were formally structured in the state, although in practice they were generally ineffective. In Spain, trade unions known as *sindicatos*, labor courts, and the social security system became the structures that linked the state to the workers. A similar system was established under Vargas in Brazil, and labor unions filled this function in Mexico under Cárdenas and thereafter were manipulated by the government party. Thus, individuals in a corporate state do not enjoy the freedom expected of citizens in a liberal democracy; instead they participate in carefully controlled state associations.

Howard Wiarda (1978: 416–417) reminds us that while it is often assumed that corporatism as a concept and an ideology died with the fall of fascist regimes at the end of and after the Second World War, recent literature suggests that it is in fact alive and flourishing. Philippe C. Schmitter recalls the statement of the corporatist ideologue, Mihail Manoilesco, who in his *Le Siècle du corporatisme* (1934) stated that "the twentieth century will be the century of corporatism just as the nineteenth was the century of liberalism" (Schmitter 1974: 85). The sixteen essays in Malloy's collection (1977), the case studies by Kenneth Erickson on Brazil (1977) and David Chaplin on Peru (1976), and general treatments by Wiarda (1973) and Frederick Pike (1974) seem to attest to this fact.

Corporatism as a tradition of Latin American politics has been questioned by Linn A. Hammergren. She argues that this corporatism has not necessarily been an ingredient of development in the region but that, instead, the regimes characterized as corporatist turned to authoritarianism in response to the instability of central institutions (Hammergren 1977: 443–444).

Schmitter has elaborated the most useful definitions and descriptions of corporatism. He laments the varied usages of the concept in the literature and alleges that "it can be found everywhere and, hence, is nowhere very distinctive . . . it becomes, at best, uniquely descriptive rather than comparatively analytic" (Schmitter 1974: 86). He attempts to give corporatism a more useful connotation, believing that corporatism displaced a decaying pluralism and served as a "system of interest representation" necessary to the perpetuation of a stable bourgeois regime and its needs of capitalism and state control:

> The more the modern state comes to serve as the indispensable and authoritative guarantor of capitalism by expanding its regulative and integrative tasks, the more it finds that it needs the professional expertise, specialized information, prior aggregation of opinion, contractual capability and deferred participatory legitimacy which only singular, hierarchically ordered, consensually led representative monopolies can provide. [Schmitter 1974: 111]

Schmitter is not optimistic about the prospects for state corporatism, however. Everywhere it reveals itself as more costly to maintain through repression, and further, it faces new demands for participation that cannot be met without undermining the established hierarchies of authority.

Corporatism thus is a conservative response to the liberal ideals of free enterprise and democratic political practice. Experimentation with corporatism outside Latin America allowed for a preservation of bourgeois class rule and national capital under authoritarian leadership. In Portugal and Spain, corporatism collapsed only after a generation of repression to maintain internal order. In Latin America, corporatism assumed, somewhat formally in Brazil and informally in Argentina and Mexico, a model based on the Iberian experience, and in the past two decades there has been an interest in corporatism as theory and explanation on the part of political scientists and other specialists on Latin America who have attempted to justify military intervention as a legitimate strategy to contain competing political and economic interests and promote capitalist development in the name of the state and private business. Corporatism also was a response to efforts in many parts of the hemisphere to promote development through some form of socialism, and further, it served as a counterforce to ideas about dependent capitalist development.

Dependent and Autonomous Capitalist Development

Ideas about dependency have led to both reformist and revolutionary strategies of development. An understanding of dependency and its strategies necessitates a look, first, at its origins and the evolution of the thinking, and, second, at its central premises (see Chilcote, 1974 and 1981, for an overview).

The origins of dependency can be traced to a variety of sources. Gary Howe (1981) suggests that its characteristics stem from seventeenth-century mercantilist thought. Carlos Johnson (1981) believes that the basic postulates of dependency theory have reoccurred throughout capitalist history, and he illustrates his position by referring to the reformist ideology of the Russian Narodniks, or popular socialists, of the nineteenth century. More commonly, the origins of dependency are identified in the work of Raúl Prebisch and the Economic Commission for Latin America (ECLA) after the Second World War (Baer 1969).

Economists such as Aldo Ferrer, Celso Furtado, and Osvaldo Sunkel have promoted the idea that *desarrollismo*, or developmentalism, is essentially a means to deter international capital through import substitution and build an infrastructure of resources that will allow local dominant classes greater participation in the process of capital accumulation. These economists have tended to view the dominant nations of the capitalist world, especially the United States, as the center or core of capitalist development whereas Latin America is part of the more backward periphery. As discussed earlier, Pablo González Casanova (1969) offered a corollary to this thesis, suggesting that a center and periphery exist within a nation; he illustrated his model, called internal colonialism, by referring to Mexico. In another work, González Casanova (1970b) went a step further in his belief that the discrepancy between the exploitative dominant center of Mexico and the exploited dependent periphery will someday be resolved by the actions of an emerging national bourgeoisie. There is an emphasis on the progressive role of a national bourgeoisie as a class that promotes autonomous capitalism within a nation in most of the early writings on underdevelopment.

The belief that a national bourgeoisie might promote autonomous development in the face of imperialism was associated with populism and nationalism; for example, in Brazil during the early 1960s. However, evidence that the multinationals were penetrating Latin America and taking over the industrialization provoked economists such as Theotonio Dos Santos and others to criticize the ECLA theses and promote the "new" dependency (Dos Santos 1968, 1970). Dos Santos also was seeking an alternative to the position of the Latin American Communist parties, in particular the two-stage thesis that the working class should support the national bourgeoisie in the initial drive toward capitalism and later promote the second stage of the socialist revolution. Dos Santos was representative of the radical "dependentistas" who sought to expose the reformist ideals of the people who favored a capitalist path.

One of the radical dependentistas who most successfully presented the critique of reformism was André Gunder Frank. In a seminal article (1966a) and a book on Latin America (1967a), he focused on the metropolis-satellite structure of the capitalist system, and through reference to the case studies of Brazil and Chile, he applied his thesis that capitalist development in Latin America brings about underdevelopment. He emphasized commercial monopoly rather than feudal and precapitalist social formations as the means whereby national and regional metropolises exploit and appropriate the surplus of satellites. In this way, capitalism on a world scale results in a developing metropolis and an underdeveloped periphery.

Despite their popularity, these ideas have been attacked by scores of critics, most notably Ernesto Laclau (1971) and Bill Warren (1973) who exposed the exaggerated attention to the impact of the market rather than production. It should also be mentioned that Frank's writing carried on a tradition of independent socialist thought presented in the journal *Monthly Review* and in particular books by Paul Baran (1957), Paul Sweezy (1942), and Samir Amin (1974, 1976). Walter Rodney (1974) also applied the same ideas to show how Europe underdeveloped Africa. These writings consistently attack reformism of all types while revising and updating Marxist theory to focus on the changing needs of the world capitalist market. Classical Marxists have faulted them for their attention to circulation rather than production of commodities and for their inattention to social classes and class struggle.

Many of the new dependentistas, including Dos Santos, not only attacked reformist strategies but returned to the Marxist view of Lenin and Trotsky, who analyzed the growing influence of imperialism throughout the world. Kenzo Mohri (1979) locates the ideas of dependency in the writing of Marx. During the middle 1860s Marx shifted his position from the belief that industrial capital would permeate backward societies and establish the material conditions of capitalism in Asia to the view, explicitly set forth in his writing on the Irish question, that "a new and international division of labor, a division suited to the requirements of the chief centers of modern industry, springs up and converts one part of the globe into a chiefly agricultural field of production, for supplying the other part which remains a chiefly industrial field" (Marx 1967: 1:451). Thus, Marx was moving toward an analysis similar to contemporary writings on dependency.

Lenin also referred to the relationship of dependent nation and periphery. In *Imperialism: The Highest Stage of Capitalism*, he affirmed, "Not only are there two main groups of countries, those owning countries, and the colonies themselves, but also the diverse forms of dependent countries which, politically, are dependent, but in fact, are enmeshed in the net of financial and diplomatic dependency" (Lenin 1967: 1:742–743).

Various lines of thinking have appeared in Trotskyist writings about Latin America. Essentially, Trotsky believed in a strategy of permanent revolution, arguing that the internationalization of revolution was necessary in order for the transition to socialism to be completed in individual countries. His law of uneven development suggested that backward countries could skip intermediate stages and catch up to advanced countries. His law of combined development held that developing countries might simultaneously follow the path of backward and advanced countries; modes of production could be combined so that advances in industrialization might occur and coexist with remnants of feudalism. Trotsky also stressed that industrialization in underdeveloped countries would lead to imperialist domination rather than to autonomous control by a national bourgeoisie. The Argentine intellectual and Marxist, Silvio Frondizi, who wrote on dependency as early as 1947 and drew upon Trotsky's thought, claimed that the consequence of imperialist domination would be the greater economic dependency of backward nations on advanced ones. Donald Hodges (1974) argues that Frondizi thus anticipated the new dependency assumptions of Dos Santos and others.

An analysis of dependency also has evolved that examines the compatibility of dependency and capitalist development in certain situations in Latin America. Instead of suggesting or even advocating socialism as an alternative to the dependent conditions described by Frank and other writers opposed to capitalism, this alternative perspective tends to look to the progressive impact of capitalism itself. Two major, yet contrasting, views have appeared in the writing of two Brazilian thinkers, Fernando Henrique Cardoso and Ruy Mauro Marini.

According to his own account, Cardoso attributes his thinking on development and underdevelopment to the early writing of Lenin. Lenin saw imperialism as a new form of capitalism, an advanced stage in which monopolistic capital replaces competitive capital. Furthermore, financial and industrial capital combine under imperialism as the banking system in the capitalist mode of production assumes a dominant role. Imperialism thus becomes the highest form of capitalism in the form of monopoly capital, and the rapid development of productive forces under monopolistic controls necessitates expansion by the advanced capitalist countries toward control of raw materials and markets in foreign areas. Cardoso argues that the consequence of this imperialism was the integration of dependent economies into the international market: "The reproduction and amplification of inequality between advanced economies and dependent economies developed as a by-product of the very process of capitalist growth" (Cardoso 1972: 85). He argues that despite Lenin's insights, important changes have occurred in the relationship between imperialist and dependent nations and Lenin's characterization is no longer adequate to explain contemporary capitalist accumulation and external expansion. Instead, one must look at the impact of the role of the multinational corporation after the Second World War and rethink previous ideas of finance capital and its control over industry.

New forms of economic dependency have appeared in Latin America, according to Cardoso. Not only are multinationals investing in industry within the dominated economies rather than in traditional agriculture and mining, but they are also joining with local capital. The result is that "*development* and *monopoly penetration* in the industrial sectors of dependent economies are not incompatible . . . there occurs a kind of *dependent capitalist development*" (Cardoso 1972: 89). Elsewhere, Cardoso (1973) refers to this result as "associated capitalist development."

Cardoso emphasizes that he does not mean to imply that this new form of imperialism unifies class interests in the dominated countries, but his notion exposes what he believes to be the fallacy of Frank's development of underdevelopment thesis. He argues that in some situations development may occur alongside dependency. This phenomenon is not found throughout the Third World, but it is found when "corporations reorganize the international division of labour and include parts of dependent economies in their plans of productive investment" (Cardoso 1972: 94).

Ruy Mauro Marini argues that the Second World War resulted in a crisis in the international economy brought about by the dislocation of forces between imperialist powers and by the emergence of new forms of capital accumulation. The United States responded to this crisis by reorganizing the world capitalist economy through such instruments as the International Monetary Fund and the World Bank. Consequently, a large commercial surplus in the United States was distributed through the international market, and there evolved a new stage of capitalist development and superexploitation in Latin America, what Marini describes as *subimperialism*.

Subimperialism is

> a form which the dependent economy assumes in order to arrive at the stage of monopoly and finance capital. Subimperialism implies two basic components: on the one hand, a . . . national productive apparatus, and, on the other, . . . a relatively autonomous expansionist policy, which is not only accompanied by a greater integration in the imperialist productive system, but also is maintained under the hegemony exercised by imperialism on an international scale. [Marini 1978b: 34–35]

Marini suggests that subimperialism in Brazil not only was economic in nature but also resulted from "class struggle in the country and from the political project defined by the technocratic-military team which assumed power in 1964, combined with the conjunctural conditions in the world economy and in world politics" (Marini 1978b: 35). With these assumptions, Marini emphasizes the Brazilian state and its ability to rationalize a subimperialist policy more effectively than that which could be imposed within Brazil by national and foreign capital. Capitalist groups and their interests were combined with the political interests of power in the hands of the military-technocratic rulers who controlled the state apparatus. Capitalism in Brazil thus assumed a progressive form only through its relationship to international capital:

> Thrown into the orbit of international finance capital, Brazilian capitalism did everything to attract the monetary flow, and since it did not have the capacity to assimilate and integrate so much productive capital, it then had to re-integrate it within the international movement of capital. With its dependent and subordinate state style, Brazil entered the capital export stage, as well as the plundering of raw materials and energy sources in the exterior, like petroleum, iron, and natural gas. [Marini 1978b: 35]

Marini then argues that subimperialism is one way in which a dependent country like Brazil may resolve, at least temporarily, its own internal contradictions. Dependent capitalism, he believes, is unable to expand and accumulate along the path of capitalist development in more advanced nations. Industrialization is limited by a weak internal market, a traditional export economy, and the importation of products from the metropolis. Overexploitation of labor accompanies these conditions in the form of lengthening the workday and intensifying the use of labor power (Marini 1974). Marini, however, identifies with the Frank model of stagnation and underdevelopment; in this regard, he is at odds with Cardoso, and a debate between the two has ensued (Serra and Cardoso 1978, Marini 1978a).

Two lines of the debate are identified by Colin Henfrey (1981). First, Marini draws on laws of dependent capitalism in his analysis of class formation, whereas Cardoso denies that such laws are applicable to dependency. Second, ideological differences are apparent since Marini has attacked Cardoso as being bourgeois oriented and opposed to socialist revolution, and Cardoso has condemned Marini's advocacy of armed struggle as dangerous. Henfrey concludes, however, that this debate is "circular"; that Marini's portrayal of dependent capitalist class formation is deterministic, or "undifferentiated," in terms of simple commodity production and capitalist accumulation; and that Cardoso's empirical descriptions fail to explain "what they describe, in the absence of a clearly guiding theory and related analytic concepts" (Henfrey 1981: 25–26).

Whatever the usefulness of reformist and revolutionary strategies around the ideas of underdevelopment and autonomous and dependent capitalist development, critics on the left generally believe that the time has come to transcend theories and conceptions of dependency and search for alternative strategies that may lead backward nations in the direction of socialism and communism. In particular, they have attacked the belief that a break with dependency will necessarily lead to autonomous capitalist development or that dependency is compatible with capitalist development. Howe, Henfrey, Carlos Johnson, and other writers affirm this position in an issue of *Latin American Perspectives* (Summer-Fall 1981) and suggest a variety of directions to which we might turn.

Even Cardoso has recently abandoned the case for dependency by criticizing dependentistas for limiting their analysis to describing economic and social deformations created by the expansion of capitalism on the periphery and for failing to offer strategies to achieve the alternative society to the bourgeois one they condemn (Cardoso 1979).

The idea of dependency particularly influenced the thought of mainstream North American intellectuals, many of whom sought alternatives to the modernization and diffusionist theory premised on the idea that capitalism and technology could be carried from advanced to backward areas in the promotion of capitalist development. These intellectuals also juxtaposed analysis of dependency to notions of corporatism and authoritarianism that were being used to explain the rise of right-wing military regimes throughout Latin America. The weaknesses and problems of mainstream theory about dependency, however, were easily perceived. Academicians tended to indiscriminately apply ideas on dependency to their empirical research. Often the origins of the dependency idea were overlooked or ignored and new jargon and terminology introduced. The result was confusion and a plea for some orderly progress (Cardoso 1977, Fagen 1977).

In summary, explanations of dependency have suggested possibilities for underdevelopment as well as for development. Clearly, no unified theory has emerged as the emphasis on dependency has permeated both mainstream and radical thought. Weaknesses in the formulations about dependency also are obvious: They fail to take into account class struggle and tend to obscure attention to imperialism; they tend to emphasize relations of exchange (trade and market) instead of class relations based on how goods are produced while exaggerating questions of nationalism and development; and finally, they tend not to offer strategies for achieving development, especially socialist development.

Socialism and Communism

There are many strategies for change that evolve from movements advocating socialism and communism. The divergences among these movements relate to the contrasting ideas of Lenin, Stalin, Trotsky, and Mao, all of whom based their thought on the writings of Karl Marx.

Marx emphasized the contradictions in European capitalist development and in particular focused on the English model. He noted the negative consequences for backward nations faced with the exploitation of capital but assumed that eventually, the less developed nations would overcome their growing pains and develop in the image of England. Most observers believe that Marx meant that historical stages in the development of production could not be skipped and, thus, capitalist development must precede the transition to socialism. Evidence for this position can be found in the *Communist Manifesto* (1848), in Marx's writings on India (1853), and in passages in the *Grundrisse* (1857–1858).

Other observers believe that in his writings on Ireland, Marx implied that capital accumulation in advanced nations would lead to investment in backward areas, which would bring about underdevelopment rather than development. In a letter of November 30, 1867, to Engels, Marx advocated self-determination, agrarian revolution, and protective tariffs for Ireland against England. Kenzo Mohri suggests that Marx had shifted from his view that industrial capitalism would provide the material basis for the development of new production in the less advanced areas of the world to a position in which those areas were seen as being headed toward destruction and decline (Mohri 1979: 35).

Lenin was influenced by Marx in his application of ideas to Russia, but there were some differences between the two. Lenin was especially interested in the political and revolutionary ideas Marx advocated in the late 1840s when he believed a bourgeois revolution, followed by a proletarian one, could occur in an underdeveloped country. Although Marx later turned his attention to England as an example of an advanced country, Lenin called for the seizure of power by the proletariat prior to the implementation of a bourgois democratic revolution. In *Two Tactics of Social Democracy in the Democratic Revolution* (1905), Lenin envisaged a bourgeois democratic revolution under proletarian leadership whereas Marx had argued that the proletariat would lead only a socialist revolution. Marx stressed political rather then military struggle, but both Marx and Lenin argued that depending on conditions, both legal and illegal means of struggle could be employed. Marx desired a mass political party of the proletariat while Lenin promoted a vanguard party of the proletariat composed of professional revolutionaries; Marx urged a majority coalition of working class parties while Lenin advocated a majority coalition of proletariat and peasantry.

Trotsky believed that the proletariat could seize power in backward countries as well as in advanced ones. He also advocated the concept of "permanent" revolution, a concept he attributed to Marx, and the idea that revolution could not compromise with dominant class rule or stop at the bourgeois democratic stage; if it did so, it would not even achieve bourgeois democratic aims. Lenin believed that a bourgeois democratic revolution must precede the establishment of a proletarian dictatorship, and Trotsky argued that the workers had to lead the revolution to assure that the historic aims of bourgeois democracy be met. Both men favored revolutionary struggle, both urged the formation of a vanguard party of professional revolutionaries, both opposed a mass party of the proletariat, and both sought a coalition of the working class with the peasantry rather than with the liberal bourgeoisie.

After the Russian revolution, strong revolutionary movements appeared in other countries such as Bulgaria, Czechoslovakia, Finland, Germany, Hungary, Poland, and Yugoslavia, but this revolutionary wave came to an end during the period of civil war in Russia itself. The counterrevolutionary inclinations of social democracy brought workers moderate reforms but not power; thereafter Nazi bands arose to promote national socialism and fascism. Under Stalin, the new privileged layer of bureaucrats gradually began to acquire control over all sectors of society, thereby undermining the political and economic power exercised by the working class. Ernest Mandel, a Trotskyist, described this development: "Stalinism is the expression of the *bureaucratic degeneration* of the first workers' state, where a privileged layer usurped the exercise of political and economic power" (Mandel 1977: 114).

After the victory of the Chinese revolution in 1949, forms of bureaucratic privileges similar to those in Stalinist Russia appeared, thus limiting participation of workers and peasants. The Cultural Revolution of the 1960s, which was led by a section of the bureaucracy, appeared to be a response to these privileges. For Mandel, Maoism was "a variety of the Stalinist deformation of Marxism-Leninism . . . the expression both of the victory of a socialist revolution and the bureaucratically deformed nature of this revolution (Mandel 1977: 119).

Given these ideas, it is not surprising that a myriad of revolutionary movements advocating socialism and/or communism have appeared in Latin America. Marxism and Leninism have exerted a great deal of influence on the left, and Stalinism generally was associated with the traditional Communist parties—especially during the era of the Comintern but also after the Second World War—until his death in 1953 and the denunciations of his personality cult by the Twentieth Congress of the Soviet Communist party in 1956. Trotskyism has been influential in certain countries, especially Mexico, where Trotsky resided in exile until his death in 1940, and also in Argentina, Bolivia, Chile, and Peru. Maoism was evident in the splits within some Communist parties during the early 1960s, especially in Brazil and Peru.

Donald Hodges (1974) has classified contemporary revolutionary movements into the categories of Apro-Marxism or democratic socialism, communism, Trotskyism, Fidelism, and Guevarism. His very useful synthesis reveals the strains in and divergence among these movements as reflected in differences in the thought of Marx, Lenin, Trotsky, Stalin, and Mao as well as in the experiences and conditions in Latin America. The discussion below identifies the principal lines of thought.

Since the turn of the century social democracy and democratic socialism have stimulated debate. For example, Karl Kautsky, a renowned Marxist, addressed pacifist inclinations, and Lenin, a militant Marxist and Bolshevik leader of the Russian revolution, focused on the means of achieving socialism. Influenced by the prospect of an evolving socialism through parliamentary coalitions, especially in Germany, Kautsky engaged Lenin in a bitter polemical debate about the nature of imperialism; Lenin, of course, defended the thesis that in view of the Russian experience, revolution should be employed. Under Stalin, the Soviet-directed international organization of Communist parties, the Communist International (Comintern), revised the revolutionary line to encourage political support of the progressive bourgeoisie and electoral alliances of Communist parties with progressive forces. One such popular front actually resulted in victory for the Radical candidate, Pedro Aguirre Cerda, in Chile's 1938 elections, and such alliances, under the leadership of the socialist and Communist parties, ushered Salvador Allende to power in 1970.

Allende and his socialist party had belonged to the Second International, which had advocated socialism through parliamentary means; namely, achieving power and socialism by means of a parliamentary majority in government. Allende, together with other politicians such as Venezuela's Rómulo Betancourt, Costa Rica's José Figueres, and Peru's Víctor Haya de la Torre, was known variously as a democratic socialist, social democrat, and democratic leftist. Allende, the most radical of these personalities, set forth a basis for socialism, but in one way or another, they all tended to seek political compromise while sacrificing their revolutionary ideals.

Bourgeois democratic governments supported by Marxists came into power in Mexico from 1934 to 1940, in Bolivia in 1952, in Guatemala in 1944, in Costa Rica in 1948, and in Venezuela in 1958. Although Víctor Haya de la Torre won a plurality in the Peruvian presidential elections of 1962, a military coup nullified the elections. Juan Bosch's Revolutionary Democratic Party, or Partido Revolucionario Democrático (PRD), won elections a year later in the Dominican Republic, but his movement was ended by the U.S. military intervention in 1965. Hodges suggests that the thought of Haya best represents these social democratic tendencies. Haya emphasized the negative consequences of capitalism in Latin America, believing that underdevelopment was the result of an imperialist and foreign bourgeoisie intent upon repatriation of profits abroad, a class of landowners that perpetuated semifeudal conditions in the countryside, and a petty bourgeoisie that could not evolve as a national bourgeoisie and promote autonomous capitalism. Haya advocated the formation of a multiclass party of petty bourgeoisie, proletariat, and peasantry. He believed that armed struggle was a viable strategy, but he resorted to electoral politics as a means to power. Once in power, he believed that the state should encourage but control private enterprise and foreign capital. Yet he opposed imperialism in theory and tended not to align with the more disciplined Communist parties.

The Communist parties of Latin America formed after the Russian revolution. They tended to follow the Russian example, an allegiance that was evident after the Comintern was established in 1919. Traditionally, the Communist parties in Latin America followed a policy of alignment in a popular front of bourgeois forces or coalition in a united front of progressive forces favoring socialism, although there were examples of attempts at armed struggle (in El Salvador in 1932 and Brazil in 1935), and a minority of leftist parties followed the Cuban revolutionary example after 1959. The Haitian, Guatemalan, Venezuelan, and Paraguayan parties pursued this line at various times; the Colombian party used a dual strategy of armed and electoral struggle; and the parties in Argentina, Brazil, Chile, Mexico, and Peru tended to follow the peaceful road. In Brazil, this tendency resulted in numerous splits and considerable intraparty struggle both before and after the 1964 military coup (Chilcote 1974), and the Chilean party was a victim of brutal repression in the 1973 military overthrow of Allende. The Communist parties that have advocated a peaceful transition to socialism have usually called for a bourgeois democratic stage prior to socialism, although the official Soviet position suggests that a single leap to socialism is possible. Their emphasis has been on mobilizing the working class under leadership of the petty bourgeoisie (that is, professionals and intellectuals). Party discipline, then, serves to hold these elements together.

Once Leon Trotsky reached Mexico in 1936, his influence spread rapidly throughout Latin America, and his theory of permanent revolution was of particular significance to the leftist movements in the area. This theory stressed that a democratic stage is not necessary prior to the socialist transition, especially in backward countries where a dictatorship of the proletariat can be established immediately; and the permanent character of the revolution cannot be completed on national foundations alone but must develop in the context of world class struggle. Although this theory provided a framework for the Trotskyist movement in Latin America, divergencies in thought have appeared.

Hodges, who has contributed a most useful analysis of Trotskyism, distinguishes between the proletarian and national liberation tendencies: The proletarian tendency opposes alliances with revolutionary nationalist movements except when the hegemony of the proletariat is assured, and the national liberation tendency favors such an alliance, provided that a proletarian vanguard can be operated independently. Although the national liberation line dominated throughout Latin America from 1949 to 1963, the two tendencies meant that most countries had at least two Trotskyist parties. Both tendencies were represented in Bolivia's revolution of 1952. Bolivian Guillermo Lora's faction broke with the Fourth International in 1956 and played an independent role until 1969 when it joined the International Committee of the Fourth International, which aggregated groups led by José Altamire in Argentina, Ricardo Napuri in Peru, and others in Brazil and Venezuela. These groups followed the proletarian tendency while another bloc, led by the Argentine Jorge Abelardo Ramos, the Peruvian Ismael Frias, the Uruguayan Alberto Methol Ferré, and several Chilean Trotskyists, favored the national liberation tendency.

The roles of the national bourgeoisie and the petty bourgeoisie constituted the major divisive issues of Latin American and especially Argentine Trotskyism. Division over these issues was evident in the writings of three major Argentine thinkers: Hugo Bressano (Nahuel Moreno) and Silvio Frondizi, who represented the proletarian view and were critical of the national bourgeoisie as well as of the petty bourgeoisie as revolutionary allies, and Ramos, who defended these classes for their revolutionary potential. In 1947 Frondizi contrasted U.S. imperialism with that of England, and he analyzed the interlocking interests of imperialism and the national bourgeoisie and criticized the thesis of dual society that attributed backwardness to feudalism. These views were aimed against the strategy of the Communist parties that favored collaboration with the national bourgeoisie against the landed oligarchy and became dominant in later writings on dependency.

Fidelism is characterized, according to Hodges, by the strategy of a united front that supports a liberation struggle in which unity of forces, rather than leadership by a vanguard party, becomes a principal objective. The idea of Fidelism is rooted in the July 26 movement that Fidel Castro founded in March 1956 after breaking from the Cuban Orthodox party. Once the Cuban revolutionary movement came to power, other such groups were formed: for example, the Peruvian APRA Rebelde, which split from Haya de la Torre's APRA in October 1959, and the Venezuelan youth wing of Betancourt's Acción Democrática, which became the Movement of the Revolutionary Left, or the Movimiento Izquierda Revolucionaria (MIR), in April 1960.

Throughout Latin America, heterogeneous movements pursued this direction, including student groups that broke from populism, socialist parties supporting the Cuban revolution (in Chile, Uruguay, Ecuador, Peru, and Argentina), some Trotskyist-influenced groups (the left wing within Peronismo in Argentina, for example), progressive church movements (Camilo Torres in Colombia), and revolutionary nationalist groups in the armed forces (Brazilian sergeants prior to 1964).

Although Fidelism tolerated populist politics and strategy in an initial phase of struggle, Gueverism emerged as a second stage in which emphasis was placed on popular support for guerrilla struggle through a coalition of peasants and workers. Whereas Fidel had included the national bourgeoisie and petty bourgeoisie in the Cuban revolution, Ché denied their revolutionary potential.

These two thrusts complemented each other, depending on the conditions in various periods. The impetus of Fidelism allowed for a coalition of forces to oppose Batista in Cuba, yet Guevarism, or the guerrilla warfare advocated by Ché and Fidel, provided the means to achieve the insurrectionary objectives of the revolution. Once in power, a unity of the new and old left evolved through the eventual merger of the members of the July 26 movement with the Communist Popular Socialist party, or Partido Socialista Popular (PSP).

Guevarism was premised on three principles: Popular forces can defeat a regular army; revolutionary conditions can be created through the insurrectional foco; and in underdeveloped areas, armed struggle should take place in the countryside. Ché's theory of the insurrectional foco (a liberated zone where guerrilla forces concentrate activities) was controversial, especially after his death in Bolivia in 1967. This theory allowed Ché to downplay the vanguard party during the insurrectional period and to concentrate on a military and political struggle to defeat an army. Ché also believed in continental revolution to defeat imperialism, and, according to Hodges, his theory was "remarkably similar to Trotsky's own theory of permanent revolution" (Hodges 1974: 167).

In addition to Cuba and Bolivia, Guevarism influenced a number of other movements in Latin America. The guerrilla forces of Yon Sosa and Luis Turcios Lima in Guatemala, the Venezuelan Armed Forces of National Liberation, or Fuerzas Armada de Liberación Nacional (FALN), and the Colombian National Liberation Army, or Ejército de Liberación Nacional (ELN), were active for many years in the countryside, for example. In the face of counterinsurgency, rural guerrilla warfare became less visible in many parts of Latin America, and after Ché's death the guerrilla forces moved to the city. The Tupamaros in Uruguay, the Montoneros in Argentina, and various groups in Brazil, Colombia, and elsewhere were able to attract international attention through bank robberies, the seizure of radio stations, and the kidnapping of foreign diplomats.

In conclusion, while the goal of socialism may be clear in all of the lines of thought discussed above, the various programs, tactics, and strategies result in debate over which path will lead most directly and quickly to socialism in Latin America. Revolution combined with socialism is rare in Latin America. Countries like Mexico, Chile, Nicaragua, and Cuba all have struggled, with varying degrees of success and failure, toward socialism. Thus, the prospects for revolution and socialism must be examined.

7

The Transition
to Socialism

In the preceding chapters, we have discussed the failure of capitalism to meet the basic needs of a majority of Latin Americans. We have also observed the failure of capitalist countries in Latin America to achieve national sovereignty and dignity under capitalism. There have been many reformist and revolutionary movements over the course of the twentieth century, beginning early in the century when the Mexican revolution came to power. This revolution intensified capitalist modernization under the leadership of a new bourgeois class in control of a strong state. Over the years the revolution has served both domestic and foreign private enterprise well, but two-thirds of the population has been left out of the fruits of the accumulation their labor has helped to create.

In the 1930s and 1940s populist regimes came to power in Brazil and Argentina. Getúlio Vargas and Juan Perón sought to lead popular fronts that would benefit industrialists and labor without contradicting the interests of landed wealth. Unable to foster a process of accumulation, the benefits they dispersed to their various constituencies proved false, or at best only sustainable for a brief period before the benefits became engulfed by inflation.

In the latter days of the Second World War a popular reformist government came to power in Guatemala. It successfully organized two honest elections and enacted a moderate land reform, but after ten years it had not sufficiently organized and mobilized its support to defeat a CIA-organized invasion by ousted members of the military.

A second authentic, popular revolution came to power in Bolivia in 1952. A coalition of workers, miners, and people from the middle sectors, it foundered when the last group gained dominance and succumbed to co-optive U.S. policies. Within a few years after the resumption of U.S.

military assistance, the military came to power, and the experiment ended.

Following the assassination of the dictator, Rafael Trujillo, a popular reformist government was elected in the Dominican Republic in 1962. Trying not to confront the dominant classes, President Juan Bosch angered them without creating a sufficient base of support among the workers and peasants. He was overthrown by the military in 1963, and when a near-spontaneous insurrection threatened the military government in 1965, the United States intervened with 20,000 troops.

Over the decades reformist governments have fallen to military coups numerous times. In Peru in 1968, a military coup brought to power a progressive government that carried out a drastic land reform, reshaping the contours of power in an effort to create a progressive national capitalism. In 1974, not having mobilized a popular base of support, the government's economic contradictions left it naked before its creditor New York banks, which dictated terms and brought it down in 1975. In the wake of years of economic failure, these regimes, many of them brutally repressive, gave way in the mid-1980s to civilian rule. Prospects are dim that they will meet the basic needs of all of their citizens in the foreseeable future.

In Chile, the Popular Unity coalition and Salvador Allende were victorious in 1970. Pressured by a U.S. destabilization campaign and having avoided steps to consolidate power that might provoke the military, the government succumbed in 1973 to a bloody military coup, which initiated years of murder and repression.

Efforts to transcend capitalism have succeeded only in Cuba and Nicaragua. Yet, at the time of this writing, the latter country was under sustained armed attack and economic aggression and threatened with an invasion by the United States. In transcending capitalism, the process of change is necessarily economic, political, social, and cultural, and all of these dimensions are integrally linked. Although the rates of change vary and development is usually uneven, the entire process is threatened if change in any single dimension lags too far behind. For example, without change in the social institutions and cultural values that inhibit females' working outside the home, economic growth will be impeded since the economic contribution of women is of great importance because of low labor productivity.

There is also the problem of popular democracy, for in all poor countries, bureaucracies hold power through their control of scarce resources, and they maintain that power by blocking democratic participation. This tendency is overcome only by the organized strength of workers and peasants. Without this political capacity, the power gained by the leaders who represent the popular interests will eventually shift to self-interested technical and managerial elites created by the revolution. Although the dimensions of the change process cannot be separated in practice, for analytical purposes we begin by reviewing economic changes.

Ending poverty and satisfying basic needs for nutrition, health care, and housing requires redistribution of income. Most important is providing employment, and in these countries, in which agriculture is the largest productive sector, agrarian reform is essential. In addition to full employment, an effective minimum wage must be established. Social services and income maintenance are important supplements for people who are unable to work or for whom employment has not yet been created, and these measures require resources that, by one means or another, must come from reducing the share of social surplus received by private owners of the means of production. The share received by the working classes and poor peasants and the portion available to the state must be increased.

In Latin America, redistribution of income alone will at best provide for the satisfaction of only minimal basic needs. Economic growth is needed, which implies increased utilization of land and human and natural resources and a substantial rate of investment. Reducing vulnerability to changes in external economic conditions is necessary to ameliorate the instability that is characteristic of monocultural economies. Reorientation toward self-sufficiency in essential commodities, beginning with food production, lowers the need to earn foreign exchange through exports, which provides some insulation from negative shifts in the terms of trade and from the leverage of trading partners. As Clive Thomas (1974) argues, orienting production to satisfy domestic needs should have priority, and efforts should also be made to diversify exports by selling abroad the products developed most successfully for domestic consumption. Although traditional exports should be maintained to earn needed foreign exchange, efforts should be made to reduce the level of imported inputs used to produce those exports. Nonessential imports must be restricted to conserve foreign exchange.

The capitalist economies of Latin America have been shaped by the decisions of large private owners who seek to maximize profits by responding to the signals of international and domestic markets. If the sort of economic changes noted above are to be achieved, the economy must be controlled by the state, which entails redistribution of income and wealth and the elimination of the prerogatives of private property. For this reason, the state must come under the control of the worker and small-peasant classes. We do not suggest that members of these social classes possess special virtues as individuals, but economic reorientation is contrary to the interests of the propertied classes and their foreign allies, and because workers and small peasants are the direct beneficiaries of change, only these classes will accept risks and hardships to pursue the new direction. Therefore, change requires that they gain state power. These two fundamental changes, state control of the economy and control of the state by worker and peasant interests, constitute the essential elements of socialism.

There is no universal consensus concerning the complete and precise meaning of the term "socialism." There is general agreement that a socialist society is one in which the economy operates under the guidance of the state to avoid capitalist crises and to assure that workers receive the value of their contribution to production (after essential needs such as investment and national defense have been met). However, there is no agreement regarding the extent of state or other collective forms of ownership. Nor is there agreement about the role the market can play in a socialist political economy. On the right, Western European social democrats are willing to ignore or postpone the question of ownership and rely on redistributive taxation and social welfare programs, along with the tools of fiscal and monetary policy used in virtually all capitalist countries; Marxian socialists generally believe that the predominance of state ownership is essential to socialism. There is also disagreement about the political model implied by socialism. The official Marxist-Leninist parties, which hold power in the Soviet Union, Eastern Europe, China, Cuba, and elsewhere, advocate that a vanguard party must maintain a monopoly of power. This model is rejected by a wide variety of socialists, including Western European social democrats and several Communist parties, some leftist groups in the United States, and the Sandinista regime in Nicaragua.

We use the term "socialism" to refer to a political-economic system in which the economy functions according to a plan that is directed toward fulfilling the needs and interests of the working classes and peasants. This definition is inductive and pragmatic while conforming to general usage. Following Marx, we also recognize a stage of advanced socialism or communism as a real possibility for human society, though it has not yet been achieved. In a Communist political economy, social classes have disappeared; the state has ceased to have or to need coercive power; work is motivated, not by a desire for private gain or the need to survive, but by habit, a conscious voluntary contribution to society, or a desire to create; productive activity and its product are under the control of the producers; and the systemic causes of alienation have been eliminated. Our use of the term "socialism" does not refer to advanced socialism or communism but to a political-economic system in which the economy is planned in the interests of workers and peasants. Thus, we use the term to refer to a stage of a society in transition toward greater equality and the possibility of developing communism.

The transition to socialism refers to the entire process of change, from the overthrow of capitalism to the achievement of advanced socialism. It is useful to divide the process into stages. First is the acquisition of state power by representatives of worker and peasant interests. Second, state power must be consolidated so that the new regime is secured and the essentials of socialism are established. Completion of the consolidation stage introduces the period of socialist development in which the goals of advanced socialism are pursued.

Although the transition to socialism is very importantly an economic project, the political dimension of socialism is equally fundamental. In this chapter, we touch on the seizure of state power, the consolidation of state power, and socialist development. Our review of some major tendencies that have emerged in the experiences of Cuba and Nicaragua emphasizes the need to maintain the political domination of class forces whose interests lie in advancing socialism.

Class Coalitions in the Acquisition of State Power

In the countries of Latin America, many classes and interests are represented in varying proportions: workers; a petty bourgeoisie consisting of small farmers, petty capitalists, intellectuals, salaried and independent professionals, and managers; the essentially lumpen classes of marginalized day laborers, penny vendors, and scrap collectors; and (except in Cuba) the bourgeoisie, including industrial and financial capitalists, *latifundistas*, and foreign capitalists. Each class has its own relation to the existing regime. Moreover, some classes are severely divided, having different interests in relation to imperialism. As a result, the successful seizure of state power is likely to involve a de facto, if not formalized, coalition of class forces as has occurred in Cuba and Nicaragua.

High levels of unemployment and underemployment and inflation in nearly every country provoke workers, peasants, and petty capitalists to seek change. These classes, as well as elements among intellectuals and professionals, may become alienated from the regime by corruption and repression. Segments of local capital are often unable to compete with foreign capital or, as in Somoza's Nicaragua, are squeezed by a family monopoly. They may join with other classes to remove the existing government.

The nature of such class coalitions is still more unclear when unions and working class parties are either weak, poorly organized, or significantly co-opted. The working classes and peasants are usually numerically predominant among participants in guerrilla struggles and mass uprisings. Representation of a variety of sectors, including the urban petty bourgeoisie, is usually significant; for example, Orlando Núñez Soto refers to "the struggles of students, of organized women, of nurses, journalists, teachers, public employees, youth, of poor urban neighborhoods and of peasants" (Núñez 1981: 11). These forms of struggle are not focused on the work place. As Núñez Soto (1981: 10–20) mentions, sectors not defined in class terms, particularly youth, played a highly significant role in the Sandinista revolution and may again be important in other countries.

The transition to socialism begins with the acquisition of state power by representatives of worker and peasant interests. The class origins of this leadership are of no particular significance. The most well-known leaders, from Lenin to Castro, have been radicalized members of the petty bourgeoisie whose subjective class identification and, often, objective class position have changed during the course of struggle. Nor does the means by which one regime is replaced by another define revolution. The history of Latin America is filled with literally hundreds of military *golpes de estado*. These "palace revolutions" have only served to maintain the status quo of ruling classes, which represent factions of the propertied classes and their foreign allies. Real revolution is the actual restructuring of society.

Although revolution is much more than the use of force to evict a government from power, it is unlikely that the transition to socialism will be successfully launched by electoral victories. In some countries (e.g., Chile and Uruguay until 1973; Venezuela after 1958; and Costa Rica, Argentina, and Colombia for varying periods of time), elections have served as an effective mechanism to distribute power among the parties that represent the owner classes. Elections have not been a means for the transfer of state power to workers or peasants. When the possibility of such a transfer has appeared, the military has assumed power.

Running on a socialist program in the 1970 presidential elections in Chile, Salvador Allende successfully led the Popular Unity, or Unidad Popular (UP), coalition of progressive parties. He was permitted to take office. Despite a two-and-a-half-year destabilization campaign orchestrated by the CIA, the mid-term elections in March of 1973 indicated that support for the UP had grown. Having failed to defeat Allende politically by sabotaging his program, the owner classes and the United States called upon the armed forces to put an end to civilian politics. After the coup of September 11, 1973, the military response to the strength of working class organization and consciousness was the torture and murder of tens of thousands of people and an unyielding campaign of brutal repression. The experience of Latin America thus far indicates that change is possible only when the armed forces have been defeated and dismantled, as in Cuba and Nicaragua.

Cuba

Conditions that led to the successful seizure of state power in Cuba matched those discussed above in general terms. Sugar dominated the economy. Because of concentrated ownership, land was denied to 400,000 cane cutters (in a population of approximately 6.5 million), thus forcing them to survive on wages earned during the four-month harvest and suffer unemployment through the dead season. Modernization of the sugar industry was discouraged by low wages. Expansion was blocked by market constraints while economic diversification was curtailed by a reciprocal tariff treaty under which Cuba was a virtually unrestricted market for the United States. Economic stagnation in the 1950s resulted in high levels of urban unemployment, causing hardship among the working classes and frustration among the more educated middle sectors, which lacked opportunity. As the economy could not provide for the legitimate economic aspirations of much of the population to engage in productive labor and be rewarded, neither could the government be a vehicle for legitimate political aspirations. Many of Cuba's economic decisions were made in the United States. The U.S. quota of sugar purchases virtually determined Cuba's sugar production, and the fate of the Cuban tobacco industry was tied to the postal regulations established by the U.S. Congress concerning the importation of cigars in bulk quantities and in smaller packages (see Smith 1960). Cuba's foreign policy followed that of the giant to the north as well.

Thus, the government served principally as a mechanism to divide up the fixed and limited economic pie among organized interests such as sugar-plantation owners competing for crop allocations and the stronger labor unions. The bloated bureaucracy provided jobs that were lacking in the private sector for those people from families with the right political connections who did not have enough property to employ their children but did have sufficient education and social position to occupy white-collar government posts. Combined with a Mafia-run tourist industry, these structural features resulted in a society characterized by wholesale corruption. Alienation from the Batista regime was further heightened by the repression employed in an effort to defeat the revolutionary forces of the July 26 movement, or Movimiento 26 de Julio (M26J), led by Fidel Castro.

The program of M26J emphasized a commitment to the working class and the peasants but envisioned a reformist capitalism that proposed to benefit all classes except the *latifundistas*, the large landowners whose land was to be nationalized. (Most major statements of the M26J, including Castro's famous "History Will Absolve Me" speech, are included in Bonachea and Valdés 1972.) Land reform, the basis of the program, was supposed to increase rural incomes while eliminating rural unemployment. Thus, the domestic market for national industries would be expanded and protected by the state. Industrial growth and a reduced migration from the countryside to the cities would reduce urban unemployment, bring about an increase in urban wages, and also increase demand in the national market.

This plan corresponded to the developing unity of class forces against the status quo. Land reform offered opportunities for employment for the rural population, including small peasants and the *macheteros* ("sugarcane cutters") who suffered during the dead season. The promise of support and protection for national industry gave hope to urban workers and investment possibilities to the small, nationally oriented bourgeoisie (Ruiz 1968: 145). Objective conditions, principally unemployment and rural poverty and oppression, supported a working class and a peasant revolution, but organizational means were lacking. The unions, largely under the influence of the Moscow-oriented Communist party—the Popular Socialist Party, or Partido Socialista Popular (PSP)—were co-opted into the Batista regime. Political parties that claimed to be progressive—the Auténticos Ortodoxos, the Radical Union party, and the PSP—sought conciliation with the Batista regime until the armed struggle led by M26J was well under way. In Cuba's underdeveloped politics, personalism dominated over issues, and programs were subject to compromise. At various times, all of the parties had been compromised by their association with state power, and a definitive break with the political game to pursue an authentic revolution was unattractive to their leaders. In the countryside, though the sugar workers had a militant union, the peasants lacked any sort of organization.

The initial insurrectionist strategy of the M26J for the seizure of power virtually ignored class-related forms of organization and called for the creation of a dramatic event leading to a spontaneous mass uprising. This attempt, the attack on the Moncada military garrison on July 26, 1953, failed. The hope for mass insurrection persisted and pervaded the invasion by Fidel Castro in December 1956, which initiated the next strategy, guerrilla warfare. The defeat of the Batista regime was brought about through a successful campaign of military action in the countryside and urban terrorism and resistance in the cities. Although the fighters were drawn predominantly from the working class and the peasantry, the most important attempt to utilize working class organizations, a call for a general strike in April 1958, failed largely because of the refusal of M26J urban leaders to involve the PSP in planning the strike (Bray and Harding 1974: 613).

The defeat of the Batista regime, only slightly more than two years after the rural insurgency was begun, was political as well as military. The inability of the regime to deal with the insurgents or the economy, combined with its brutality against people suspected of siding with the opposition, led to the withdrawal of middle-sector support and the isolation of the regime. "The impending collapse of the Batista regime led to increasing defections in the Church as well as the legal and military systems. Members of the Catholic Church hierarchy openly denounced the Batista regime in early 1958. . . . Some of Batista's legal officials were refusing to prosecute political prisoners" (Bray and Harding 1974: 613). Thus, the seizure of state power could be seen as a victory for reform, but it was not clearly identified with a class or a class coalition.

Nicaragua

The last military occupation of Nicaragua by the United States ended on January 1, 1933, but the U.S. Marines left behind a well-trained National Guard headed by General Anastasio Somoza García. On February 21, 1934, General Augusto César Sandino attended a dinner at the Presidential Palace in Managua at the invitation of President Juan Bautista Sacasa. Following the dinner, Sandino was taken prisoner and summarily executed because he had refused to accept U.S. dominance over the political and economic life of Nicaragua and had led a peasant army against the government. Following Sandino's assassination, Somoza ordered the extermination of the forces that had fought for the popular and nationalist government advocated by Sandino.

On July 19, 1979, the brutal and corrupt Somoza dynasty headed by Somoza García's son, Anastasio Somoza Debayle, fell to a mass insurrection led by the Sandinista Front for National Liberation, or Frente Sandinista por la Liberación Nacional (FSLN). Founded in 1961, the FSLN initially operated as guerrilla bands in the harsh terrain along the Nicaragua-Honduras border. Within two years hardship and military failure led to a new strategy emphasizing political work in the cities in alliance with the traditional left. When the leftist parties entered electoral politics in 1967, the FSLN returned to the mountains. A guerrilla strategy was again followed, but it met with disaster. Beginning about 1970 the FSLN began to organize links with the masses through organizations of students, workers, and Christian groups. Peasants were also incorporated into the organization. A policy of "the accumulation of forces in silence" was followed until the end of 1974, when sporadic attacks were begun in the cities.

The FSLN survived government counterinsurgency sweeps and urban repression while making political advances. In late 1977 the regime heightened its repression in response to increased FSLN activity. Liberals, including some business groups, recognized the legitimacy of the FSLN and promoted a dialogue. The assassination of the most visible leader of the liberal opposition and editor of *La Prensa*, Pedro Joaquín Chamorro, appeared to be Somoza Debayle's answer.

In the last two years of the Somoza dynasty, the struggle grew from a series of sporadic attacks on military outposts to military control of major cities in the western part of the country. The FSLN was supported and sometimes even anticipated by mass insurrection of the people. A process of mutual escalation seemed to take place in which the people reacted to the brutality of the National Guard with harassment and street fighting. The guard increased its repression, and as insurrection grew, Somoza Debayle ordered aerial bombing of the cities. Uprisings, now coordinated and led by the more experienced FSLN regulars, grew more massive until government forces were overwhelmed.

During the 1970s this process of reciprocal escalation took place in the context of economic deterioration, which helps to explain why the opposition was so broad and tenacious. In the countryside, landownership was highly concentrated. More than half, including the most fertile land, was owned by only 2 percent of the landowners. On the other hand, the holdings of the poorest 70 percent of the landowners accounted for only 2 percent of the land. More than a sixth of the rural population was made up of landless, seasonal farm workers. Income distribution followed land distribution. Landowners with holdings too small to provide subsistence and rural laborers with no land made up just over half of the economically active population in the countryside but received only 7.5 percent of rural income. Moderate and large landowners made up

3.5 percent of the rural population and received over 63 percent of rural income. The poorer half of the rural population had an average intake of 1,767 calories per day, just over two-thirds of the requirement recognized by the United Nations. The poverty of the rural population was matched by oppression in the rural structure (sources and additional data in Collins 1982: 15, 155–157).

Less than 5 percent of agricultural land was used to grow food for domestic consumption. Following earlier booms in coffee and cotton, beef production grew in importance during the 1960s. By the 1970s over 90 percent of the land used for export production was given over to cattle grazing. This less intensive use of land was also a cause of increased unemployment.

Between 1967 and 1971 the real wage in agriculture, manufacturing, and construction dropped by about 13 percent. Then, in the early 1970s, two unrelated events exacerbated the structural tendencies of the Nicaraguan political economy. The jump in world market oil prices resulted in a rise in what had been a low rate of inflation in Nicaragua. Consumer prices rose 16.8 percent in 1973 and 20.5 percent in 1974; from 1971 to 1973 the real wage had declined by about 16 percent.

The destruction of many small businesses in the December 1972 earthquake destroyed employment for many of their owners as well as for workers. The earthquake also led to a surtax on salaries in the name of reconstruction and to a substantial increase in the workweek. The earthquake also seemed to heighten the greed of the Somoza regime. Massive corruption in the diversion of international relief aid was openly visible. In addition to the economic and political impact of the earthquake on the working and middle classes, the disaster spurred Somoza to expand his interests at the expense of the other investor groups, the Bank of America and the Banco Nicaragüense. "At the same time, growing political and labor unrest caused many Nicaraguan capitalists to doubt the regime's capacity to continue to promote beneficial growth. Somoza's previously growing backing among the upper classes began to break down during the mid-'70s and the development of a unified bourgeoisie was arrested" (Booth 1983: 3; also see Booth 1982 for additional sources and data).

In the mid-1970s, internal differences over tactics developed within the FSLN. The Prolonged Popular War, or Guerra Popular Prolongada (GPP), emphasized military struggle in the countryside while the Proletarian Tendency, or Tendencia Proletaria (TP), advocated a focus on organizing urban workers. The Third Tendency, or Terceristas, favored efforts to attract the broadest base of opposition to the regime and emphasized bold actions to stimulate popular insurrection. These differences did not result in the formation of separate organizations.

In accordance with its long-term goals and the broad opposition to the Somoza regime, the FSLN enunciated a clear commitment to worker and peasant interests while leaving open opportunities for private enterprise. Less than a year before Somoza fell, all three Sandinista tendencies endorsed the program of the United People's Movement, or Movimiento del Pueblo Unido (MPU), a coalition of twenty progressive organizations formed to develop and coordinate mass organization against the regime. This program differed from that of the Broad Opposition Front, or Frente Amplio Opositor (FAO), the representative of the anti-Somoza segment of the bourgeoisie, in that it called for a radical restructuring of the economy and explicitly stated that a national economic plan would be created. The program specified the nationalization of all holdings of the Somoza family; natural resources including minerals, petroleum, and wood and the companies that exploited them; maritime, air, and mass-passenger land transport; and the domestic and foreign banking system.

In Cuba and Nicaragua, the revolutionary movements incorporated broad sectors of the population. In both countries, the programs called for political pluralism based on private ownership of the means of production with the state and the economy serving *los humildes*, or the "humble" majority. Also in both countries, the state would intervene to the extent necessary to orient the economy to contribute to the popular, nationalist goals. Both programs relied on the assumption that the private sector would constructively participate in the political and economic life of the new regimes.

The Consolidation of State Power

The composition of class forces and the immediate causes of revolutionary organization, mobilization, and struggle vary, of course, in accordance with historical particularities. Whatever those factors may be, the successful seizure of state power necessarily begins a process of struggle to determine the nature of the new regime. A contest for power often takes place among the different forces in the coalition: those who seek only a change of personalities (e.g., "Somocismo without Somoza"), those whose interests lie in some type of capitalist reformism, and the various lines and groupings committed to the interests of the working classes and peasants.

To the extent that the seizure of power involves a coalition of class forces whose long-term interests and objectives are antagonistic, the consolidation of state power will engender a polarization of class forces as the new state defines itself in action. The state is necessarily an expression of the victories, defeats, and compromises of the classes within the social formation over which it rules. Because of the ambiguity of the class content of the revolutionary movement, the struggle through which the state is defined occurs after the old regime has fallen.

In the stage of consolidation, there are many tasks to be accomplished. Order and military security must be established to create the capability to deal with the challenges of imperialism and internal counterrevolutionary forces. Economic measures must be taken toward quick recuperation from the damage to the economy during the struggle for power (which may vary considerably depending on the nature of the struggle). The reorientation of the economy must be toward national development and more equitable distribution of income while creating the means to provide needed social services and education for the entire population.

Some programs, such as mass literacy and preventive health campaigns, which can rely mainly on volunteers, can provide significant benefits at low cost. However, the new regime defines its class content, willingly or not, as it acts to deal with the economy. As the new government seeks to generate employment, to increase the nutritional levels of people without enough food, or to manage the scarce supply of foreign exchange, it must choose among a limited number of options. Some programs may be effective while not challenging property rights. The government may use means common to capitalist regimes, inducing property owners to act as the state wishes by making it profitable for them to do so; more often, conflicts arise between social needs and property rights. For example, providing immediate cash compensation to landowners for expropriation of land would be too costly if agrarian reform is carried out on a large scale. The government must usually choose between ignoring the needs of the landless or expropriating land with deferred compensation, if any. (Nicaragua is an exception as expropriation of Somoza land without compensation did not threaten the bourgeoisie.) Substantial state intervention in the economy has been common in nearly every country in Latin America and does not, itself, indicate the class commitments of the regime. These commitments can be determined by observing which social classes are the beneficiaries of state intervention.

Each choice made by the government signals the priorities of the new regime. As the class commitments of the regime are expressed in its actions, support and opposition arise from the respective winners and losers. The response of the leadership to this political polarization is of great importance. Moreover, foreign hostility tends to exacerbate difficult choices and to create crises. If past history offers any guidance in anticipating the future, a new revolutionary government can expect to encounter economic warfare ranging from a cutoff of credit to military attacks against the country's infrastructure.

To date, the experience in Latin America suggests that survival of the new regime and its program for change requires that the government accept polarization as unavoidable and direct its policies to develop its base among the workers and peasants. Unfortunately, efforts to maintain the broad coalition that defeated the old regime tend to reduce the government's capacity to provide benefits for its essential base. For example, rigorous enforcement of minimum wage laws can benefit many workers but results in a loss of business support. Restrictions on the importation of nonessential consumer goods will alienate many of the people who have been able to enjoy such luxuries in the past. Failure to impose such restrictions will reduce the amount of foreign exchange available for economic development efforts or programs oriented to the immediate benefit of the majority. These choices also affect the tendency for respective social classes to identify with the regime. When peasants take over unused private land, the government's response will essentially determine whether landless rural laborers and small peasants feel that it is their regime or that of the property owning classes.

Efforts to compromise in order to avoid polarization and maintain the broad coalition tend to weaken the support of the worker and peasant base. For example, the refusal of the Allende government to legitimize some of the factory seizures that had been carried out during the 1972 truckers' strike caused some confusion among workers supporting the Popular Unity coalition. There appears to be a self-reinforcing process: Actions to cultivate the base engender more militant opposition, and in the face of opposition to the direction it has chosen, the regime relies for support on the constituency to which it is oriented. Thus, in Cuba, renters of houses and apartments welcomed the rent reductions specified in the Urban Reform Law and developed a heightened level of commitment to the revolution as a result; landlords were injured and tended to move into opposition. A similar polarization occurred with respect to the Agrarian Reform Law in that country. U.S. resistance to the direction of the revolution became more pronounced and threatening, and the need for militant mass support was increased accordingly. The greater opposition encouraged intransigence on the part of the people whose interests had suffered, but the incentive of the government to appease the opposition declined while the need to follow policies that would assure mass support increased.

In the absence of foreign intervention, this process might conclude with the voluntary departure of the people who could not accept the future role of their social class in the new regime. As an increasingly isolated minority, they would lack an alternative course of action. However, the United States has consistently supported counterrevolution with military force. In the first third of this century, and again in 1965, the U.S. Marines invaded and occupied countries in the Caribbean and Central America. Three times in the last three decades, the CIA has organized, coordinated, and funded invading military forces. In 1954 the Arbenz government of Guatemala was ousted by elements of the Guatemalan military invading from Honduras. In contrast, the invasion of Cuba at the Bay of Pigs in 1961 was unsuccessful. The third CIA-sponsored invasion, initiated in 1981 using remnants of Somoza's defeated National Guard with support from the Honduran armed forces, was aimed at Nicaragua.

When politics are normal, varying levels of support or opposition may be manifested through acts such as voting or participating in a rally. When politics give way to military combat, a much higher level of commitment on the part of the regime's constituency is required. The reformist Guatemalan regime lacked a sufficiently strong and mobilized support to prevail. At the Bay of Pigs, the peasants who made up the local militia in the area of the invasion were willing to risk death to hold off the invaders until regular forces arrived. The Sandinista regime pursued a policy that sought to maintain a role for the bourgeoisie in the Nicaraguan revolution while developing the strong commitment of the workers and peasants necessary to defeat the sustained invasion.

To achieve power, a revolution (as opposed to a military coup) must have substantial backing from the worker and peasant classes. Governments that have even the passive support of the population do not fall to guerrilla insurgents, regardless of arms, training, or logistical assistance that may be provided by external benefactors. At the moment of victory, the breadth and depth of popular support and the strength of revolutionary organization will vary in relation to the length of the struggle, the degree of mass involvement, and the quality of the groups that have led the struggle.

The new regime enjoys some conditions that enhance mass support during the period of transition. Victory over the old regime itself brings a feeling of confidence and political efficacy to the people who were active in the struggle. It imparts joy and a sense of optimism to those who sympathized with the struggle. For those who identified with the revolution, there is relief from fear of the repressive forces of the old regime. Except for those who fought for the old regime, there is a sense of relief that the conflict is over.

At the outset of the new regime, workers and peasants experience psychological and some material benefits from the ascendancy of their social classes. As laws and programs are fashioned that reflect their interests, they experience a new relation to society. Although some caution or cynicism may remain, there is a lessening of alienation and a growing sense of belonging and perhaps ownership, similar in some respects to the way the propertied classes felt when they were dominant. This sense of identification with society and with the revolution is strengthened by the elimination or attenuation of situations in which workers and peasants have been subordinate (i.e., relationships with landlords or employers).

The victory may also lead to immediate, tangible improvements that increase political support. Revolutions generally do not gain the mass support necessary for victory unless unemployment is high, and in the semi-industrialized countries of Latin America, existing productive capacity is often underutilized. These conditions are exacerbated by revolutionary struggle. Following the victory, the new regime can increase the purchasing power of people with low levels of income. This expansion of demand will tend to quickly increase economic activity, setting into motion underutilized productive facilities and reducing unemployment.

Unless offset by the physical destruction and disruption of agriculture caused by the revolutionary struggle, a relative prosperity is thus begun, though it will last only until further expansion requires new investment. Some relatively inexpensive government programs such as literacy campaigns and vaccination and other elementary health programs can also aid in developing mass support.

Despite these favorable conditions, maintaining the necessary level of political support is difficult for the new regime because the immediate benefits the revolution can provide are limited by a scarcity of resources. The process of change brings with it problems and mistakes that cause temporary economic losses. Resources will probably be further limited by actions against the new regime such as credit blockades and calculated disruptions of foreign trade. Other needs such as defense and economic reconstruction may compete with consumption for resources.

The widespread longing for change and the active opposition to the existing regime, which brought the revolution to power, do not necessarily enable the working class and the peasantry to understand the difficulties that are inherent in the transition to socialism. Illiterate poor peasants and day laborers know the ways in which they have been exploited and cheated by the landowners who rented land to them or bought their labor. But they may not understand why the new regime refuses to divide large farms and parcel out the land to individual families. Organized urban workers in the advanced sector of the economy know of the great wealth possessed by the few people who occupy the exclusive residential districts, and they are bitterly aware of the repression or the manipulation of their unions. But they may have an unrealistic conception of the real possibilities available to the new regime to improve their material standard of living in the short term, especially given the needs of the unemployed and the underemployed.

This lack of understanding will tend to make some of the people who make up the essential core of support vulnerable to antigovernment propaganda. Some members of the coalition against the old regime may have gained prestige during the struggle even though their primary interests may diverge from those of workers and peasants. They are in a position to cause considerable confusion and a resultant weakening of support for the new regime when problems inherent in the change process develop.

Education of the workers and peasants, the essential base of the revolution, is necessary to minimize confusion and disaffection caused by the difficulties of the consolidation phase. The new regime must impart an understanding of the national reality, the needs of the country, the resources available, the limitations and obstacles, and the conditions that are beyond the control of the leadership. This understanding can do much to diffuse the tension caused by the difference between expectations and immediate possibilities. It reduces the natural tendency to attribute the situations people experience in their daily lives, such as shortages, to the new government. In this way, education reduces the regime's vulnerability to external destabilization. Moreover, the diffusion of a knowledge of national needs helps worker and peasant class groups to place their own particular situations and interests within the perspective of the nation as a whole. Open discussion of errors and mistakes committed by the government is a significant aspect of popular education. Such sharing can reduce wishful thinking and contribute to a more concrete understanding of the specific problems that must be faced and the efforts of the government to confront them.

This educational effort is also necessary for the creation of a new ideological hegemony. Underlying every political system is the hegemony of the ideological framework that previously established the legitimacy of the ideologies which are in accordance with the interests of the dominant classes and the needs of the prevailing system of production. Embedded in each ideology are definitions of key political economic and philosophical concepts (i.e., freedom as property rights; freedom as secure access to basic physical and cultural necessities; freedom from alienated labor). The ideological framework establishes the legitimacy of the demands on the system emanating from the dominant classes, demands that are in accordance with the needs of production. It denies the legitimacy of other demands, which contradict the needs of the system of production, so it keeps the problems of the subordinate classes from becoming public issues. Groups are motivated to formulate demands within the terms of the ideological framework and thus to reinforce it, even as they struggle for the interests of the subordinate classes.

For instance, in the capitalist United States, representatives of workers' interests cannot argue for income maintenance programs such as unemployment insurance by rationalizing that such programs increase the bargaining power of workers over owners. Instead, they assert that such programs benefit business (i.e., the capitalists) by making up for the loss of demand when unemployment increases. Similarly, in Nicaragua, with its mixed economy under the political hegemony of workers and peasants, the private sector does not argue against controls on prices by asserting that permitting speculation will increase the merchants' profits while reducing the purchasing power of the real wage and helping to bring down the popular government. Instead, they condemn price controls on the basis that they discourage production and thus damage the national reconstruction effort. In addition, the ideological framework facilitates the processing of conflicting demands by shaping them in a fashion that permits compromise among competing interests, which the framework defines as legitimate.

Revolutions do not come to power unless the dominant ideology has been substantially discredited by the actual daily life experience of the masses. However, fragments of the old ideology tend to survive, and thus, education is needed to counter those that can cause confusion, especially during the consolidation phase.

More important in the longer term, the establishment of a new ideological hegemony is a necessary part of the creation of a new political system. The process of struggle itself does not elaborate and disseminate the new framework. This is an important task in the consolidation of state power. By establishing the fundamental priority of worker and peasant interests in the new political economic system, counterrevolutionary proposals are stripped of their legitimacy. The boundaries of politics are drawn.

In the consolidation of state power phase, a balance must be struck between the exigencies of the moment, which demand unity, and the development of a political process in which all legitimate interests can be articulated. This balance is continually changing as the threat from remnants of the old regime is alleviated and the ability to withstand external aggression is developed. At the moment of victory, centralization of power is necessary. The first actions of the new regime must be by decree. As long as the survival of the revolution is seriously threatened, unity has a high priority, and the logic of the situation weighs heavily in favor of national needs over less-than-national interests.

Despite the need for centralization and the dominance of national needs in the stage of consolidation of state power, an important task during this stage is to lay the foundation for a more decentralized mass participation and the articulation of subnational interests. The establishment of a new ideological hegemony is essentially the creation of a base for the articulation of diverse interests within the worker-peasant coalition. The definition of a common terrain and common terms for dialogue and criticism is necessary to avoid isolation of the regime during the stage of socialist development, a problem to which we will return.

In Cuba, the reformist program elaborated by M26J during the struggle for power did not get a full trial because the political contradictions of the consolidation phase intervened. Regardless of the strongly and consistently expressed commitment of Castro to the poor, and to workers and peasants to carry out agrarian and other reforms, the class content of the revolution only became clear in the concrete actions of the new government. The earliest measures, such as reduction of urban rents and utility rates, were inconclusive since they could be signs of an opportunistic populism, easily reversible when the correlation of class forces was reversed. Implementation of the agrarian reform was far more serious. It struck at the distribution of wealth and power in society, redefining property rights in the process. From that point, resistance grew among the bourgeoisie and elements of the petty bourgeoisie, which had supported the replacement of Batista and an attack on corruption but would not accept a society run by and for social classes other than their own. After an offer of a co-optive loan was rejected, the United States undertook a campaign of diplomatic pressure. Before the end of the regime's first year in power, small planes sporadically attacked Cuba from U.S. territory. These attacks peaked with the invasion of the Bay of Pigs but continued in a secret war throughout the 1960s.

During the consolidation phase, the Cuban leadership was consistent and uncompromising in its commitment to the economic reforms it had promised. Its response to attack was counterattack. When factory owners reduced or stopped production, the government occupied the factories to maintain employment. When U.S.-owned oil refineries refused to refine Soviet crude oil as required by preexisting Cuban law, they too were taken over. When the U.S. government eliminated the Cuban sugar quota, U.S. enterprises in Cuba were nationalized. Throughout the process, the government continually explained the developing situation. Each measure against the revolution was met with a heightened mobilization of the regime's supporters. These actions and others had the effects of hardening and deepening the opposition of the people who were not committed to the egalitarian goals of the revolution while solidifying a willingness to defend the regime on the part of its supporters.

A compromise such as the acceptance of an International Monetary Fund loan offer, made only four months after coming to power, would have reduced immediate economic difficulties. However, the austerity requirements of the offer would have prevented the regime from carrying out its program to immediately benefit workers and peasants, and the regime's capacity to survive intimidation and attack depended on that program. Instead, the Cuban government relied on its program to provide immediate benefits to peasants and workers, and when its measures brought threats and attacks by the counterrevolutionary opposition, the regime responded with still stronger actions.

Nationalization was a major weapon used by the Cuban leadership against its enemies. The inability of the regime to efficiently operate the nationalized enterprises was extremely costly as takeovers of firms occurred rapidly in the first two years. The government lacked personnel with training or experience in management and planning, and even educated people loyal to the revolution were in short supply. Other measures such as expensive housing programs, subsidized wages on agricultural cooperatives, and subsidized prices in rural peoples' stores (*tiendas del pueblo*) were also costly in economic terms in the long run. Archibald Ritter (1974) has suggested that because of ignorance, the Cuban leadership may have been unaware of the costs and consequences of these actions and may have been incapable of trying a more sophisticated carrot-and-stick approach to getting the behavior they desired from the private sector. Nonetheless, the value of these measures for the successful political consolidation of the revolution was highly significant, possibly critical to the survival of the new regime.

Nicaragua responded in a different way to the challenges of the consolidation of state power. For at least four years, beginning in 1981, the country faced a prolonged attack organized and sponsored by the CIA. At least until 1985 this invasion differed from earlier ones in that it did not involve a large landing force aimed at an immediate military victory. Instead, frequent raids across the Honduran border were carried out in combination with a sophisticated destabilization program. The policy of the United States appears to have been guided by a plan formulated by the Heritage Foundation, a right-wing policy group close to the Reagan administration: "Nicaraguan workers continue to have an emotional attachment to the revolutionary movement. This attachment can be expected to weaken as the economy deteriorates . . . economic shortcomings might provoke at least limited civil unrest by the end of the current harvest season (May-June 1981)" (Giovanni 1980: 3).

Military attacks were directed at disrupting the harvest in the northern regions of the country, destroying economic infrastructure, and forcing the government to allocate resources to defense and away from programs that would strengthen popular support. Nicaraguan government officials estimate that the raids by the "contras" caused $237 million damage to the country's economic infrastructure during the four-year period beginning in 1981. According to President Daniel Ortega, nearly three-fourths of the construction industry and half of the transport resources were diverted to the war effort. These estimates of the economic cost of the attacks do not include the loss of potential production. By 1985 fully 40 percent of the government budget was being allocated to defense (*Washington Report on the Hemisphere* 1985: 5).

In addition to the costs of the military attack, the United States used its vote and influence at the World Bank, the International Monetary Fund, and the Inter-American Development Bank to deny loans and assistance to Nicaragua. U.S. economic sanctions caused substantial losses in trade and loans (Nicaraguan officials estimate $354 million in 1983 alone), and other U.S. actions were also directed against Nicaragua. The U.S. government pressured private corporations in the United States from doing business in and with Nicaragua.[9]

Efforts were made to manipulate religious sentiment. Right-wing fundamentalist religious sects sent delegations to Nicaragua, and miraculous visions were proclaimed (e.g., a statue of a saint was said to be "weeping for the sadness of the country"). The U.S.-based Institute for Religion and Democracy cultivated the increasingly antigovernment Bishop Obando y Bravo, inviting him to visit the United States in 1982. A diplomatic effort was also undertaken to isolate the regime from international support.

The United States also used the contra war to exacerbate ethnic conflict in Nicaragua. The Atlantic Coast region, in which the indigenous Miskito population resides, had previously been under British rather than Spanish rule, and cultural differences had been reinforced by religious differences when Moravian and Capuchin missionaries came to dominate the Atlantic Coast area in the late nineteenth century. Without road, rail, or telegraph communication, isolation had maintained the identity of the Miskito people as a nation distinct from the Catholic "Spaniards" of Nicaragua to the west.

These differences led to hostility when the initial policies of the Sandinista government failed to consider the distinct history, economy, and culture of the people of the Atlantic Coast region. These mistakes were exploited by the United States. Several thousand Miskitos were induced to go north into Honduras, and beginning in late 1981 attacks by the contras were launched against Nicaraguan territory. The government responded by evacuating the Miskito population near the Honduran border, which heightened the friction. In twelve months beginning in December 1981, two documented incidents occurred in which Miskitos were killed by Sandinista soldiers. A total of approximately twenty-five Indians died, and seventy disappeared. No further deaths or disappearances occurred, at least through late 1984 (Americas Watch Committee 1984). By early 1985 relations had improved to the extent that the Nicaraguan government had permitted Brooklyn Rivera, the leader of one Miskito contra faction, to return to Nicaragua to meet with his followers, and the government had begun a process of negotiations toward granting some degree of autonomy to the Miskitos.

In the face of the military and economic aggression, the Sandinista leadership followed an economic program based on the principle of making the private sector function for social purposes. Nationalization was limited almost entirely to property formerly owned by Somoza and his associates, most of whom had fled the country when the new regime came to power. Approximately 79 percent of agricultural production, 69 percent of manufacturing, and 62 percent of commerce and services remained in private hands (Harris 1985). The government used a variety of economic policies that are common in capitalist economies to stimulate private economic activity. The state provided enough credit to the private sector to supply all operating capital requirements as well as funds for new investment. Despite the shortage of foreign exchange, businesses received a preferential exchange rate to import intermediate goods, parts, and new equipment.

The basic concept of the Sandinista economic model proposed that while capitalism functions with a logic favoring minority propertied classes, it is possible to make a still privately owned economy function in the interest of the majority.[10] The place of private ownership is perhaps best signified by the Agrarian Reform Law initiated in 1979. Unlike comparable laws elsewhere, no limit was imposed on the amount of land that could be owned by an individual. The government insisted that ownership carry with it a responsibility to employ property productively, but the regime was not hostile to profit. State policy was designed to make private enterprise profitable, an essential precondition for the private sector to function. Policies such as a flat tax of about 40 percent on net profit were imposed. Through these mechanisms, a substantial portion of the surplus value appropriated from the working classes would be returned to them through the state. This pragmatic, or instrumental, view of property was also reflected in provisions of the Agrarian Reform Law under which state farms, which could not be made to operate efficiently, would be distributed to individuals and cooperatives. In the first year of the law's implementation, over 300 farms in the public sector were denationalized (Collins 1982).

Along with an approach to production based on state guidance and encouragement of privately owned enterprise, state policy sought to influence distribution toward the interests of workers and peasants. The minimum wage law was modified, and, for the first time in Nicaragua, it was enforced. Limits were established on land rents charged to small farmers, and price controls and a limited amount of rationing were employed in the allocation of staples. A state distribution system for consumable goods was created as much to enforce the price controls as to handle distribution. The concept was that with staples available through the state system at prices set by the government, private merchants would be unable to charge substantially more without losing customers to the state system. Government distribution was largely handled by small private stores whose owners were judged by local block committees to be honest.

These policies attempted to make incomes derived from wages and from the profits of small producers adequate to purchase at least basic necessities. Another aspect of the distribution policy was a sharp increase in the social wage, services, and benefits provided without any relation to employment. During the regime's first three years, a literacy program mobilized thousands of young people and succeeded in reducing illiteracy from about 50 percent to 12 percent. The education budget grew from 1.32 percent of the GNP to 4.25 percent. The total number of students doubled to 1 million, and the number of adult education students rose from near zero to almost a quarter million. The health budget more than tripled. The number of vaccinations administered increased from 810,000 to 1,740,000, and clinics providing basic care were established throughout the country. In particular, the rate of child mortality from dehydration caused by intestinal parasites was sharply reduced. Infant mortality declined from 121 per 1,000 to 94 per 1,000.

The program of the Sandinista regime raised two fundamental questions: the first initially economic and the second more broadly political. First, would private owners respond favorably to the incentives offered by a government that gave priority to worker and peasant interests? That is, would capitalists operate their enterprises at a rate that would bring them the greatest return? Would they maintain the land, stock, plant, and equipment? Would they expand operations when capital was available and investment was justified by considerations of profitability? During the first four years of the Nicaraguan revolution, the performance of the private sector was mixed in regard to operation and maintenance while investment of privately held capital was nil. Funds loaned to business people by the state to assist and stimulate production were often illegally converted into foreign currencies, which were then sent abroad. Because the state sector made investments to expand production while the private sector abstained, the state sector grew in relation to the private.

To fulfill the economic role assigned to the private sector in the Sandinista strategy, it would appear that members of the propertied classes had to behave as individuals rather than as members of a class. From the perspective of the individual capitalist, or even a very large family financial interest or corporation, it would appear that the state is part of the environment in which the enterprise must function. Although a financial interest may in fact be very influential, rarely does it "own" a government. The predominant perspective of the individual capitalist is to accept the environment largely as a given (and to function within it) even while trying to influence the state. The capitalist, functioning as an individual, tends to respond positively to incentives such as those offered by the Sandinista regime, which provided opportunities for secure, profitable investment. In contrast, the perspective of the capitalist class is preoccupied with control over the state, maintenance of the system of private property, and enhancing its economic and social position and rewards. Class-oriented behavior during the period of consolidation of state power leads to resistance to the regime in all forms, including forgoing potential profits to disable the economy.

The second basic question was political. Was it possible to reduce class-oriented behavior on the part of the bourgeoisie in order to make the mixed economy function while simultaneously increasing class consciousness among workers and peasants in order to consolidate the political and military support upon which the survival of the regime and its progressive direction depended?

As suggested earlier, government actions to benefit one constituency tend to alienate others, particularly when resources are as limited as those available to the Sandinista regime. The effort to establish a mixed economy required some measures to reassure and encourage the private sector, and other measures, which would have had the opposite effect, were precluded. For example, the expansion of credit and the initiation of new programs tend to be inflationary because they expand the money supply without immediately resulting in increased production. This problem could have been temporarily ameliorated to some extent by appropriating and rationing the distribution of stocks of consumer goods on hand (balancing the expanded money supply by making more goods available to be purchased). Foreign exchange earnings could have been more fully employed to import the parts and intermediate goods needed to maintain production while refusing to honor debts contracted by the Somoza regime. However, these measures would have assured the defeat of the effort to provide a positive environment for private enterprise.

Instead, the debts were honored. Almost 40 percent of foreign exchange earnings was used for debt service in 1982, and payments in 1983 were projected to be 27 percent of the government budget (*Barricada inter-*

nacional, March 21, 1983: 4). Although agricultural production increased, the continuing decline in the prices of these exports on world markets reduced foreign exchange earnings. This loss, together with the partially successful U.S. credit blockade, resulted in an inability to make some purchases needed by the industrial sector, and in 1982 industrial production declined about 6 percent. Efforts to reduce inflation centered around austerity. Inflation ran at 35.3 percent in 1980 and 23.9 percent in 1981. In 1980, for example, the real wage fell by 16 percent (*Instituto histórico centroamericano* July 1982: 10, 12).

The mixed economy strategy imposed constraints on the capacity of the government to provide immediate material benefits to workers and peasants, and the clarity of the regime's commitment to the interests of workers and peasants was also obscured to some extent. At the same time the effort to maintain political pluralism provided channels for public criticism as well as for the dissemination of antigovernmental propaganda. The Council of State functioned as a consultative body subordinate to the National Directorate. It included representatives of all sectors, those who opposed as well as those who supported the Sandinistas. This institution allowed for the articulation of all interests and made possible a dialogue on major policies. At the same time it offered legitimacy to organized political opposition, but beginning in early 1981 the Sandinista regime censored the most overt instances of false or distorted information designed to destabilize the government. In the absence of improvements in the material conditions of most of the working class and peasantry, the Sandinistas relied heavily on the capacity of workers and peasants to understand their own long-term interests in relation to the regime and to correctly interpret the developing situation.

The Sandinista regime tenaciously held to a vision of political pluralism based on a mixed economy in spite of the apparent contradictions and dangers. There are reasons for this policy direction aside from ideological preferences. The Sandinista leadership had the benefit of the Cuban experience. The difficulties and costs of assuming the task of economic management provided a strong incentive to avoid nationalization (particularly since the rate of illiteracy in Nicaragua was considerably higher than in Cuba, and the pool of personnel, who were both capable and trustworthy, available to the regime was even smaller). Overly ambitious economic programs in Cuba had caused a great deal of waste in the use of resources. The low level of development in Cuba had proved a powerful obstacle to socialist planning, and the Nicaraguan economy was more backward than that of Cuba twenty years earlier.

There were additional conditions that served to constrain the tendency to secure the survival of the regime by eliminating political opposition, expropriating the economic base of the bourgeoisie, and taking direct control of the larger enterprises. The Sandinista government had inherited a desperate economic situation and required immediate aid from a broad spectrum of sources. The war had left great physical devastation (an estimated $480 million), caused principally by Somoza's air force, including the destruction of most productive facilities. One season's crops had been lost because the war had prevented planting. The new regime had inherited a foreign debt of approximately $1.6 billion, and Somoza had sacked the treasury shortly before his departure, leaving only $3.5 million in exchange reserves. For these reasons, the maintenance of trade relations was vitally important, and foreign loans and gifts were urgently needed.

Moreover, the Soviet Union showed no signs of making a major aid commitment to Nicaragua. In 1980 and 1981 the socialist countries (including Cuba) purchased only 5.7 percent of Nicaragua's exports and provided only 1.6 percent of imports (*Instituto histórico centroamericano* July 1982: 7, 12). In the 1980–1982 period Western European donations to Nicaragua totaled $97 million (43.5 percent) while those from Latin America and the socialist bloc amounted to $64 million (28.7 percent) and $62 million (27.8 percent), respectively. Latin America extended the largest amount of credits, $243 million (*Barricade international*, March 7, 1983: 4). Therefore, avoiding the loss of aid, which was contingent upon the continuation of a mixed economy and political pluralism, was an important consideration for the Sandinista leadership.

The strength of the Catholic church in Nicaragua was also a factor. Priests working in poor communities and layworkers had played an active part in the struggle against the Somoza regime, and a substantial proportion of the Sandinistas were Catholics. When large parts of the bourgeoisie had joined the opposition to Somoza, the hierarchy had followed. Bishop Obando y Bravo had actively spoken out against the repression of Somoza forces and had called for a dialogue with the opposition. Thus, at the time of the victory of the Sandinista revolution, the church enjoyed considerable prestige because of its unity with the people as well as its traditional base. As the private sector withdrew from the revolution and began active opposition, Bishop Obando followed. Polarization throughout Nicaraguan society was mirrored by a division within the church. The hierarchy, traditionally associated with the bourgeoisie, maintained that affiliation, and Catholics who had sided with the poor supported the government. Had it wished to abandon the model of a mixed economy and political pluralism, the Sandinista regime would have incurred a significant loss of support if it had done so before the contradictions of the model had become intolerable. Instead, if polarization was inevitable, the regime had to rely on an erosion of the prestige of the hierarchy in favor of the "popular church" as the process developed.

Both the Cuban and the Nicaraguan revolutions came to power leading a rather broad coalition of class forces against the old regime. Both enunciated programs based on state guidance of a predominantly private economy and political pluralism. In one sense, the Sandinista program was somewhat more radical than that of M26J. The former was more specific in asserting the dominance of "the logic of the majority" over the interests of property when conflicts could not be avoided. Nonetheless, within two years of coming to power a majority of the Cuban economic system had been nationalized. Within three years the concept of pluralism had been rejected in favor of a Leninist political organization based on the vanguard party. For at least five years the Sandinista regime resisted pressures to secure its survival by nationalizing the economic base of the bourgeoisie and eliminating its political organization and its propaganda instruments. It used nationalization only to punish instances of flagrant economic sabotage.

In response to military aggression, the Nicaraguan government introduced censorship and made a small number of usually short-term political arrests. However, no effort was made to eliminate the organizations of political opposition. On the contrary, in November 1984 elections were held to select a president and vice-president and members of a ninety-six-seat Constituent Assembly. According to the report of an official observer team of the Latin American Studies Association, "by Latin American standards (the electoral process) was a model of probity and fairness" (LASA 1984: 32).[11]

Several measures favored the six opposition parties. All of the parties received substantial public funding for their campaigns as well as free media time. Had the single-member-district formula been used, under which candidates would have had to win at least a plurality to be elected, there would have been little opposition representation in the assembly. The proportional-representation system that was chosen favored minority parties, so the opposition parties gained thirty-five seats in the assembly. Moreover, another provision of the electoral law allowed the defeated presidential candidates of the opposition parties to hold seats in the assembly so they could represent their parties.

Differences in the international conditions faced by the Cuban and Nicaraguan revolutions during the consolidation stage help to partially explain their different actions. In the early 1960s the United States was capable of isolating Cuba from economic relationships with virtually the entire capitalist world. The United States had emerged from the Second World War in a position of political, economic, and military dominance, and Western Europe lacked the interest, independence, and capability to engage in foreign policies in opposition to Washington. In the twenty-year interim between the two Latin American revolutions, European economic strength increased dramatically in relation to that of the United States, and opportunities developed to break into the Latin American markets, which had been a nearly exclusive U.S. preserve during the postwar period. A relatively weaker U.S. position and the growth of Venezuelan and Mexican oil revenues also made Latin American aid available to Nicaragua, but assistance from Western Europe and Latin America seemed contingent upon Nicaragua's continuing the mixed economy strategy.

In contrast, the United States was able to bribe or coerce all of Latin America except Mexico to break diplomatic as well as economic relations with Cuba. When the United States abruptly ceased its purchases of Cuban sugar in 1960, the survival of the Cuban revolution depended upon obtaining economic and military support from a reluctant Soviet Union. Cuban domestic strategy may have been influenced by the need to realign its international position, so the Cuban regime would have been pressed to take actions to assure the Soviet Union that Cuba was not following a bourgeois reformist path, that Cuba would identify with the Soviet bloc.

We observed earlier that revolutions in Latin America have only succeeded when they have had the militant, organized support of substantial sections of their respective worker and peasant classes, but the Sandinista strategy limited the regime's capacity to provide immediate material benefits to workers and peasants. Because the regime attempted to create a secure place for the bourgeoisie, it also appeared to hamper a consolidation of the identification and militant commitment of its necessary class constituency. For these reasons, Nicaragua's strategy was vulnerable to destabilization and armed aggression.

The stage of consolidation of state power is a very dynamic period. At the time of this writing, fewer than six years had passed since the Sandinista regime had achieved power, and polarization had developed in spite of the regime's strategy. Three alternative outcomes seemed to define the range of possibilities. First, if the private sector continued to abstain from investment, then it appeared most likely that the mixed economy model would eventually give way to one in which the state assumed a larger ownership role. Thus far, that portion of the petty bourgeoisie that uses the income produced by its enterprises for its immediate livelihood has continued to operate those enterprises. Large-property owners, responsible for most investment, have failed to play the role assigned to them by the policy of a mixed economy. Most have either left the country or have given their support to the counterrevolution. Without cooperation from the bourgeoisie, the mixed economy model would become irrelevant. Therefore, an economy based on large-scale state enterprise, with a substantial sector of small individually or cooperatively owned businesses and farms, would be most likely. If the extreme pressures of continued military attacks and economic hardships reduced the government's capacity to tolerate a legitimized opposition, then political organization based on a de facto Leninism would be likely. These internal developments would probably be accompanied by a shift in external support, with increased assistance from the Soviet bloc and some reduction in aid from other sources.

Despite nearly four years of contra aggression, this direction was not followed. On the contrary, a relaxation of political censorship and other restrictions was initiated at the beginning of the 1984 election campaign period and continued afterward. In early 1985 a broad amnesty was extended to virtually all contras, including the leadership, permitting them to return to Nicaragua to engage in struggle on a political level.

Second, if the state of emergency and its attendant hardships continued over several years, weariness could lead to a disaffection of the masses. If the Sandinistas persevered in maintaining their initial policy and the bourgeois opposition continued while workers and peasants became apathetic, the externally based counterrevolution could achieve a military victory. It was likely that this possibility would be recognized by the leadership, who would then respond by expropriating the bourgeoisie and following the scenario suggested above.

Third, success of the mixed economy strategy in its present form appeared to be the least probable scenario. It would be considerably more likely that the United States would completely reverse its policy and adopt a posture of cautious support similar to that of such social democratic regimes as Sweden. In those changed circumstances, a portion of the Nicaraguan bourgeoisie might choose to accommodate itself to the mixed economy model. These capitalists would then act in their individual rather than in their class roles and seek to maximize their profits within the framework established by the government. Without externally imposed economic obstacles, Nicaragua's natural endowment of resources would suggest good prospects for long-term economic development. In the absence of economic hardship or threat of external aggression, Nicaragua might well achieve a functioning mixed economy with political pluralism within the Sandinista ideological hegemony. This unlikely outcome would continue to contain the contradiction between the interests of property owners and the logic of the majority.

The Stage of Socialist Development

With the successful completion of the consolidation of state power, the new regime is secure from internal counterrevolution. The economy is yet to be transformed, being still based primarily in agriculture and possibly mining. Production and distribution are predominantly carried out in large numbers of small enterprises, and labor productivity is generally low. Although the economy suffers from poor coordination and inefficiency, it does function more or less in accordance with a plan. The priority of the interests of the producing classes has been established in the direction of the economy and in the ideological framework of the new state. The revolution has successfully led to the stage of socialist development.

This socialism, a product of capitalism in the periphery, has a contradictory nature. On one hand, it is a regime of seemingly limitless possibilities. The contradictions of imperialism and uneven development have brought about a mobilization of class forces sufficient to overthrow the old regime. Idleness of potentially productive land and people had been widespread; now a government committed to the interests of workers and peasants is in power. It has the power to put an end to the market's irrational allocation of resources, and wasteful luxury at the expense of the majority can be brought to an end. Production can be turned to meeting basic needs. The very severity of the conditions that brought about revolution appears as a lever of change. Change is imperative, justified by desperate need. Moreover, the conditions themselves and the process of struggle create an active political will for justice on the part of the exploited and the oppressed.

At the same time the new regime is bounded by constraints. Economic transformation presents many difficulties. Capitalist countries in the Third World are likely to have a shortage of almost everything. Many countries in Latin America are dependent on the importation of food as well as manufactured goods, and agriculture as well as manufacturing is likely to be oriented toward the use of imported inputs. Trained technical and managerial personnel are lacking, and orientations toward industrial production are not diffused throughout the population. Important economic sectors are likely to be disrupted when foreign owners, buyers, or tourists reject the changes the revolution is seeking. Some production must be diverted away from current consumption and into investment if accumulation is to take place. Given the low amount of surplus produced, accumulation will usually require austerity.

Paradoxically, socialist development is most certain of eventual success where it appears weakest at the outset—in the economy. Notwithstanding the difficulties and problems noted above, economic growth is a virtual certainty even though it requires time and sacrifice. The rate of growth depends on conditions such as the level of the economy at the beginning; the natural resource endowment, both that which has been developed and that which is easily available for development; the degree of vulnerability to economic blockade; and the educational and cultural levels of the population. When natural resources are scarce, development will be slower, but with investment in human resources, the population can eventually achieve the capacity to produce much of the society's needs and to export to finance necessary imports. The records of the Soviet Union, China, Cuba, and Democratic People's Republic of Korea, and other socialist countries demonstrate that growth, diversification, and eventual industrialization can be achieved. The experiences of these countries have included a variety of policies. Many mistakes have been made and problems encountered; the level of sacrifice has sometimes been high. Nonetheless, even countries as poor as China have used economic planning successfully to achieve economic development.

The long-term goal of socialist development is advanced socialism or communism. Communist society as conceptualized by Marx differs fundamentally from capitalism and is similar to some precapitalist societies in that exchange is absent from the economy. Primitive communism was characterized by simple production for use. Production was motivated by survival needs of the producer and his or her family unit. Social roles included activities to meet the needs of the group, and such contributions to the group had no connotation of exchange.

In the evolution of human societies, a greater complexity of production brought forth a division of labor and eventually class divisions based on ownership of the means of production. Economic behavior within the nuclear family conforms to social roles, but elsewhere, self-interest and exchange in the market are dominant. The owners of the means of production are motivated by profit to organize workers to produce. Labor is performed for a wage, which is needed to fulfill individual and family needs. The divisions based on property have resulted in a concentration of wealth and power, and exploitation and oppression.

In the Marxian conception of advanced socialism, individuals relate to their society as they relate to their nuclear family. Unlike primitive communism, production is complex and requires a division of labor. People do not directly consume what they or the members of their immediate social group produce. Most of their labor contributes to production for people whom they do not know, and they receive most of the goods they consume from others.

However, advanced socialism, or postcapitalist communism, resembles primitive communism in that exchange does not govern economic activity. Like primitive communism, work that meets the needs of people outside the nuclear family is embedded in the social roles available to the population. Neither power nor individual consumption is related to individual ownership or work. Consumption is self-regulated, and access to the benefits available in society as well as social prestige depend upon other aspects of each person's conduct or characteristics. With the removal of material gain from its place of importance in motivating behavior, other dimensions of the human personality can be developed. Of course, this advanced socialism requires production sufficient to satisfy the expectations for consumption that are present in the society. Since there has been no actual experience of advanced socialism, it remains a matter of conjecture whether human personality and society can transcend the known limitations of human history.

The progression from the consolidation of a socialist regime to the achievement of advanced socialism is a project whose length is measured in generations. Short of this historical transcendence lies the goal of a prosperous, independent society that we refer to as developed socialism. In a developed socialist society, the productive forces (including technology, physical plant and equipment, and the cultural-technical level of the work force) have advanced sufficiently to provide for society's needs and for further accumulation while eliminating the need for the most arduous physical labor and reducing the workweek so that time is available for participation in decision making as well as educational and cultural development and recreation. Developed socialism differs from communism in that individual consumption is allocated through wages and salaries, which are unequal "according to work." Substantial differences remain in the income, influence, and prestige associated with various social roles, but access to these roles is more or less equal. Although the state retains coercive power, participatory mechanisms prevail throughout social institutions. The need for a Leninist vanguard party has been overcome through a diffusion of communist ideology, based on the successes of socialist development.

On the day the old regime fell, the political dimension of the revolution may have seemed its greatest strength. Ironically, the achievement of developed socialism is ultimately most threatened by the danger of political distortion. We have noted that the class coalition that overthrows capitalism in peripheral areas tends to contain elements, such as local capitalists who are being squeezed by foreign capitalists or a greedy family dictatorship, whose interests do not lie with a transition to socialism, and we have suggested that the survival of the revolution and its progressive direction depend upon the consolidation of a mobilized base of support among those classes whose interests do lie in socialism. Similarly, the coalition that carries forward the project of socialist development contains strata—such as higher-level managers, political cadres, and scientific, technical, and other intellectual workers—whose interests lie in continued economic growth but not in sociopolitical transformation.

The dangers of political distortion are a consequence of the conditions of revolution arising from the contradictions of imperialism and uneven development. Given the nature of capitalist societies in the Third World, a vanguard directs the project of socialist development on behalf of a working class that is not numerically predominant. Although the working class usually is represented in the party in a higher proportion than in society, the role and position of the political vanguard providing direction and coordination are distinct from those of the workers. The party manages the demands of the small peasants, intellectual workers, and managers as well as the workers. The state tends to assume vast economic power in order to bring underutilized land into production. To promote industry and rapid economic growth, investment is increased at the expense of consumption. Power is used to secure the survival of the new regime and to strive for a sometimes too ambitious rate of economic growth.

The power of the party tends to be exercised without accountability. There is a gap between the ultimate constituency of socialist development and the present nature of society. Moreover, most of the classes that support the revolution are lacking in political experience and are therefore initially incapable of meaningful political participation, especially beyond the local level. During the time that is needed to develop the political capacity of the working class and the peasantry, there is a tendency for the party to degenerate, that is, the original motives of the revolutionaries may be replaced by a self-serving interest. And the power acquired through this process may be turned toward maintaining power and bureaucratic privilege.

The period from the consolidation of state power to the achievement of developed socialism is one of tension between the task of economic transformation and efforts to bring about sociopolitical transformation. The progressive direction of change during the consolidation of power phase required a dominance of those class forces that were in favor of socialism. Similarly, continued progress toward sociopolitical transformation requires the maintenance of a progressive coalition of class forces.

The problem of socialist development is the tendency of conservative class forces to arise from within. One instance is the above-mentioned tendency for the party to become isolated and self-serving. The other major source of conservatism lies in the nature of the economic development project in the context of the inheritance of capitalism in the periphery nations. The capitalist accumulation process is broken by crises. Nonetheless, it is an effective mode of production for the development of the metropolitan centers. The bias of the market in favor of the strongest financial and industrial powers tends to bring about uneven development. The concentration is conducive to growth, at least until the monopoly stage is reached. Growth is facilitated by the entrepreneur's or his manager's brutal suppression of the workers' consumption in pursuit of maximum profit.

The political revolution that brings about the period of socialist development inherits conditions in which accumulation is facilitated by many of the same measures. Detailed centralized planning has proved to be effective in mobilizing unutilized resources, but it tends to result in waste and inefficiency. Difficulties in centrally coordinating the allocation of resources lead to delays and stoppages. Managers dedicated to maintaining production are sometimes driven to subverting the plan to do so. The market tends to exercise an effective discipline over managers with respect to controlling costs of production. When managers have the authority to purchase production inputs in the market and have an incentive to minimize costs, production tends to be carried out more efficiently, at least in the narrow sense of the term. The market also tends to be a more effective agent of quality control than planners' performance specifications. Similarly, work discipline tends to be higher when wages are linked to performance, particularly when labor consists of simple repetitive tasks in which there is little differentiation in the quality of work performed. Payment for such work according to piece rates is the most effective as well as the most brutal basis for remuneration. And while alienation induced by job insecurity tends to lower worker productivity, the authority of managers to discipline and dismiss workers imparts fear, a negative but frequently effective work incentive.

Thus, policies and practices that reflect a single-minded pursuit of economic growth tend to replicate many of the worst aspects of industrial capitalism. Moreover, as the level of the economy advances, technical education and training grow in importance. Developing a cadre of technical personnel is facilitated by offering strong incentives, which make possible a privileged consumption level that tends to create a cultural isolation of this technical cadre from other workers. Advancing science and engineering, which contribute to higher productivity, is also facilitated by focusing educational resources on the students who perform best in primary and secondary schools. The parents of these students are most often the members of the educated strata and those whose political position provides access to better early education. Thus, an emphasis on increased productivity through technological advancement tends to contribute to the creation of roles that are isolated from other strata of the producing classes and with which privilege is associated. And the educational system tends to become a mechanism through which these privileged positions can be passed on from parents to their children. Thus, the conditions of socialist development arising from revolution against peripheral capitalism tend to create a managerial/technical class. The interests of this class lie in continued economic transformation according to a strategy that limits measures that are oriented toward greater sociopolitical equality.

This course corresponds in large measure to the experience of the Russian revolution. Because of the hostility of its international environment, industrialization was imperative. Moreover, all segments of the leadership appear to have held a rather narrow and rigid concept of productive forces (Sweezy 1980: 58), and economic transformation was seen almost exclusively in terms of industrialization. The countryside was the source of surplus to support industry. The peasantry, which was the necessary producer of this economic surplus, was written off politically as a backward social class for which there was no place in the socialist future. Presiding over a period of severe austerity during the years of the Second World War, the Party followed a model of tight economic and political centralization. Although highly centralized planning served well to mobilize resources after recovery from the devastation of the war and the development of a more complex economy, the deficiencies of overcentralization became apparent. However, reform efforts have been limited, and given the structure of power in the Soviet Union, it would appear that progress in the sociopolitical area of socialist development will require the emergence of an autonomous movement of the working class and the peasantry.

Considering the conditions of Russia at the time of the revolution, it is not surprising that the major accomplishments of the Communist regime have been in the realm of economic transformation. Russian society had by no means fulfilled the possibilities of capitalism, the point at which a brief and direct path to developed socialism would have been a real possibility. Socialism in the Soviet Union has served as a mode of development to reach that level.

Maoism is an alternative to the Soviet model of socialist development. China has oscillated between a program drawing upon the Soviet approach to economic modernization (1949–1956, 1960–1966, 1975 to the present) and a strategy that emphasizes mobilization to achieve economic development (1957–1959, 1966–1975). Although often favoring heavy industry, the Chinese leadership has given greater consideration to balancing the needs of heavy industry with those of agriculture and light industry. During the periods of mobilization, efforts were made to counteract the tendency toward uneven development by diffusing industry throughout the country, based on the use of indigenous as well as modern technology. Ideological campaigns were carried out against most forms of hierarchy, and collective management was encouraged. The professionalization of knowledge was attacked in favor of egalitarianism, and intellectuals were subjected to considerable harassment and repression. Students, managers, and other people in roles that were subject to cultural isolation were required to perform manual labor, usually in the countryside. Although these policies suppressed the managerial, technical, and intellectual strata, whose tendency toward elitism most concerned Mao, they did not bring about a democratization of power.

In general, China has continuously achieved high rates of economic growth since 1949. However, the stresses of intensive mobilization eventually resulted in a reaction that permitted the people who favored a more traditional approach to come to power. The new leadership has rejected Maoist policies, giving greater priority to the promise of rapid growth through the importation of modern technology than to Mao's hope of achieving a mass-based egalitarian socialist development. In the post-Mao period a centralization of political power has continued while greater use has been made of the market and individual material work incentives. It would appear that the political, managerial, and technical strata in China will consolidate their power and obstruct progress in the sociopolitical dimension of socialist development.

In Cuba, toward the end of the consolidation of state power (approximately 1962–1965), a debate took place concerning the direction of Cuban socialism (Silverman 1971). One approach, *auto-financiamiento*—in which state enterprises finance investment through retained earnings—emphasized the limits imposed by Cuba's level of development. It argued for use of the market, traditional one-person managerial responsibility, and individual material incentives to establish discipline in the economy and to achieve the most productive allocation of resources. The other approach, *presupuestario de financiamiento*—central budgeting, articulated most prominently by Ché Guevara—argued that emphasis on the market would only reproduce the existing deformities of Cuba's economy and society.

Proponents of the more conservative market socialism argued that Cuba's choices were constrained by the level of development of productive forces. They felt that Cuba was not sufficiently developed to sustain a high level of centralized economic planning and that market mechanisms still had an important role to play in the allocation of resources. With an economy characterized by a large number of small enterprises, planning was not feasible, as it would be under the economic concentration of advanced capitalism. Without the capacity for social control of production through planning, control through the discipline of the market and the use of individual material incentives to motivate work would be needed.

Guevara disagreed, denying the relevance of conditions within Cuba. Instead, he focused on consciousness as a source of direction for management and motivation for workers. He argued that imperialism had reached an advanced stage on a world scale and an advanced level of consciousness had been developed in reaction to it, even in under-developed neocolonial countries. Therefore, this consciousness could serve as a resource in the building of socialism. According to this approach, the conservative influence of the market and the corrupting influence of individual material incentives could be avoided. With a strong central direction of the economy, resources could be allocated in accordance with an integrated development plan by setting prices without relation to production costs. Thus, Guevara argued that revolutions arising from the contradictions of imperialism and underdevelopment could proceed directly toward advanced socialism, simultaneously constructing socialism and communism.

In Cuba, the strategy of "moral incentives" advocated by Guevara was followed from 1966 through 1970. Most state enterprises were grouped into a few large *combinados*, or combined industries, to make direct central allocation more manageable (instead of a buying and selling of intermediate goods among enterprises under the more autonomous direction of their managers). The link between the individual's work performance and individual consumption was severed by a number of measures. To facilitate the movement of personnel, employees and workers received the highest wage or salary they had ever earned, even when assigned to a position with a lower pay scale. Workers often were not docked for absences from work. It was hoped that the example of those workers who made an extraordinary effort would influence the slackers to do their share. Under the pressure of an increasing volume of pesos in circulation combined with a constant or declining quantity of goods available for purchase, money lost most of its power as an incentive. With over 30 percent of production devoted to investment, little beyond necessities was available for consumption, and almost everything for sale was rationed to assure that everyone received a share of the scarce commodities. People were called upon to contribute labor, either directly in agriculture or by taking over the work of fellow workers who had gone to cut sugarcane, plant vegetables or coffee, or perform other agricultural tasks. Workers whose efforts were especially great were publicly honored with awards of recognition.

It was hoped that these voluntary efforts and a high rate of investment would bring about rapid economic growth, which would enable the state to increase consumption in general and the free-goods sector in particular. It was hoped that consciousness would grow through the experience of receiving more free goods as a result of voluntary work contributed by a large part of the population. In this way, Cuba was to maintain an egalitarian sociopolitical transformation while overcoming the economic inheritance of peripheral capitalism.

The policies of various revolutions have usually been articulated in terms of broad approaches to socialist development, seemingly flowing from abstract conceptions. It is more likely that particular concrete conditions and problems shape decisions that, taken together, form the overall path that is followed. The Cuban strategy of moral incentives was explained by Fidel Castro as a way to "create wealth with consciousness" in order to avoid arriving at "selfishness amidst abundance," a critical reference to the Soviet model. The moral incentives strategy rejected the concept of constraints on social relations imposed by the level of a society's productive forces, which specified that a more advanced consciousness could come about only with the achievement of economic advances (i.e., consciousness created by wealth). Although the Soviet Union had not achieved abundance, the Cuban leadership seemed to imply that Soviet economic advances had been achieved at a cost in the quality of sociopolitical life that was both too high and unnecessary.

The choice of unorthodox and risky policies was probably influenced by the situation Cuba faced at the time. There was a need to expand agricultural exports to finance the importation of a broad range of capital goods needed for the mechanization of agriculture and the development of other sectors of the economy, and aside from forced labor, the mobilization of voluntary labor through the moral incentives policies appeared to be the only feasible way to accomplish the necessary expansion of the agricultural work force (see Silverman 1973, Edelstein 1981: 240).

Cuba's experience with the moral incentives strategy as a means of increasing productive labor was mixed. A great deal of labor was contributed, but much of it was offset by a loss of work through absenteeism and a reduced intensity of labor on the part of workers who could not put forth consistent effort without the direct link between quantity and quality of work on the one hand and pay on the other. Centralized allocation proved to be effective in setting the resources of Cuban society into motion, but the government's inability to effectively coordinate production led to intolerable shutdowns caused by delays in the delivery of materials, parts, and intermediate goods. In this respect, moral incentives was a major cause of the disorganization of the Cuban economy.

The moral incentives strategy in Cuba did minimize the differences in levels of consumption and access to culture and education. It emphasized revolutionary and patriotic commitment as valued individual attributes, which were rewarded to some degree in the allocation of consumer goods and in selection for higher education. In this sense, the official commitment to egalitarian sociopolitical transformation was diffused throughout Cuban society. However, together with the emphasis on economic growth and the austerity caused by the reduced proportion of production that was devoted to current consumption, the strategy functioned in a contrary political direction. Although worker participation in decision making in the work place had never been significant in Cuba, the increased centralization of planning reduced the possibility of greater work place democracy, and hierarchy in the work place may have increased as the unions fell to neglect. One consequence of the high priority placed on the drive for rapid accumulation was a decline in the quality of political direction and organization because, in numerous work places and communities, many of the most capable party cadres were recruited for administrative and management positions. The open dialogue on socialist development also fell victim to the perceived need for unity of the mobilizational strategy. The 1968 trial of a "microfaction" of a few people who had deviated from the direction of official policy had the effect of drawing the lines of acceptable political differences quite narrowly (see Huberman and Sweezy 1969: chap. 11).

The moral incentives strategy was associated with a campaign begun in 1963 to work toward the goal of a harvest of 10 million tons of sugar in 1970. In 1970, 8.5 million tons were actually produced, short of the goal but a new record. The largest harvest until that time had been 7.2 million tons in 1952. By the end of the 1970 harvest, the population had grown impatient with austerity, the stresses of mobilization, disorganization, and their inability to have any influence over the failures of centralized economic planning that affected them.

A new policy direction was initiated to correct the deficiencies of the moral incentives strategy and to comply with mass popular feelings. Its major economic features included greater autonomy for the enterprises, less detailed central economic direction, and the reestablishment of the link between work and consumption. Bonuses were created for managers and workers based on the quality of individual work and the performance of the enterprise as a whole. Investment was reduced to 23 percent of the GNP to permit a higher level of consumption. In the late 1970s the sphere of private economic activity was expanded. Whereas the legitimate private sector had been limited to small farmers, it came to include electricians, plumbers, and some other people who were trained and licensed by the state.

Many goods were either removed from the rationing system or made available on the free market at higher prices than charged on ration. Additional consumer goods, including some luxury goods, became available for sale. Under the policies of the revolutionary government, small private farmers had always been permitted to sell small quantities of vegetables to individuals, but in 1980 state-run markets were established in the cities so private farmers could offer their surplus produce to city dwellers. Legitimizing private trade alleviated the failure of the state to provide adequate and timely repair and maintenance services, which had been a source of widespread annoyance and frustration. Making more nonessential and even luxury goods available for purchase reduced both the black market and the dissatisfaction of people who had found nothing on which to spend their money. At the same time these policies legitimized greater inequality in consumption. In this sense, they appeared to reduce the priority of egalitarian sociopolitical transformation.

However, in a more fundamental sense, the new policies provided for the institutionalization of political mechanisms that were important for the long-term commitment to sociopolitical transformation. Institutions for mass participation in decision making were created. (A valuable description of these institutions functioning at their best is provided by Harnecker 1980.) For the first time in modern Cuba, before or after the revolution, the unions were democratized by competitive elections and a secret ballot. Monthly meetings were established that gave workers the opportunity to directly question the decisions of management as well as working conditions. These production assemblies also had the authority to distribute housing owned by the enterprise and some durable consumer goods. Also, the quality of the political leadership was strengthened by the return of capable cadres to party work.

In 1974 a major step in the movement toward decentralization and democratization occurred with the establishment of the Organs of Popular Power, or Organos de Poder Popular (OPP), organized on municipal, provincial, and national levels. On the local level, representatives are chosen by secret ballot in competitive elections from among nominees selected at open meetings. The electoral districts are quite small, usually composed of 800 to 2,500 residents, so that candidates are often known personally by the voters. OPP representatives serve as volunteers, continuing their employment. They receive expenses when they travel on public business, but otherwise they serve without pay. They have regular office hours each week to receive reports of problems, complaints, and suggestions from constituents, and they report on their activities in an open meeting of the district every three months. They are subject to recall for inadequate performance. The municipal assemblies, which are made up of these local representatives, choose representatives to the provincial and national levels on a ratio of one representative for each 10,000 and 200,000 people, respectively.

Each level of the OPP has responsibility for the operation of all production and services functioning on a comparable level. For example, a municipal assembly oversees the operations of local schools, hospitals, stores, theaters, hotels, restaurants, radio stations, auto repair shops, courts, etc. The provincial assemblies supervise the administration of regional bus systems, electric power grids, and so on. The National Assembly oversees the operation of the national ministries, such as those operating heavy industries, the planning apparatus, etc. The division of functions is such that although a local hospital falls under the jurisdiction of a municipal assembly, technical assistance provided to hospitals by the national health ministry is the responsibility of the National Assembly. In 1980 greater accountability of local enterprises and institutions was further encouraged by the sanctioning of public criticism by citizens. A consumers' journal, *Opina*, was created to carry out this function.

Cuba's experience with the high degree of centralization and egalitarian distributive policies of the moral incentives strategy suggests that such measures work poorly, especially after the task of mobilizing idle resources has been completed. Moreover, at least in a context of austerity, they tend to lead to increased hierarchy, authoritarianism, popular disillusionment, and isolation of the political leadership.

The economic and educational policies adopted in Cuba since 1970 tend to emphasize individual material rewards. Although unions can allocate some consumer durables for purchase on credit at a discount for especially meritorious workers, the most important determinant of access to consumer goods is salary. Higher salaries are paid for jobs that require higher levels of skill, education, or training; those that entail a higher level of responsibility; and those that involve hardship.

The sociopolitical implications of the incentive system are somewhat mixed. On the one hand there are opportunities to establish licensed service businesses through which a person can independently sell her or his skilled labor on the open market. At the same time no one in Cuba can strike it rich, purchase a part of the means of production, and henceforth live off the labor of others. No one need fear that lack of income will deny access to medical care, to free education for his or her children, or other basic services. A family headed by an unskilled service worker will have little more than the very basic necessities. A family with the income of two professional workers is able to own a private automobile and to purchase some luxury goods.

Success in education offers the possibility of obtaining positions of responsibility or prestige and of having a higher quality of consumption. Admission to advanced schooling is based on prior academic record, not on political recommendations. Children whose parents have more education are more likely to have a high level of education achievement. To this extent, there are positions of privilege, and the offspring of the people who occupy these positions have an advantage in succeeding their parents in them. On the other hand differences in income have no effect on educational opportunity and little impact on cultural opportunities. Because of the extent of equality of access to these keys to advancement in both political and economic structures, the recruitment system for the higher-level positions in Cuba is among the most open and egalitarian to be found anywhere.

As long as there are positions in society offering higher levels of those things that are held to be valuable, there will be a tendency toward the establishment of elite strata and mechanisms through which positions in these strata can be passed on from generation to generation. In Cuba, the OPP and other participatory institutions develop the capacity and the experience of the population in decision making. This latter element will probably strengthen the ability of the Cuban working class to combat tendencies toward bureaucratic isolation of the government and to press for the use of resources to support further sociopolitical transformation as opportunities become available through economic development.

Thus far the Cuban revolution has succeeded in providing for the basic needs of the Cuban people. In contrast to conditions before the revolution, which are still prevalent throughout major portions of Latin America, there is no hunger in Cuba today. The Cuban health care system is the best in the Third World and better than most in developed countries. Health care is universally available, and refining the health care system is an almost obsessive priority of government policy. With adequate-to-good nutrition and medical care, including prenatal and well-baby programs, infant mortality in Cuba is 16 per 1,000 live births, less than a third of what it was before the revolution and about the same as that of developed countries. Life expectancy has increased to over seventy-three years. Cuba now has achieved the highest level of education in Latin America. Not only literacy but completion of school through the sixth grade is nearly universal among the adult population.

Economically, the Cuban economy has become increasingly more diversified. Although sugar continues to account for approximately 80 percent of foreign exchange earnings, a larger proportion and variety of domestic needs are produced in Cuba. Inputs such as chemical fertilizers and mechanical harvesters, needed for sugar production and other agricultural uses, are produced domestically. Agriculture is substantially mechanized and therefore requires far less labor than before. Moreover, the emphasis on education has led to the creation of a scientific and an engineering infrastructure that supports rapid progress in the introduction of more sophisticated techniques in agricultural and industrial production and in management. "Cuba's leap into twentieth-century science and engineering in only one generation has hurtled the island in most fields far beyond its Latin American neighbours. And in some applied areas—for example, sugar-cane by-product research—Cuba has jumped to world leadership" (Ubell 1983: 745).

Although Cuba has substantial financial and trade relations with all of the advanced capitalist countries except the United States, relations with the Soviet Union and Eastern European countries are of great importance. Cuba purchases oil from the USSR at a cost far below the price on the capitalist market. Although the price of sugar has fluctuated drastically on the capitalist market, the Soviet Union has purchased it at a constant price of slightly over thirty cents (U.S.) per pound, which has sometimes been more than five times higher than the capitalist world price. Moreover, when the capitalist market price rose briefly to an unprecedented eighty cents per pound, the Soviet Union suspended some delivery commitments to allow Cuba to benefit from the erratic market. These economic benefits of Cuba's relations with the USSR obviously reinforce that country's powerful influence in Cuba.

Despite the leverage the Soviet Union has gained through its economic role, the relationship between Cuba and the USSR does not parallel the dependent metropolis-periphery relationships among capitalist countries. In addition to differences such as the absence of any foreign ownership in the Cuban economic structure, there is a fundamental political difference. The ruling classes in the capitalist countries in the periphery are situated atop systems of exploitation. Although they sporadically have differences with the rulers of the metropolitan countries, their interests are nonetheless aligned in the maintenance of these systems in opposition to the interests of the majorities in their own countries. In Cuba, there is no gap between the leadership and the masses such as has arisen in some countries of Eastern Europe.

It is still too soon in the evolution of Cuba's experience of socialist development to predict whether that country will avoid the tendencies toward the growth of a privileged bureaucratic technical/managerial coalition or whether efforts to empower the masses through institutions that provide experience in decision making will prevail. If the political capacity of the working classes is successfully developed, Cuba may achieve developed socialism with a progressive correlation of class forces capable of moving toward the possibility of communism without the need for further class struggle.

It would appear that the model in the Soviet Union and much of Eastern Europe has led to the creation of a state dominated by bureaucratic political and technical/managerial classes. At its worst, this class coalition opposes egalitarian sociopolitical change, except what is necessary to co-opt pressure from the working classes. Nonetheless, more complex and sophisticated economies are emerging that are increasingly hampered by overcentralization and bureaucratic insensitivity. Educational levels have been raised so that the populations are becoming increasingly intolerant of authoritarianism and of alienating conditions in the work place and other aspects of social life. That is, socialist development may succeed in bringing about an economic transformation that overcomes the uneven development of capitalism in the periphery but fails to maintain the dominance of the interests of the producing classes. The result then is a society of postcapitalist bureaucratic state socialism that must succumb to the overthrow of its ruling class if it is to go further in its sociopolitical transformation. The recent experiences of the Soviet Union and Eastern European countries suggest that economic development creates internal contradictions that have the potential to create a new working class movement oriented toward the further development of socialism (Singer 1982).

8

Prospects for
Capitalism and Socialism

Most theories of development and underdevelopment concern the impact of capitalism upon the growth and well-being of societies and peoples everywhere. Some of these theories address the impact of socialism, either in its idealized form or in situations in which it currently is practiced. Development and underdevelopment are ideas in literature that often reflect a degree of modernization or backwardness, of urban industrialization or rural poverty. Whatever the theories and ideas about development and underdevelopment, however, it is clear that these concepts can be understood only in reference to the experience of capitalism and socialism. Thus, in assessing the prospects for Latin America, we focus on capitalism and socialism.

Capitalism consists of commodity production, that is, production for sale on the market so that capitalist enterprise and the bourgeois or capitalist-owning class can control and benefit from the surplus value of commodities produced by workers. Under capitalism, of course, the means of production are privately owned, and the objective of capitalists is the maximization of profits. Capitalism also seeks to ensure the accumulation of capital so as to ensure the progressive growth of the capitalist firm or economy. Capitalism emerged in a manufacturing stage, which spanned the sixteenth through the eighteenth centuries, and an industrial stage, marked initially by free competition in the late eighteenth and most of the nineteenth centuries and later by imperialism in the 1880s. Imperialism implied a concentration of capital in industry and banking, which resulted in monopoly capitalism. At the turn of the twentieth century, this monopoly capitalism was characterized by finance capital—that is, bank capital—which penetrated industry (Lenin 1967: 1: 673–777). Since the end of the Second World War, monopoly capitalism has also been identified by a high degree of corporate capital in the hands of multinational firms whose capital extends to the international level (Baran and Sweezy 1966). Ernest Mandel (1978) has proclaimed this to be a stage of "late capitalism."

In the United States, the economy is characterized by oligopoly. In virtually all major industries over 80 percent of production is carried out by three or four firms. The largest domestic corporations are also dominant in foreign investment and in the production of military equipment, an industry that is even more concentrated than domestic enterprise in general. Economic power is the source of political power as electoral campaigns require resources that are available only to people who have the support of a significant segment of the owners of corporate wealth. Since U.S. policy, particularly foreign policy, is determined by a corporate consensus that favors maintaining and expanding operations, imperialism must be viewed as a natural product of the U.S. political economic system.

What are the consequences of capitalism for Latin America? It is clear that North American corporations exercise considerable influence over the political economy of most nations in the area. The profit rates of U.S. operations in Latin America are far higher than those of domestic investment. Control of Latin American resources through ownership and lack of competition among the limited number of purchasers of Latin American products result in high profits on imports to the United States. North American exporters to Latin America enjoy monopoly power in many areas, which results in high prices. Moreover, the operations of North American businesses within other nations are growing at a much higher rate than those of domestic business.

Socialism strives for the replacement of a bourgeois society by a classless one in which the individual drive for wealth is replaced by solidarity on behalf of the collective society and social and economic equality for all. Under socialism, production for need replaces production for profit. Rather than producing goods for exchange on the market, production will be distributed to satisfy the needs of all members of society. Society will seek to eliminate all social and economic antagonisms and to establish a more harmonious world.

The achievement of a socialist society in Latin America and elsewhere would eliminate the private means of production. It is clear that such a change would be resisted vigorously by the power of U.S. corporations engaged in foreign activities, for socialism in Latin America would mean sharp constraints and lower profit rates on direct private foreign investment. Profits on trade would be reduced since the monopoly and monopsony power of the multinational corporations would be broken. Foreign control of Latin American resources and markets, a goal often as important as immediate profits to North American firms, would be out of the question, even if limited or indirect participation were permitted. The prospect of the nationalization of existing holdings and the loss of opportunities for future growth and super profits would cause the corporations to fight to maintain the status quo.

The break with capitalism is a difficult and seemingly impossible task. Nevertheless, the prospects for such change are not altogether bleak. Cuba has demonstrated that the achievement of socialism is possible in Latin America, Nicaragua is struggling in that direction. Yet Chile under Allende failed in its efforts to transform itself through electoral means and reforms along a "peaceful road" to socialism. Although the particular ways in which socialist governments have gained power are likely to be duplicated, it is highly probable that other Latin American nations may break out of the imperialist system in the near future.

One might speculate on the consequences that might arise if socialism were to spread throughout Latin America. Even though imperialism is at the heart of the monopoly capitalist system, it is useful to consider the implications of an end of empire, especially in Latin America, for the U.S. economy and people. Might not one consequence be economic recession and unemployment in the United States, resulting in dissatisfaction with the system's inability to deal with severe social and economic problems so that the defeat of corporate power would be part of a strategy to restructure U.S. society? Might not such conditions necessitate changes in U.S. relations with Latin America?

The impact of such a change would not be severe for a majority of the people in the United States. Although lower profits would directly affect owners of corporate stocks and bonds, it should be noted that over three-fourths of these holdings are owned by a group that composes only 1.6 percent of the population (Lundberg 1968: 13). This group is so wealthy that its ability to consume would be affected little, if at all, by a lower return on investment.

For the overwhelming majority of North Americans, the implications of socialism in Latin America are unclear. The major problem of the U.S. economy is a tendency toward stagnation—unemployment and unused plant capacity (Baran and Sweezy 1966: passim). Because of the lack of price competition, cost-cutting technological advances in the United States have resulted in higher prices in relation to costs for the large corporations because they have not been forced by competition to pass savings on to workers and consumers. These potential surplus profits are available for investment, but a demand that is sufficient to provide profitable investment opportunities to absorb the surplus is not generated spontaneously. Although government spending, motivational advertising, and waste serve to stimulate demand and to absorb some of the surplus, the economy is characterized by a persistent tendency toward stagnation.

Exports provide one possibility for absorbing production that U.S. workers cannot consume, and purchase of this excess abroad opens up opportunities for investment and jobs within the United States. The people who argue the importance of imperialism to the United States point to the purchase of U.S. products in the Third World as one way in which the U.S. economy benefits. Opponents of this perspective respond that exports are insignificant (less than 5 percent) in relation to the U.S. GNP. However, the appropriateness of this comparison is in dispute since the GNP includes government expenditures, personal and professional services, trade, and activities of banks, real estate firms, and stock brokers. In relation to the output of U.S. farms, factories, and mines, exports are far more significant.

Regardless of how significant exports are for the U.S. economy now, the future of exports to a socialist Latin America is an important question. Trade with Cuba was stopped by the U.S. government in an attempt to undermine the revolutionary government there, and for many years the Cuban government has expressed a desire for negotiations toward the restoration of bilateral trade. Similarly, in 1983 the United States unilaterally reduced the Nicaraguan sugar quota by 95 percent and closed Nicaragua's six trade consulates in the United States. The Nicaraguan government has expressed a desire to diversify trade more or less equally among the United States, other advanced capitalist countries, other Latin American countries, and the Soviet bloc.

The coming of socialism to Latin America need not preclude trade any more than has socialism elsewhere. The United States has engaged in trade and even provided military assistance to at least nominally socialist countries (e.g., Yugoslavia) for many years, and arrangements with the Soviet Union and China should destroy any lingering doubt about the possibility of U.S. trade with socialist nations. Although the loss of U.S. monopoly power would result in lower profits on exports, and though some industries such as shipping might not be able to operate at competitive rates and would be hurt, Latin America would still be in need of much that is produced in the United States.

Of course, we are not suggesting that the prevailing trade patterns would continue. Lower prices in Latin America for U.S. goods would be one benefit of the overthrow of imperialist penetration, and the resultant savings would be important in the Latin American development effort. As these efforts succeed, the eventual diversification of production would require a drastic change in trade patterns. The U.S. economy has been oriented to appropriating minerals and commercial crops from other nations and exporting food, finished goods, and agricultural commodities. As the nations of Latin America escaped from the need to sell their resources to acquire what they do not presently grow or manufacture, the U.S. economy would have to be shaped to match the new situation. However, development initially must occur in the context of the distorted economies created during the imperialist period, and in the course of development, needs for industrial equipment and other sophisticated products increase. Higher prices for Latin American exports would enable these nations to purchase more foreign products. The U.S. economy would benefit from this market to the extent that goods could be offered at prices that are competitive with those of other industrial nations.

It is easy to see the relationship of U.S. exports and employment levels in the United States, and the impact of eliminating restraints on competition for internal U.S. markets is equally clear. U.S. political and economic power has been used to prevent competition of foreign manufacturers with U.S. enterprise. Although most primary products can now be imported duty free into the United States if they are in a raw or an unprocessed state, a wide variety of tariffs and restrictions are in effect on the same products if they have been processed. Other ways of restricting competitive imports are also employed. For example, the U.S. government pressured Brazil (reportedly through threats to cut Brazil's aid allocation) to impose an export tax on Brazilian powdered coffee. Using cheap, broken coffee beans, Brazil had been able to take over about 14 percent of the U.S. instant-coffee market so political pressure was used to destroy the advantage of Brazilian producers (Magdoff 1969: 163).

The effect of a radical change in economic patterns on markets for U.S. goods both in Latin America and in the United States is of direct significance because demand is important for the U.S. economy. Sufficient surplus for investment is continuously generated. An additional potential for creating surplus exists, requiring only a growth in demand, which would make additional investment profitable. Predictions regarding the impact of a radical change on internal and Latin American markets for U.S. goods requires a weighing of the factors discussed above.

Two other areas require consideration, and both are still problematic. First, what would be the domestic effect in the United States of the loss of opportunities for direct private foreign investment? Such opportunities have been viewed as an escape valve for surplus capital, but even though initial investment usually creates a net capital outflow and absorbs excess capital, the growth of U.S. holdings abroad today is financed by profits earned on foreign operations and by capital raised locally in the host country and abroad from government loans and from foreign private banks. As we noted earlier, repatriated profits are far larger than new investments of U.S. capital going abroad, so foreign investment aggravates the problem of surplus capital in the United States. Though profit on foreign operations is equal to more than 25 percent of the profit on domestic enterprise, U.S. capital invested abroad is well under 10 percent of domestic investment. Additionally, the development efforts of socialist governments in Latin America would probably provide vast opportunities for long-term loans.

Second, the impact on the U.S. economy of a loss of its control of Latin American mineral resources must be considered. In the twentieth century the United States has become an importer of both rare and common minerals as the country does not have some minerals and supplies of others have been reduced or exhausted. At the same time requirements of the U.S. economy have increased. Consequently, U.S. imports of iron ore equal more than 40 percent of domestic production, imports of oil about a third. In regard to strategic materials such as chromium, nickel, niobium, and cobalt, reliance on imports is still greater. Most of these minerals are imported from the Third World, but not from Latin America. If confronted by socialist governments throughout the Third World, it is likely that the United States could continue to acquire these materials at least in the immediate period of Third World development, though at somewhat higher prices than currently are paid. Higher prices for imported minerals would also stimulate domestic production of low-grade ore reserves in the United States, which are not currently profitable because of the availability of cheap foreign high-grade ore. Longer-range considerations regarding resources are more problematic.

The impact of the rise of socialism and the end of imperialism in Latin America has a commanding importance for the foreign operations of North American corporate owners. We have observed that change would come only with the defeat of corporate, financial power, either through successful revolution in the nations of Latin America or through radical political change within the United States. In all probability, the process of being forced out of Latin America by revolutionary movements and governments would bring about a very significant political change. However assuming no dramatic change, a weighing of the considerations discussed above does not yield a clear projection of how the material standard of living for the non-stock-owning majority of North Americans would be affected by revolution in Latin America.

If the end of empire were brought about by or associated with the defeat of corporate power in the United States, a majority of the people in the United States would benefit. In terms of material standard of living, the poorest three-fifths of the U.S. population, which now receives approximately one-third of the total personal income, would benefit from income redistribution to a greater extent than they would lose from any negative consequences to the economy. Moreover, change in the United States would open possibilities for marked improvement in the quality of life. In this regard, instead of suppressing change in Latin America, people in the United States could benefit greatly from observing and learning about Latin American political and economic experiments.

In recent decades revolutionary ferment in Latin America has given rise to extraordinary artistic and literary achievements of great international importance. The Latin American novel has attained stature in world literature, and parallel contributions have been made in film. The Nueva Cancion, or New Song movement, has successfully integrated aspects of the indigenous roots of Indo-America with the contemporary themes of protest and the struggle to build the future. Clearly, current superiority in technology and wealth should not prevent the United States from being open to the values and achievements of Latin American societies.

Although the United States is more able to provide material goods for mass consumption, a life-style that is less dominated by the striving for commodities could well provide greater satisfaction and more mean-ingful lives for the country's citizens. Moreover, there are indications that natural resources such as minerals are not sufficiently abundant in the earth's crust for even half of the world's population to match the U.S. consumption level.

The prospect of unlimited economic growth for the United States is also seriously in question. It would appear that as demand for a finite quantity of resources reaches the limits of supply, consumption in the United States will be at the expense of Third World development more directly than ever before, and increasing military force will be required to ensure the extraction of resources. Even if current U.S. consumption patterns continue, and assuming that the Third World is prevented from industrializing, the viability of consumerism as a way of life is in doubt. During the 1970s, the United States, Europe, the USSR, Japan, and South Africa used over 90 percent of the world's copper production. U.S. industries alone consumed half the world production of aluminum, a quarter of the smelted copper, about 40 percent of the lead, and a third of the nickel, zinc, and chromium. Even with control of Third World reserves and with technological innovations and some greater effort at recycling, inadequate resources or environmental pollution caused by expanded industrial production may well place limits on U.S. economic growth.

It was noted that in Cuba, an effort is being made to eliminate the role of consumption as a central motivating force in favor of other values. Although this goal will not be achieved in the near future for the population as a whole, it represents one alternative to the sense of meaninglessness that is common in the United States and to the danger of an environmental crisis caused by pollution or resource depletion. Cubans can pursue this course because the government has its political base in the masses of workers and peasants; the situation in the United States is far different. As a rich country, it does not need to make the demands on its population that the Cuban development effort requires. However, under the control of a ruling class based on the economic power of ownership, with a population that is dominated by the consumerist ethos, and with an economic system that demands mass consumption, most people in the United States are not at present in a position to use the lessons the Cuban experience may offer. Nonetheless, Latin America will probably develop a variety of alternatives to the present U.S. structures and institutions. The very existence of these alternatives will be a challenge and a force for change.

In general, people in the United States sympathize with one alternative, the revolution in Nicaragua, a course they also followed initially in the case of Cuba. The Nicaraguan insurrectionary struggle began in 1927 with the battle of Augusto César Sandino against U.S. Marines and ended with the victory of the Sandinistas over the Somoza dynasty, which had ruled for almost half a century. The struggle was popular, nationalist, and against imperialism. In the phase of reconstruction that followed in the wake of victory, the Sandinistas began to consolidate their coalition of forces in the direction of socialism. But in 1985 Nicaragua was not socialist. Its plans included the revitalization of capitalism through both state and private ownership and production. The objective was a planned economy combined with the hard work, discipline, and sacrifice of the people.

For U.S. policymakers, however, the direction was all too clear, and faced with the possibility of insurrection throughout Central America, the Reagan administration moved quickly in early 1981 to end aid to Nicaragua. The challenge to the U.S. empire and hegemony over Latin America had to be resisted at all cost, even if that meant toppling a military-dominated regime. Support for Guatemala's right-wing military dictatorship was also part of the U.S. design. The grand strategy was to build an alliance with Mexico and Venezuela in order to preserve stability and prevent socialism from penetrating further in the Caribbean and Central America. In South America, military regimes in Argentina, Brazil, and Chile had consolidated their power over long periods of time, and despite the appearance of a democratic opening and elections, there appeared to be no immediate threat to U.S. interests there.

The foreign policy of the Reagan administration represented a slight departure from the objectives of trilateralism that had influenced the presidency of Jimmy Carter. The Trilateral Commission was founded in 1973 by David Rockefeller, chairman of Chase Manhattan Bank. At that time some 300 people from international business, banking, government, academia, media, and labor were brought together to forge a partnership of the ruling class interests in North America, Western Europe, and Japan and to preserve capitalism in a world of disorder. The significance of trilateralism was apparent after the election of Carter in 1976 when he appointed twenty-five trilateralists, including Zbigniew Brzezinski (founding director of the commission) and others to fill high positions in his administration. Toward the end of his term of office, Carter seemed intent on leading the West on a military crusade in the Caribbean and Central America, and the Reagan administration, which included such trilateralists as Vice-President George Bush and Defense Secretary Caspar Weinberger, followed in this path. Under Carter, trilateralists had pushed for and overcome right-wing opposition to the Panama Canal treaties, the Zimbabwe settlement, and aid to Nicaragua. Under Reagan, trilateralists had to accommodate to a more aggressive, anti-Communist stance.

It is evident that these policy differences represented "contradictions within the ruling class, contradictions internal to the capitalist system, and, most important, contradictions between trilateral goals and people's needs and aspirations" (Sklar 1980: 556). Whatever the contradictions, it is clear that trilateralism continues as a major influence in world affairs. Its objective is to coordinate and control resources, technologies, and markets in order to ensure the survival and prosperity of capitalism and to promote the accumulation of capital on an international scale.

Thus, the prospects for socialism in Latin America are dependent on several considerations. First, there are the differences and struggles within the ruling classes. Second, any change in the new international strategy of trilateralism must be assessed. Finally, in the face of these forces, the success of socialism will ultimately depend on revolutionary developments and the degree to which exploited and repressed peoples are willing and able to take power in their own hands, correct injustices, provide for basic needs, and ensure the material progress and commitment of all people.

Notes

1. Although these figures provide a reasonably accurate presentation of differences in the condition of the "average" Latin American and the "average" North American, a few points of clarification are necessary. The situation in Latin America is probably worse than the figures indicate as data collection of health and welfare statistics for many areas is poor. Moreover, in most cases we have had to use sources such as the *Statistical Abstract of Latin America* (Wilkie and Haber 1983) that rely on the governments themselves for information, and there is an ever-present tendency for governments to portray things as better than they are.

Also, averages are highly misleading. Inequality in both the United States and Latin America is great, but it is particularly extreme in Latin America. For example, a 1977 study by the Economic Commission for Latin America (Wilkie and Haber 1983: 187) indicates that the poorer 70 percent of the populations in Latin America received only 27.8 percent of national income while the richest 10 percent received 44.2 percent. The poorest 20 percent had a per capita income of only $55 (all figures cited are in 1960 dollars) while the richest 10 percent had a per capita income more than thirty-five times that figure. The average annual per capita income of the bottom 70 percent was only $167. For these more than 250 million people, conditions were far worse than for the upper 10 percent who had full access to food, housing, medical care, and schooling. Average figures for each country also hide large differences in the conditions of urban and rural Latin America.

In addition to the gross differences within each country, which are obscured by the aggregate figures, we should not forget the very great differences among countries. For example, the average per capita income in Haiti is about one-tenth that in Venezuela. Differences in quality of life indices are comparable. We are very uneasy when we refer to "Latin America" as a whole in this book, and we do so only because the qualifications necessary to account for the differences among countries would continually interrupt the train of thought being followed.

2. Baran identified at least three types of economic surplus: actual surplus ("the difference between society's actual current output and its actual current consumption"); potential surplus ("the difference between the output that *could* be produced . . . and what might be regarded as essential consumption"); and planned surplus ("the difference between society's 'optimum' output . . . and some chosen 'optional' volume of consumption")—see Baran (1957: 22–42).

3. English (Kahn and Llobera 1981) and French (Meillassoux 1980) economic anthropologists have popularized the mode of production approach, but the empirical work on Latin America has only recently become available in English— see Bartra (1975), Rodriguez (1980), Rojas (1980), Sindico (1980), and Montoya (1982).

4. According to de Janvry's analysis (1981), the importance of the external market in Latin America undermines the significance of wages, which are important only as a cost of production. The cost must be minimized to the greatest possible extent to maximize profits and to keep exports competitive. The agricultural wage is important as a cost in the production of crops for export. It is also important as a cost in the production of food crops, and therefore it is a factor in determining manufacturing wages. Thus, there is intense pressure to keep the agricultural wage at a minimum. There are no sources of motivation to counter this pressure because of the lack of importance of internal demand to the health of the economy. Moreover, rural conditions generally accord virtually total power to the owners of the large farms and plantations. The result is an agricultural wage that cannot meet the costs of subsistence and reproduction of the laborer. Agricultural workers sustain themselves and their families with the food they grow on the small plots they rent or sometimes own. Although these plots may seem feudal in nature, they serve to subsidize the modern commercial sector.

5. In the twentieth century Latin America has experienced considerable industrial growth. However, because of the dominance of foreign involvement in this industrialization, the creation of a truly *national* manufacturing bourgeoisie has been difficult, although strong bourgeoisies such as in Brazil have emerged in conjunction with foreign interests and capital and through state incentives, credits, and advantages.

6. Brazil, with its substantial resources and manufacturing base, is a notable exception. In 1984 exports exceeded imports by about $13 billion, and the country was largely self-sufficient in foodstuffs, minerals, and energy, although the high cost of importing petroleum after 1973 brought recession and problems.

7. The student may wish to unravel the complexities of these observations through further reading. Goodman and Redclift (1983), for example, offer case studies on Brazil and Mexico as they analyze the agrarian transition to capitalism that occurred in Latin America during the past generation. In discussing Latin America, John Taylor (1979) shows the irrelevancy of most theories, beginning with modernization, to an analysis of emerging capitalism, and he concludes that emphasis on a modes of production approach is especially useful. Harry Bernstein (1979) offers a provocative critique of theories of development and underdevelopment, and Anthony Brewer (1980) provides the best critical overview of the major theories and thinkers.

8. A summary of U.S. intervention abroad was presented on September 17, 1962, by Secretary of State Dean Rusk to a joint meeting of the Committees on Foreign Relations and Armed Services of the U.S. Senate (1962). Nearly 200 interventions were listed to show that there was precedent for the use of such

force without congressional authority; Rusk was defending U.S. involvement in the abortive Bay of Pigs invasion by Cuban exiles during April 1961.

9. The *Washington Report on the Hemisphere* provides a succinct summary: "In April 1981, U.S. bilateral assistance was cut off, including PL480 credits for purchase of wheat and edible oils. Export-Import Bank credits were also suspended. In April 1982, the Standard Fruit Company unilaterally cancelled its exclusive contract to market Nicaraguan bananas abroad. In October 1983, the EXXON tanker fleet, which was contracted to transport Mexican crude to Nicaragua, halted its shipping on the grounds that the risk from contra attacks was too great. Also in 1983, the U.S. government unilaterally reduced Nicaragua's sugar import quota for the U.S. market from 58,000 tons to 6,000. This meant that 52,000 tons which had been sold at the preferential price of 17 cents a pound had to be put on a saturated world market at prices around six cents a pound, an aggregate loss of $15 million annually in foreign exchange" (1985: 5).

Technical assistance in running the election came from two members of the Swedish Electoral College and from France. Financial aid, principally for paper and electronic calculators, was provided by France, Norway ($800,000), Sweden ($400,000), and Finland ($450,000). None of the donors complained that its aid was misused.

Ortega received 67 percent of the valid votes (of which 7 percent were improperly marked), the three parties to the left of the Sandinistas received 3.8 percent, and the three to the right received 29.2 percent.

The LASA observer team reported that "a close inspection of the platforms of the seven parties listed on the November 4 ballot reveals that the Nicaraguan voter had a wide range of options on major issues—considerably wider, for example, than in recent elections in El Salvador and Guatemala. With regard to foreign policy, the FSLN government was flanked by one party attacking it for aligning Nicaragua too closely with Soviet foreign policy (the Popular Social Christian Party), and another party attacking it for not bringing the country closer to the Soviet camp (the Communist Party of Nicaragua). On economic strategy, the Democratic Conservative Party called for greater latitude for the private sector, while the Marxist-Leninist Popular Action Movement advocated complete nationalization of private enterprise. People concerned about the military draft could also choose several alternative policies to the right of the FSLN, including that of the Democratic Conservative Party, which wants to abolish conscription altogether" (LASA 1984: 21).

10. Contrary to popular conceptions, only in bourgeois ideology is there a single view regarding the role of the private sector (in capitalism, a compulsion to leave all enterprise in private hands if there is any possibility that it can be profitable). There is a preference in Marxian thought for collective rather than individual ownership, but only when the conditions are adequate for effective collective administration and control. As we indicate in discussing the debate about economics centralization in Cuba, this is a controversial subject. The more orthodox Marxian position tends to hold that when productive forces are at a low level of development, public ownership is generally premature and private ownership still has a positive role to play.

11. The election rules were created through a three-year negotiation process involving all thirty-three major political groupings in the country, including both the political parties that participated in the elections and those that boycotted them, all trade union federations, all church groups, and the organizations

representing private enterprise. The electoral process was supervised by a five-member independent commission headed by a U.S.-trained political scientist who was twice elected to the presidency of the National University of Nicaragua. According to the LASA report, "the Supreme Electoral Council functioned in a professional and impartial manner, both before and during the electoral campaign" (LASA 1984: 13).

There was no censorship of the thirty-nine private radio stations, and press censorship was incomplete. Each party had free, uncensored, uninterrupted time during prime time on both of the country's two television channels and on all state-run radio stations. As for misuse of its control of government, the report concluded a lengthy analysis of the question, "in this campaign the FSLN did little more to take advantage of its incumbency than incumbent parties everywhere (including the United States) routinely do, and considerably less than ruling parties in other Latin American countries traditionally have done" (LASA 1984: 23).

Glossary

Throughout this book we have attempted to explain and clarify the meaning of terms as they evolved in the conceptualization and theory of our discussion. However, we generally do not redefine and explain terms after they first appear in the text. Thus, the list of terms below may help the reader.

Accumulation. The process whereby the capitalist sells his commodities and converts the money from the sale into capital.

Agrarian bourgeoisie. Modern landowners who run farms with machinery, pay salaries to workers, and make profits.

Agrocommercial bourgeoisie. Merchants whose activities relate to the purchase and sale of agricultural products. Often their activities overlap with those of the agrarian bourgeoisie.

Associated dependent capitalism. Situation in the periphery in which the domestic bourgeoisie ties itself to capitalism, associates with international capital, and stimulates capitalist accumulation. Accumulation and expansion of local capital thus depend on the dynamic of international capitalism (cf. *Dependency*).

Backwardness. Characterization used by Baran and others to describe conditions of exploitation and underdevelopment in some countries.

Bourgeois democratic revolution. The stage of parliamentary democracy or social democracy in which proletarian forces support bourgeois rule and reformist action en route to socialism.

Bourgeoisie. The capitalist class, the class of owners of the means of production, and the employers of wage labor under capitalism.

Capitalism. Characterized by the formation of a bourgeois class that owns and controls the means of production and a class of producers that owns only its labor and must sell its labor power to the owners of the means of production in order to survive.

Circulation of capital. Capital, for example, commodity capital within the sphere of circulation, that is on the market. Usually refers to trade, market, and circulation of capital.

Class. An aggregate of people who share a similar position in relation to the means of production. Alternatively, a group or groups characterized by similar socioeconomic criteria such as income and status. Marx believed that under capitalism, society would eventually polarize into two classes, the bourgeoisie and the proletariat. Max Weber described class in a market situation and emphasized status groups within a class. These writers and others refer to many classes. A ruling class, for example, is an economic class that rules politically; it tends to be a class of varied interests that become cohesive. Other classes may include the monopolistic, agrarian, mining, industrial, and commercial bourgeoisies; the petty bourgeoisie; the new middle class or new petty bourgeoisie; proletariat; peasants; and lumpen proletariat.

Colonial dependency. Situation in which the land, mines, and labor of a colony are tied to the mother country through trade monopolies.

Commercial capitalism. An incipient form of capitalism, involving commercial activities and trade with the capitalist-oriented market (cf. *Merchant capital*).

Communism. A type of society characterized by the elimination of a commodity and money economy; the disappearance of inequality, classes, and the state; the overcoming of alienation in work; and the creative use of work and leisure.

Competitive capitalism. Capitalism with "free" competition, usually under small-scale enterprise, in contrast to the tendency to concentrate capital through cartels, trusts, and holding companies under monopoly capitalism.

Dependency. Situation in which accumulation and expansion of capital are undynamic, the result being dependency on the dominant countries that can expand and be self-sustaining (cf. *Associated dependent capitalism, Colonial dependency, Financial-industrial dependency, New dependency*).

Dependentistas. Those who advocate a dependency theory, framework, or relationship (cf. *Dependency*).

Development of underdevelopment. The thesis of André Gunder Frank and others that capitalism generates economic growth in the metropolitan center through the appropriation of the economic surplus of the satellites, thereby contributing to stagnancy and underdevelopment in the periphery.

Diffusionist development. The view that political and economic democracy, nationalist development, and modernization will result from the diffusion of capital and technology from advanced to backward nations.

Dual society. A society considered to have two separate economies, one feudalistic in the countryside and the other capitalistic in the cities.

Economic surplus. As defined by Baran, the difference between a society's output and its consumption.

Enclave economy. An economy in which foreign capital has penetrated into the local productive processes in the form of wages and taxes to ensure exports of raw materials or goods.

Feudalism. Pertaining to the feudal system of lords and serfs, prominent during medieval times and evident in precapitalist social formations in later periods (cf. *Precapitalist social formations*).

Finance capital. Bank capital that penetrates and dominates industry.

Financial-industrial dependency. A situation in which big bank and industrial capital dominated and expanded outside the hegemonic centers during the period from the end of the nineteenth century to the Second World War.

Forces of production. Productive capacity, including plants and machinery, technology, and labor skills (cf. *Means of production, Mode of production*).

Imperialism. As defined by Lenin, monopoly capitalism, the highest stage of capitalism, usually associated with the appearance of cartels, trusts, and holding companies and the growth of industrial monopolies; alternatively, the military and political expansion of aggressive nations beyond their borders (cf. *Monopoly capitalism*).

Import substitution. Protection of domestic industry through the implementation of tariffs and the encouraging of local industry to meet demands for consumer goods.

Industrial capitalism. Associated with the rapid development of manufacturing during the late nineteenth century and indicative of an advanced stage of capitalism.

Infrastructure. The economic structures in which the relations of production and material foundations are found and upon which, according to Marx, the legal and political superstructures arise; as used by the ECLA economists, the roads, power, and other resources that permit industrialization.

Internal colonialism. A relationship similar to the colonial relationship between nations but involving dominant and marginal groups within a single society (for example, according to González Casanova, the monopoly of the ruling metropolis in Mexico over the marginal Indian communities).

Labor power. Capacity of work, including skills, owned by the class of producers who, under capitalism, must sell it to the owners of the means of production in order to survive.

Lumpen. Lumpen proletariat of unemployed idle persons, etc.

Manufacturing bourgeoisie. Capitalist owners of manufacturing enterprise (cf. *Bourgeoisie*).

Means of production. The tools, land, buildings, machinery, and raw materials with which workers produce goods for themselves and the society (see *Mode of production, Forces of production*).

Merchant capital. An elementary form of capital associated with the introduction of money and the appearance of the merchant in international commerce.

Metropolis. Capitalist centers that dominate over peripheral areas and countries known as satellites. More generally refers to the chief or capital city of a country.

Mode of production. The mix of productive forces and relations of production in a society at a given time in history. Modes may include primitive communism, feudalism, capitalism, and communism (cf. *Forces of production, Means of production*).

Monoculture. National economies that produce and export a single commodity or rely on the extraction and export of some raw material.

Monopoly capitalism. A form of capitalism characterized by the rise of cartels, trusts, and holding companies and the growth of industrial monopolies.

Monopsony. A condition of a market characterized by dominance of a simple buyer.

Multinationals. Large firms, sometimes monopolies, that control production and market of their activities in various countries and parts of the world—similar to transnational firm (cf. *Transnationals*).

National bourgeoisie. The domestic class of "progressive" capitalists within a nation whose interests presumably are not tied to international capital but are associated with the development of national resources and industrialization.

New dependency. Dependency characterized by capital investment of multinational corporations in industries oriented to the internal market of underdeveloped countries in the period after the Second World War (cf. *Dependency*).

Peripheral capitalism. As defined by Prebisch and others, an imitative capitalism in the backward countries in which capitalism is unable to reproduce itself and capital accumulation is incompatible with the consumer society (cf. *Capitalism*).

Periphery. Nations, usually associated with the Third World or less developed areas in Asia, Africa, and Latin America, that are considered to be dependent on the dominant center of advanced capitalist nations.

Petty bourgeoisie. A class between the bourgeoisie and the proletariat. Small capitalists who directly or indirectly control their means of production but, unlike large capitalists, do not usually possess much capital.

Petty-commodity production. The production by professional artisans of commodities that they exchange freely for products they need.

Precapitalist social formations. A stage of development where the forces and relations of production are not yet dominated by capitalism. Could involve simple commodity production, feudalism, and other forms. Usually evident where the accumulation of surplus is not the main goal of producers and where the producers are not separated from the means of production.

Primitive accumulation. The process whereby the possession of the means of production is taken from the workers or producers in the early stages of capitalism, thus breaking down the precapitalist social formation.

Proletariat. A class of workers who only own their labor and must sell this to the owners of the means of production in order to survive.

Relations of production. The division of labor that puts productive forces in motion (cf. *Means of production*).

Reproduction of capital. Process in which a capitalist society, in order to continue producing, must reproduce itself by replacing equipment, raw materials, and other essentials used in production. In production, workers consume the means of production or raw materials that go into their product; with their wages, they also consume in order to obtain food and shelter; and the capitalist consumes labor power or pays for the labor that is used in the production process.

Serf. A person bound to the soil and subject to the will of the owner (cf. *Feudalism*).

Service sector. Persons employed in the public sector involving unproductive labor that does not produce commodities.

Socialism. Collective and public rather than individual and private ownership of the means of production and appropriation of the surplus product (cf. *Transition to socialism*).

State. Originally evolved when the functions of people in primitive communal societies were assumed by separate groups of people such as armies, judges, and hereditary rulers. Hegel, Marx, and Engels saw the state as emerging from the civil society as a separate entity of apparatuses and activities. An instrumentalist approach to the study of the state emphasizes that the state is only an instrument manipulated by the ruling classes, whereas the structuralist approach stresses that the bourgeois ruling class is unable to dominate the state and the state unifies and organizes the interests of that class through structures or apparatuses such as the army, police, and judiciary.

Structuralism. The approach of political economists to analyzing the world in terms of centers and peripheries, metropoles and satellites; alternatively, in some Marxist writings, the repressive, political, and ideological apparatuses of the capitalist state.

Subimperialism. As defined by Marini, a situation in which the prospects for industrialization in a dependent capitalist economy are not great, and therefore the economy attempts to expand by pushing beyond its national borders and dominate the economies of weaker neighbors.

Superstructure. The legal, political, religious, philosophical, or ideological forms that, according to Marx, arise out of the infrastructure or economic base of society (cf. *Infrastructure*).

Surplus production. The production of workers beyond their requirements for subsistence.

Third World. As defined in this volume, a condition of exploitation and oppression, a lack of technology and development, underdevelopment brought about through colonialism and imperialism, and dependency on the dominant capitalist world system.

Transition to socialism. Period in which a workers' state replaces the capitalist state, the means of production come under collective rather than private ownership, and proletarian democracy replaces bourgeois democracy, though remnants of capitalism such as a money economy may persist.

Transnationals. Firms of various sizes that are able to internationalize their operations. In contrast to multinationals, which tend to be large enterprises, transnationals may also be small in size (cf. *Multinationals*).

Underconsumption. Traditionally, a condition in which domestic consumption is unable to absorb the products of industrialized nations, thus necessitating imperialism in the search for markets in the exploited colonies and outlying areas; more recently, an explanation for underdevelopment in backward countries in which a bourgeoisie's consumption is limited.

Bibliography

Aguilar, Alonso
1963   *Latin America and the Alliance for Progress.* Pamphlet Series, 24. New
            York: Monthly Review Press.
1965   *Pan Americanism from Monroe to the Present: A View from the Other
            Side.* New York: Monthly Review Press.

Allende, Salvador
1972   "Chile." Washington, D.C.: Embassy of Chile. Speech Before the
            United Nations General Assembly, December 4.

Americas Watch Committee
1984   *The Miskitos in Nicaragua 1981–1984.* New York and Washington,
            D.C.: Americas Watch Committee.

Amin, Samir
1974   *Accumulation on a World Scale: A Critique of the Theory of Under-
            development.* 2 vols. New York: Monthly Review Press.
1976   *Unequal Development: An Essay on the Social Formations of Peripheral
            Capitalism.* New York: Monthly Review Press.

Apter, David
1965   *The Politics of Modernization.* Chicago: University of Chicago Press.

Baer, Werner
1969   "The Economics of Prebisch and ECLA." In Charles T. Nisbet, ed.,
            Latin America: Problems in Economic Development, pp. 203–218. New
            York: Free Press.

Baran, Paul
1957   *The Political Economy of Growth.* New York: Monthly Review Press.

Baran, Paul A., and Paul M. Sweezy
1966   *Monopoly Capital: An Essay on the American Economic and Social
            Order.* New York: Monthly Review Press.

Bartra, Roger
1974   *Estructura agraria y clases sociales en México.* Mexico City: Era.
1975   "Peasants and Political Power in Mexico: A Theoretical Approach."
          Latin American Perspectives 2 (Summer): 125-145.

Bell, Daniel
1960   *The End of Ideology.* Glencoe, Ill.: Free Press.

Bemis, Samuel Flagg
1943   *The Latin American Policy of the United States.* New York: W. W.
          Norton.

Bernstein, Harry
1979   "Sociology of Underdevelopment vs. Sociology of Development?"
          In David Lehman, ed., *Development Theory: Four Critical Essays*, pp.
          77-106. London: Frank Cass.

Bodenheimer, Susanne J.
1970   "The Ideology of Developmentalism: American Political Science's
          Paradigm-Surrogate for Latin American Studies." *Berkeley Journal of
          Sociology* 15: 95-137.

Bonachea, Rolando E., and Nelson P. Valdés, eds.
1972   *Revolutionary Struggle 1947-1958: Volume I of the Selected Works of
          Fidel Castro.* Cambridge, Mass.: M.I.T. Press.

Booth, John A.
1982   *The End and the Beginning: The Nicaraguan Revolution.* Boulder, Colo.:
          Westview Press. Rev. ed. 1985.
1983   "Toward Explaining Regional Crisis in Central America: The Socio-
          economic and Political Roots of Rebellion." *Mesoamerica* 2 (March),
          pp. 2-3.

Bottomore, T. B.
1964   *Elites and Society.* Baltimore: Penguin Books.

Bray, Donald W., and Timothy F. Harding
1974   "Cuba." In Ronald H. Chilcote and Joel C. Edelstein, eds., *Latin
          America: The Struggle with Dependency and Beyond*, pp. 579-734.
          Cambridge, Mass.: Schenkman Publishing Company.

Bresser Pereira, Luiz Carlos
1984   *Development and Crisis in Brazil, 1930-1983.* Boulder, Colo.: Westview
          Press.

Brewer, Anthony
1980   *Marxist Theories of Imperialism.* London: Routledge and Kegan Paul.

Cantor, Norman F., ed.
1963   *The Medieval World: 300-1300.* New York: Macmillan Company.

Cardoso, Fernando Henrique
1972   "Dependency and Development in Latin America." *New Left Review*
          74 (July-August): 83-95.
1972-1973 "Industrialization, Dependency, and Power in Latin America." *Berke-
          ley Journal of Sociology* 18: 79-95.

1973   "Associated-Dependent Development: Theoretical and Practical Implications." In Alfred Stepan, ed., *Authoritarian Brazil: Origins, Policies, and Future*, pp. 142–176. New Haven: Yale University Press.
1977   "The Consumption of Dependency Theory in the United States." *Latin American Research Review* 12(3): 7–24.
1978   "Las desventuras de la dialéctica de la dependencia." *Revista Mexicana de Sociología* 40: 9–55.
1979   "Development Under Fire." Unpublished paper. Mexico City: Instituto Latino-americano de Estudios Transnacionales. May.

Cardoso, Fernando Henrique, and E. Falleto
1969   *Dependencia y desarrollo en América Latina*. Mexico City: Siglo XXI Editores.
1979   *Dependency and Development*. Berkeley: University of California Press.

Chaplin, David, ed.
1976   *Peruvian Nationalism: A Corporatist Revolution*. New Brunswick, N.J.: Transaction Books.

Chilcote, Ronald H.
1974   "A Critical Synthesis of the Dependency Literature." *Latin American Perspectives* 1 (Spring): 4–29.
1981   "Issues of Theory in Dependency and Marxism." *Latin American Perspectives* 8 (Summer-Fall): 3–16.
1984   *Theories of Development and Underdevelopment*. Boulder, Colo.: Westview Press.

Citizens' Board of Inquiry into Hunger and Malnutrition in the United States
1968   *Hunger, U.S.A.* Boston: Beacon Press.

Cockcroft, James D., André Gunder Frank, and Dale Johnson
1972   *Dependence and Underdevelopment: Latin America's Political Economy*. Garden City, N.Y.: Doubleday.

Colletti, Lucio
1977   "The Question of Stalin." In Gary L. Olson, ed., *The Other Europe*, pp. 226–248. Brunswick, Ohio: King's Court Communications.

Collier, David, ed.
1979   *The New Authoritarianism in Latin America*. Princeton: Princeton University Press.

Collier, Ruth Berins, and David Collier
1979   "Inducements Versus Constraints: Disaggregating 'Corporatism.'" *American Political Science Review* 73 (December): 967–986.

Collins, Joseph (with Frances Moore Lappe and Nick Adams)
1982   *What Difference Could a Revolution Make?* San Francisco: Institute for Food and Development Policy.

de Janvry, Alain
1981   *The Agrarian Question and Reformism in Latin America*. Baltimore and London: Johns Hopkins University Press.

Domhoff, G. William, and Hoyt B. Ballard, eds.
1968   *C. Wright Mills and the Power Elite*. Boston: Beacon Press.

Dos Santos, Theotonio
1968   *El nuevo caráter de la dependencia.* Cuadernos de Estudios Socio-económicos (10). Santiago: Centro de Estudios Socio-económicos (CESO), Universidad de Chile.
1970   "The Structure of Dependence." *American Economic Review* 60 (May): 231–236.

Dozer, Donald M., ed.
1965   *The Monroe Doctrine: Its Modern Significance.* New York: Alfred A. Knopf.

Edelstein, Joel C.
1981   "The Evolution of Cuban Development Strategy, 1959–1979." In Heraldo Muñoz, ed., *From Dependency to Development*, pp. 225–266. Boulder, Colo.: Westview Press.

EPICA Task Force
1980   *Nicaragua: A People's Revolution.* Washington, D.C.: EPICA Task Force.

Erickson, Kenneth P.
1977   *The Brazilian Corporative State and Working Class Politics.* Berkeley: University of California Press.

Esteva, Gustavo
1978   "Y si los campesinos existen?" *Comercio Exterior* (Mexico City) 28 (June): 699–732.

Evans, Peter
1979   *Dependent Development: The Alliance of Multinational, State, and Local Capital in Brazil.* Princeton: Princeton University Press.

Fagen, Richard R.
1977   "Studying Latin American Politics: Some Implications of a Dependencia Approach." *Latin American Research Review* 12(2): 3–27.

Feder, Ernest
1971   *The Rape of the Peasantry.* Garden City, N.Y.: Anchor Books.

Flores, Edmundo
1963   "Land Reform and the Alliance for Progress." Policy Memorandum 27. Princeton: Center for International Studies.

Foster-Carter, Aiden
1978   "The Modes of Production Controversy." *New Left Review* 107 (January-February): 47–77.

Frank, André Gunder
1966a   "The Development of Underdevelopment." *Monthly Review* 18 (September): 17–32.
1966b   "Functionalism, Dialectics, and Synthetics." *Science and Society* 30 (Spring): 136–148. Reprinted in his *Latin America: Underdevelopment or Revolution*, pp. 95–107.
1967a   *Capitalism and Underdevelopment in Latin America: Historical Studies of Chile and Brazil.* New York: Monthly Review Press.

1967b   "Sociology of Development and Underdevelopment of Sociology."
            Catalyst 3 (Summer): 20–73. Reprinted in his *Latin America: Under-*
            development or Revolution, pp. 21–94.
1969a   *Latin America: Underdevelopment or Revolution.* New York: Monthly
            Review Press.
1969b   "The Underdevelopment Policy of the United Nations in Latin
            America." *NACLA Newsletter* 3 (December): 1–9.

Furtado, Celso
1970   *Economic Development of Latin America: A Survey from Colonial Times*
            to the Cuban Revolution. London: Cambridge University Press.

Gil, Federico G.
1971   *Latin American–United States Relations.* New York: Harcourt Brace
            Jovanovich.

Giovanni, Cleto Di
1980   "U.S. Policy and the Marxist Treaty in Central America." In *Heritage*
            Foundation Backgrounder (October 15): 3–5. Cited in *NACLA Report*
            on the Americas 16 (January-February, 1982): 23, 45.

González Casanova, Pablo
1969   "Internal Colonialism and National Development." In Irving Louis
            Horowitz et al., eds., *Latin American Radicalism*, pp. 118–139. New
            York: Vintage Books.
1970a   *Democracy in Mexico.* New York: Oxford University Press.
1970b   *Sociología de la explotación.* Mexico City: Siglo XXI Editores.

Goodman, David, and Michael Redclift
1983   *From Peasant to Proletarian: Capitalist Development and Agrarian*
            Transition. New York: St. Martin's Press.

Graziano da Silva, José F. (with Barbara A. Kohl)
1984   "Capitalist 'Modernization' and Employment in Brazilian Agriculture,
            1960–1975: The Case of the State of São Paulo." *Latin American*
            Perspectives 11 (Winter): 117–136.

Gurley, John W.
1979   *Challengers to Capitalism.* 2d ed. New York: W. W. Norton.

Hamilton, Nora
1982   *The Limits of State Autonomy: Post-Revolutionary Mexico.* Princeton:
            Princeton University Press.

Hammergren, Linn A.
1977   "Corporatism in Latin American Politics: A Reexamination of the
            'Unique' Tradition." *Comparative Politics* 9 (July): 443–461.

Harnecker, Marta
1980   *Cuba: Dictatorship or Democracy?* Westport, Conn.: Lawrence Hill and
            Company.

Harrington, Michael
1976   *The Twilight of Capitalism.* New York: Simon & Schuster.

Harris, Richard L.
1978   "Marxism and the Agrarian Question in Latin America." *Latin American Perspectives* 5 (Fall): 2–28.
1985   "The Revolutionary Process in Nicaragua." *Latin American Perspectives* 12 (Spring): 3–21.

Hayter, Teresa
1971   *Aid as Imperialism.* Baltimore: Penguin Books.

Henfrey, Colin
1981   "Ideological, Theoretical, or Marxist Practice? Dependency, Modes of Production, and Class Analysis of Latin America." *Latin American Perspectives* 8 (Summer-Fall): 17–54.

Hibbert, A. B.
1953   "The Origins of the Medieval Town Patriciate." *Past and Present* 3 (February): 15–27.

Hilton, R. H.
1952   "Capitalism—What's in a Name?" *Past and Present* 1 (February): 32–43.

Hirschman, Albert O.
1961   *Latin American Issues: Essays and Comments,* pp. 3–42. New York: Twentieth Century Fund.

Hodges, Donald C.
1974   *The Latin American Revolution: Politics and Strategy from Apro-Marxism to Guevarism.* New York: William Morrow and Company.

Horowitz, Irving L., Josué de Castro, and John Gerassi, eds.
1969   *Latin American Radicalism: A Documentary Report on Left and Nationalist Movements.* New York: Vintage Books.

Howe, Gary Nigel
1981   "Dependency Theory, Imperialism, and the Production of Surplus Value on a World Scale." *Latin American Perspectives* 8 (Summer-Fall): 82–102.

Huberman, Leo, and Paul M. Sweezy
1969   *Socialism in Cuba.* New York: Monthly Review Press.

Huntington, Samuel P.
1965   "Political Development and Political Decay." *World Politics* 17 (April): 386–430.

Imaz, José Luis de
1970   *Los que mandan (Those Who Rule).* Albany: State University of New York Press.

Instituto Histórico Centro Americano
1982   "The Dilemmas Confronting the Sandinista Revolution Three Years After the Victory." *Envio* (Managua) 13 (July).

Johnson, Carlos
1981   "Dependency Theory and Processes of Capitalism and Socialism."
        Latin American Perspectives 8 (Summer-Fall): 55–81.

Johnson, John J.
1958   *Political Change in Latin America: The Emergence of the Middle Sectors.*
        Stanford: Stanford University Press.
1964   *The Military and Society in Latin America.* Stanford: Stanford University
        Press.

Johnson, John J., ed.
1962   *The Role of the Military in Underdeveloped Countries.* Princeton:
        Princeton University Press.

Kahn, Joel S., and Joseph R. Llobera, eds.
1981   *The Anthropology of Pre-capitalist Societies.* London: Macmillan Press.

Laclau, Ernesto
1971   "Feudalism and Capitalism in Latin America." *New Left Review* 67
        (May-June): 19–38.

Lambert, Jacques
1959   *Os dois Brasis.* Rio de Janeiro.
1967   *Latin America: Social Structures and Political Institutions.* Berkeley and
        Los Angeles: University of California Press.

Latin American Studies Association (LASA)
1984   *Report of the Latin American Studies Association Delegation to Observe
        the Nicaraguan General Election of November 4, 1984. LASA Forum*
        special edition (November).

Lenin, V. I.
1967   *Selected Works.* 3 vols. Moscow: Progress Books.

Le Riverend, Julio
1967   *Economic History of Cuba.* Havana: Book Institute.

Lewis, Gordon K.
1963   *Puerto Rico: Freedom and Power in the Caribbean.* New York: Monthly
        Review Press.

Lipset, Seymour Martin
1963   *Political Man.* Garden City, N.Y.: Doubleday.

Lundberg, Ferdinand
1968   *The Rich and the Super-Rich: A Study in the Power of Money Today.*
        New York: Bantam Books.

Magdoff, Harry
1969   *The Age of Imperialism: The Economics of U.S. Foreign Policy.* New
        York: Monthly Review Press.

Malefakis, Edward E.
1970   *Agrarian Reform and Peasant Revolution in Spain.* New Haven: Yale
        University Press.

Malloy, James M., ed.
1977   *Authoritarianism and Corporatism in Latin America*. Pittsburgh: University of Pittsburgh Press.

Mandel, Ernest
1968   *Marxist Economic Theory*. Vol. 1. New York: Monthly Review Press.
1977   *From Class Society to Communism: An Introduction to Marxism*. London: Ink Links.
1978   *Late Capitalism*. London: Verso.

Marcuse, Herbert
1968   *One-Dimensional Man: Studies in the Ideology of Advanced Industrial Society*. Boston: Beacon Press.

Marcussen, Henrik Secher, and Jens Erik Torp
1982   *Internationalization of Capital—Prospects for the Third World: A Re-Examination of Dependency Theory*. London: Zed Press.

Marini, Ruy Mauro
1974   *Dialéctica de la dependencia*. 2d ed. Mexico City: Serie Popular Era, Ediciones Era.
1978a   "Las razones del neodesarrollismo (respuesto a F. H. Cardoso y J. Serra)." *Revista Mexicana de Sociología* 40: 57–106.
1978b   "World Capitalist Accumulation and Sub-imperialism." *Two Thirds* 1 (Fall): 29–40.

Marx, Karl
1967   *Capital: A Critique of Political Economy*. 3 vols. New York: International Publishers.

Meillassoux, Claude
1980   "From Reproduction to Production: A Marxist Approach to Economic Anthropology." In Harold Wolpe, ed., *The Articulation of Modes of Production*, pp. 189–201. London: Routledge and Kegan Paul.

Miliband, Ralph
1969   *The State in Capitalist Society*. New York: Basic Books.

Mohri, Kenzo
1979   "Marx and 'Underdevelopment.'" *Monthly Review* 30 (April): 32–42.

Montoya, Rodrigo
1982   "Class Relations in the Andean Countryside." *Latin American Perspectives* 9 (Summer): 62–78.

Nichols, David
1972   "Ruling Class as a Scientific Concept." *Review of Radical Political Economics* 4 (Fall): 35–69.

NACLA (North American Congress on Latin America)
1971   *Yankee Dollar: The Contribution of U.S. Private Investment to Underdevelopment in Latin America*. Berkeley: NACLA.
1978   "Program of the United Popular Movement (MPU)." *NACLA: Report on the Americas* 12 (November-December): 36–37.

Novack, George
1970   "The Permanent Revolution in Latin America." *Intercontinental Press*
           8 (November 16): 978–983.

Núñez Soto, Orlando
1981   "The Third Social Force in National Liberation Movements." *Latin
           American Perspectives* 8 (Spring): 5–21.

O'Connor, James
1970   *The Origins of Socialism in Cuba*. Ithaca: Cornell University Press.

O'Donnell, Guillermo A.
1973   *Modernization and Bureaucratic Authoritarianism: Studies in South
           American Politics*. Berkeley: Institute of International Studies, Uni-
           versity of California.

Organski, A.E.K.
1965   *The Stages of Political Development*. New York: Alfred Knopf.

Palloix, Christian
1975   *L'Internalisation du capital*. Paris: Maspero.
1977   "The Self Expansion of Capital on a World Scale." *Review of Radical
           Political Economy* 9 (Summer): 1–28. Translation of Chapter 2 and
           Appendix 1 of his *L'Internalisation du capital*.

Petras, James, ed.
1965   "Ideology and United States Political Scientists." *Science and Society*
           29 (Spring): 192–216.
1973   *Latin America: From Dependence to Revolution*. New York: John Wiley
           and Sons.

Petras, James, and Maurice Zeitlin, eds.
1968   *Latin America: Reform or Revolution?* Greenwich, Conn.: Fawcett
           Publications.

Pike, Fredrick B.
1974   "Corporatism and Latin American–United States Relations." *Review
           of Politics* 36 (January): 132–170.

Poulantzas, Nicos
1976   *The Crisis of the Dictatorships: Portugal, Greece, Spain*. London: NLB.

Pratt, Julius W.
1959   *Expansionists of 1898: The Acquisition of Hawaii and the Spanish Islands*.
           Gloucester, Mass.: Peter Smith.

Prebisch, Raúl
1980   "The Dynamics of Peripheral Capitalism." In Louis Lefeber and Lisa
           L. North, eds., *Democracy and Development in Latin America*, pp. 21–
           27. Studies on the Political Economy, no. 1. Toronto: Society and
           Culture of Latin America and the Caribbean.

Quijano, Aníbal
1971   *Nationalism and Capitalism in Peru: A Study in Neo-imperialism*. New
           York: Monthly Review Press.

Rey, Pierre-Philippe
1973   *Les alliances de classes.* Paris: Maspero.

Ritter, Archibald H.M.
1974   *The Economic Development of Revolutionary Cuba.* New York: Praeger.

Rodney, Walter
1974   *How Europe Underdeveloped Africa.* Washington, D.C.: Howard University Press.

Rodriguez O., Gustavo
1980   "Original Accumulation, Capitalism, and Precapitalistic Agriculture in Bolivia." *Latin American Perspectives* 7 (Fall): 50–66.

Rojas, Antonio
1980   "Land and Labor in the Articulation of the Peasant Economy with the Hacienda." *Latin American Perspectives* 7 (Fall): 67–82.

Rostow, Walt W.
1962   *Stages of Economic Growth: A Non-Communist Manifesto.* London: Cambridge University Press.

Ruddle, Kenneth, and Mukhtar Hamour, eds.
1972   *Statistical Abstract of Latin America: 1970.* Los Angeles: University of California Latin American Center.

Ruiz, Ramón Eduardo
1968   *Cuba: The Making of a Revolution.* Amherst: University of Massachusetts Press.

Schmitter, Philippe C.
1972   "Paths to Political Development in Latin America." In Douglas A. Chalmers, ed., *Changing Latin America: New Interpretations of Its Politics and Society,* pp. 83–105. *Proceedings of the Academy of Political Science* 30(4). New York: Columbia University.
1974   "Still the Century of Corporatism?" *Review of Politics* 36 (January): 85–131.

Serra, José, and Fernando Henrique Cardoso
1978   "Las desventuras de la dialéctica de la dependencia," *Revista Mexicana de Sociología* 40: 9–95.

Sherman, Howard
1972   *Radical Political Economy: Capitalism and Socialism from a Marxist-Humanist Perspective.* New York: Basic Books.

Silverman, Bertram
1971   *Man and Socialism in Cuba: The Great Debate.* New York: Atheneum Publishers.
1973   "Economic Organization and Social Consciousness: Some Dilemmas of Cuban Socialism." In J. Ann Zammit, ed., *The Chilean Road to Socialism,* pp. 391–418. Sussex: Institute of Development Studies.

Sindico, Domenico E.
1980   "Modernization in Nineteenth-Century Sugar Haciendas: The Case of Morelos (from Formal to Real Subsumption of Labor to Capital)." *Latin American Perspectives* 7 (Fall): 83–99.

Singer, Daniel
1982   *The Road to Gdansk.* New York: Monthly Review Press.

Sklar, Holly, ed.
1980   *Trilateralism: The Trilateral Commission and Elite Planning for World Management.* Boston: South End Press.

Smith, Robert Freeman
1960   *The United States and Cuba: Business and Diplomacy, 1917–1960.* New York: Bookman Associates.

Stavenhagen, Rodolfo
1970   *Agrarian Problems and Peasant Movements in Latin America.* Garden City, N.Y.: Doubleday Anchor.
1975   *Social Classes in Agrarian Societies.* Garden City, N.Y.: Anchor Books.

Stein, Stanley J., and Barbara H. Stein
1970   *The Colonial Heritage of Latin America: Essays on Economic Dependence in Perspective.* New York: Oxford University Press.

Sunkel, Osvaldo
1972   "Big Business and 'Dependencia.'" *Foreign Affairs* 50 (April): 517–531.

Sweezy, Paul M.
1942   *The Theory of Capitalist Development: Principles of Marxian Political Economy.* New York: Monthly Review Press.
1980   *Post-Revolutionary Society.* New York: Monthly Review Press.

Sweezy, Paul M., and Charles Bettelheim
1971   *On the Transition to Socialism.* New York: Monthly Review Press.

Taylor, John G.
1979   *From Modernization to Modes of Production: A Critique of the Sociologies of Development and Underdevelopment.* New York: Macmillan.

Thomas, Clive
1974   *Dependence and Transformation.* New York: Monthly Review Press.

Ubell, Robert
1983   "Cuba's Great Leap." *Nature* 302 (April 28): 745–748.

United Nations. Economic Commission for Latin America
1970   *Economic Survey of Latin America: 1969.* New York: United Nations.

United States Senate. Committee on Foreign Relations and Committee on Armed Services
1962   *Hearing, Situation in Cuba,* 87th Cong., 2d sess., September 17, pp. 82–87. Reprinted in *Studies on the Left* 3:2 (1963): 54–59.

Vaupel, J. W., and Jean P. Curham
1969   "The Making of Multinational Enterprise." Cambridge, Mass.: Harvard University Division of Research.

Veliz, Claudio, ed.
1965   *Obstacles to Change in Latin America.* London: Oxford University Press.

Vicens Vives, Jaime
1976   *An Economic History of Spain.* Princeton: Princeton University Press.

Wallerstein, Immanuel
1974   *The Modern World System.* New York: Academic Press.
1979   "Underdevelopment and Phase-B: Effect of the Seventeenth Century Stagnation on Core and Periphery of the European World-Economy." In Walter L. Goldfrank, ed., *The World-System of Capitalism: Past and Present*, pp. 73–84. Political Economy of the World-System Annuals, 2. Beverly Hills, Calif.: Sage Publications.
1980   "The Future of the World-Economy." In Terence K. Hopkins and I. Wallerstein, eds., *Processes of the World-System*, pp. 167–180. Political Economy of the World-System Annuals, 3. Beverly Hills, Calif.: Sage Publications.

Warren, Bill
1973   "Imperialism and Capitalist Industrialization." *New Left Review* 81 (September-October): 3–44.

Warren, Bill, ed.
1980   *Imperialism: Pioneer of Capitalism.* London: Verso.

Washington Report on the Hemisphere
1985   "Nicaragua: Economic Future Grim." 5:12 (March 19).

Wiarda, Howard J.
1973   "Toward a Framework for the Study of Political Change in the Iberic-Latin Tradition: The Corporative Model." *World Politics* 25 (January): 206–235.
1977   *Corporatism and Development: The Portuguese Experience.* Amherst: University of Massachusetts Press.
1978   "Corporatism Rediscovered: Right, Center and Left Variants in the New Literature." *Polity* 10 (Spring): 416–428.

Wilkie, James W., and Stephen Haber, eds.
1983   *Statistical Abstract of Latin America.* Vol. 22. Los Angeles: UCLA Latin American Center, University of California.

Zeitlin, Maurice
1984   *The Civil Wars in Chile.* Princeton: Princeton University Press.

Index

Acción Democrática (Venezuela), 91
Advertising, 20, 51
AFL-CIO. *See* American Federation of
    Labor-Congress of Industrial
    Organizations
Africa, 82
Agency for International Development
    (AID), 54, 73
Agrarian reform, 42, 95, 104, 105, 112
Agrarian Reform Law (Cuba), 105, 109
Agrarian Reform Law (1979) (Nicaragua),
    112, 113
Agrarian revolution, 87
Agriculture, 7, 39, 63, 119
    commercial, 12, 24
    employment in, 19
    markets, 14, 20, 21, 24–25, 26, 29
    modernization of, 8, 12, 131
    monoculture, 8, 32. *See also*
        Monocultural economies
    plantation, 30–31, 32, 50
    production, 12, 95
    surplus, 13, 124, 128
    technology, 12, 13
    See also Exports, agricultural; Peasantry;
        Rural society; *under* Cuba; Mexico;
        Nicaragua
Aguilar, Alonso, 68
Aguirre Cerda, Pedro, 89
AID. *See* Agency for International
    Development
Aircraft, 32
Allende, Salvador, 45, 53, 54, 60, 89, 90,
    94, 98, 135
Alliance for Progress (1961), 73, 74
Allianza Popular Revolucionaria Americana
    (APRA) (Peru), 91
Altamire, José, 90
Aluminum, 139
American Federation of Labor-Congress of
    Industrial Organizations (AFL-CIO), 52
Amin, Samir, 82

Andalusia, 28, 29
Apprentices, 13
APRA. *See* Allianza Popular Revolucionaria
    Americana
APRA Rebelde (Peru), 91
Apro-Marxism. *See* Democratic socialism
Apter, David, 8
Arbenz, Jacobo, 72, 105
Argentina
    development, 60
    elite, 58–61
    government, 44, 58–61, 78, 93, 140
    guerrilla movement, 92
    income, 8
    industrialization, 42, 43, 59, 77
    infrastructure, 77
    literacy, 8
    loan repayment, 51
    middle class, 8, 60–61
    and OAS, 72
    political parties, 90
    Trotskyism, 88, 90–91
    See also under United States
Aristotle, 79
Armed Forces of National Liberation
    (FALN) (Venezuela), 92
Artisans, 13, 14, 25
Asia, 82
Associated capitalist development, 84
Austerity policies, 19, 120, 128, 130
Authoritarianism, 30, 77–78, 80, 130, 132
Auto-financiamiento, 125
Automobiles, 32

Banco Nicaragüense, 102
Banking, 20, 50
Bank of America, 102
Baran, Paul A., 3, 4, 66, 82
Bartra, Roger, 49, 50
Basic needs, 22, 95, 120, 131, 141
Basque Country (Spain), 29
Batista, Fulgencio, 68, 70, 78, 91, 99, 100

reinvestment, 51
remittances, 4
repatriated, 21, 51, 52, 60, 89
Progressive church movements, 91
Proletarian Tendency (TP) (Nicaragua), 102
Proletariat. *See* Peasantry; Working class
Prolonged Popular War (GPP) (Nicaragua),
  102
Protective tariffs, 87
PSP. *See* Communist Popular Socialist
  party
Public safety, 52
Puerto Rico, 69
Puiggrós, Rodolfo, 38

Quadragesimo Anno (Pius XI), 79
Quijano, Aníbal, 55, 56, 62, 63, 64

Racial superiority, 67
Radical party (Argentina), 59
Radical party (Chile), 89
Radical Union party (Cuba), 99
Railroads, 70, 77
Ramos, Jorge Abelardo, 90, 91
Ranches, 39
Rand Corporation, 74
Rationing, 113, 128
Reagan, Ronald, 68, 75, 140
Reformist strategy, 6, 21, 41, 43, 44, 77,
  78, 81, 93, 94
Relief aid, 102
Repression, 4, 66, 75, 79, 80, 94, 101
Rerum Novarum (Leo XIII), 79
Resources
  access to, 3, 77, 83
  allocation, 120, 123, 125
  utilization, 56, 95, 107
Retailing, 20, 50
Revolutionary Democratic Party (PRD)
  (Dominican Republic), 89
Revolutionary movements, 87, 88, 90, 91–
  92
Revolutionary strategy, 6, 21, 42, 49, 53,
  77, 78, 81–82, 83, 87, 89–90, 91, 93,
  98, 141
Rio Treaty (1947), 71
Ritter, Archibald H. M., 110
Rivera, Brooklyn, 112
Rockefeller, David, 140
Rodney, Walter, 82
Rojas Pinilla, Gustavo, 78
Roman law, 79
Roosevelt, Franklin D., 70, 71
Roosevelt, Theodore, 67, 68, 70
Rostow, Walt R., 65
Royalties, 4, 21, 52
Rubber, 33
Ruling class, 6, 26, 30–31, 32, 35, 44, 45–
  48, 50, 55, 57, 58, 59–61, 63, 140, 141
  defined, 47
Rural society, 99
  and development, 16–17
  and feudalism, 7, 12, 37(table)
  income, 101, 102

landless, 49, 50, 101
  and prices, 110
  power, 12
  traditionalism, 23, 25
  See also Dual society; *Latifundista*;
    Metropolis-periphery relations;
    Peasantry; Poverty
Rural-urban migration, 50
Rusk, Dean, 73

Saint Thomas Aquinas, 79
Sandinista Front for National Liberation
  (FSLN) (1961) (Nicaragua), 101, 102
Sandino, Augusto César, 100, 139
Santander (Spain), 29
Santo Domingo (Dominican Republic), 68
Savings, 17
Schmitter, Philippe C., 79, 80
Sears, Roebuck & Company, 75
Second International, 89
Secret ballot, 129
Self-determination, 87
Semiperipheral countries, 4
Serfs, 9, 10, 11–12, 13, 23, 24–25
Service sector, 10
Seventh International Conference of
  American States (1933), 70
Seville (Spain), 29
Sharecroppers, 49
Shipping charges, 52
Siècle du corporatisme, Le (Manoilesco), 79
Silver, 20, 28, 29, 33, 58
Sindicatos, 79
Slums, 15
Social democracy, 88, 89
Social democrats (W. Europe), 96
Social formations, 4, 5
  precapitalist, 3, 12
Socialism, 5, 19, 21, 23, 42, 66, 85, 86,
  87, 88, 89–90, 92, 135, 136, 138, 140,
  141
  advanced, 96, 120, 121, 132
  and centralized planning, 123, 124, 125–
    126, 128, 130, 132
  compared to communism, 121–122
  and consumption, 121, 124, 127
  defined, 95–96
  and development, 80, 81, 104, 109, 119–
    132
  and foreign control, 55
  goals, 120, 134
  Marxian, 96
  and political power, 96. *See also* Class
    coalitions; State power
  schools of developmental thought, 2, 3–
    5, 6, 82
  transition to, 49, 64, 83, 86, 89, 90–91,
    96–97, 98, 107, 122
  See also Chile; Cuba; Nicaragua
Social mobility, 8, 16, 42
  colonial, 30
  feudal, 10
Social structure, 35, 97
  colonial, 30–31